Africa and the Universality of Human Rights

Nijhoff Law Specials

VOLUME 107

The titles published in this series are listed at *brill.com/nlsp*

Africa and the Universality of Human Rights

By

Bertrand G. Ramcharan

BRILL
NIJHOFF

LEIDEN | BOSTON

The Library of Congress Cataloging-in-Publication Data is available online at https://catalog.loc.gov
LC record available at https://lccn.loc.gov/2022024679

Typeface for the Latin, Greek, and Cyrillic scripts: "Brill". See and download: brill.com/brill-typeface.

ISSN 0924-4549
ISBN 978-90-04-52063-9 (paperback)
ISBN 978-90-04-52064-6 (e-book)

This book is printed on acid-free paper and produced in a sustainable manner.

TO TASLIM OLAWALE ELIAS (NIGERIA)
Who pioneered the quest for the rule of law in Africa and the world
AND TO
WALTER RODNEY (GUYANA)
Who gave his life in the quest for human dignity in Africa and the world

Contents

Foreword

> All human rights are universal, indivisible and interdependent, and interrelated. The international community must treat human rights globally in a fair and equal manner, on the same footing, and with the same emphasis.
>
> Paragraph 5: Vienna Declaration and Programme of Action adopted by the World Conference on Human Rights, Vienna, 25 June 1993.

This was the rallying cry of the World Conference on Human Rights held in Vienna, Austria in June 1993. It was a rallying cry demanded by many human rights defenders and activists in Vienna in order to establish the extent and nature of the universality of human rights and to comprehensively put paid to the ideas of exceptionalism that had become current in the era preceding Vienna and whose voices could still be heard on the floors and podiums of Vienna. This was a significant statement for another reason. This was the era of renewed confidence and hope both in the capacity of the world community to put right the wrongs of the past, and for the world community to work together in the interests of each other's nations and for the good of humankind.

Emerging from Vienna a great responsibility was placed on the UN system of Human Rights to coordinate and assist states by providing a counselling and advisory services and to strengthen the multilateral instruments for the promotion, defence and strengthening of human rights across the world. The Office of the United Nations High Commissioner for Human Rights was soon established. It was in his role as Deputy High Commissioner that I first met Dr Bertrand G Ramcharan in 1998. Since then, he has established himself as an expert in international law in the service of the international institutions like the United Nations and several of its agencies. In doing so he has gathered a great deal of knowledge and understanding of the human rights situations in different parts of the world. He is held in very high regard as authoritative in human rights matters.

I had the privilege of getting to know Dr Ramcharan in my various capacities as the inaugural Chairperson of the South African Human Rights Commission, and later, in liaison with the National Human Rights Institutions that at some point I served as Chairperson of, and which was facilitated by the Office of the High Commissioner. Throughout those years, Ramcharan, including when he performed the functions of UN High Commissioner, served as advisor and guide. He and his staff facilitated our work during our regular visits to Geneva. By so doing he became a valued friend to many of us across the world especially in the support for the establishment and equipping of National Human Rights Commissions established according to the Paris Principles.

What excites me about this book is that having served simultaneously as the member of the Banjul-based African Commission on Human and Peoples' Rights, I got to get a Continental dimension of human rights promotion and application in my work as a member of the ACHPR. That work brought me and my colleagues closer to the African Union, in its earlier incarnation as the OAU. It was during our time that we managed to make a case for the establishment of the African Court on Human and peoples' Rights based in Arusha, Tanzania.

I set out herein the various instances and touchpoints one has with Bertie Ramcharan in person but also with the content of the book that he has produced. As one who has been dealing with these matters professionally for many years both as an activist, as a leader in human rights promotion and as a defender, as well as an academic, Dr Ramcharan has put at our disposal a textbook that consolidates a wide range of materials and sources in a comprehensive way that both teachers, students and activists and human rights defenders on the grounds will find value in. To the best of my knowledge, this will add to the work that is being done at the Centre for Human Rights at the University of Pretoria with the specialisation on the African human rights system, and their publications.

To the extent that this publication *Africa and the Universality of Human Rights* is a comprehensive treatment of the human rights systems and machinery applicable in Africa, he has produced a book the like of which I am yet to come across.

Dr Ramcharan's work is a masterpiece. It has come at a time when Africa is wrestling with a myriad of problems notwithstanding the instruments available to nations and societies at this time. Yes, the debate about African culture and exceptionalism has waned somewhat, though I daresay it has not been eliminated altogether. The work of the late Ghanaian Secretary-General of the United Nations, Kofi Anan in that regard is commendable. Yes, African states supported nations in the Security Council who were hellbent to teach the Brother Leader of Libya *Mu'ammar Al-Qadhafi* a lesson by invoking a No-Fly Zone over Libyan airspace under Resolution 1973 in March 2011. Yes, all manner of subterfuge was resorted to justify the invasion of Iraq under the pretext of the need for the destruction of weapons of mass destruction. Yes, the *Ruto and Sang* case at the ICC generated furious calls from African states for a mass withdrawal from the Rome Statute on the basis that the ICC was targeting African heads of state. That, together with the subsequent embarrassing diplomatic rebuff of the ICC by South Africa in the matter of the President of

Sudan, *Omar el-Bashir* by defying an order of the High Court and violating its obligations under the Treaty of Rome.

In fairness to the African states, however, it must be stated that the issue did not just end with the denunciation of the ICC. Efforts were made to provide an African instrument that would substitute the ICC, by undertaking to establish a Pan- African criminal justice instrument to cover crimes against humanity and war crimes etc. Towards that end the protocol on the Statute of the Court of Justice and Human Rights was adopted. It was to establish a new Court of Justice and Human Rights. The Malabo Protocol was to give authority to the Court to "intervene in a Member State pursuant to a decision of the Assembly in respect of grave circumstances, namely, war crimes, genocide and crimes against humanity as well as serious threats to legitimate order to restore peace and stability to the Member State of the Union ..." Now nearly seven years later both Protocols have not come into effect principally because they have not yet received the required number of ratifications by Member States.

At the time of writing Ethiopia is at war against its own Tigray Province, a state of emergency has been declared, there is a call to arms by civilians and retired army officers. It is a civil war that is bound to cause enormous human rights violations and loss of life as well as an unwelcome destabilisation of the economic well-being of ordinary citizens, not to mention the flight of refugees and asylum-seekers flocking into neighbouring states. It is a human catastrophe and a humanitarian crisis that will soon engulf the whole region. On 25 October 2021 a military coup was declared in Sudan whereby the Constitution was suspended, the civilian/military interim government was dissolved, and many government officers were detained. On the streets of Khartoum and elsewhere civilians have been protesting the coup, and a growing number has been killed. That is the story that one can tell about Africa today: in Tunisia, Mali, Guinea Bissau, Mozambique, eSwatini.

Of course, these developments beg the question, what about the comprehensive human rights instruments so ably expressed in this study? How is it that this machinery that is designed to enable the advancement of peace and human rights and the elimination of conflict, and the maintenance of Good Governance and Democracy, so carefully explained by Dr Ramcharan, is not working. The confidence of Vienna may appear to have evaporated. It is a long way from 1993 to 2021 in Africa.

Having said that peace, justice and human rights are no one-day wonder instruments. These days the clamour for the withdrawal from the Rome Statute has died down; the instruments of the AU on Principles of Governing Democratic Elections among others have not been retracted. What is missing, maybe, is that the African states need stronger monitoring mechanisms that are independent, a civil society that is equipped to hold states accountable, researchers and academic institutions that can continue to teach the young, investigate and research, publish and if needs be, to name and shame those who pay lip service to their own declarations at the AU.

For all the reasons stated above, this study by Dr Bertrand G Ramcharan is timely. It provides a concise, scholarly and yet interpretation and application of the relevant instruments that human rights defenders will find to be an invaluable guide for practitioners, students and government agencies.

N Barney Pityana GCOB
First Chairperson of the South African Human Rights Commission
Former Member of the African Commission on Human and Peoples' Rights.
Professor Emeritus of Law: University of South Africa;
Member: Academy of Science of South Africa (ASSAf).
4 November 2021

Preface

The universality of human rights is the corner-stone of the contemporary international order. It is a pillar of the United Nations Charter and of its vision for a world of peace, justice, development, and the rule of law grounded in respect for the human rights of every person.

In a lecture on "The Human Crisis", delivered at Columbia University on 28 March, 1946, the celebrated Algerian-born writer and philosopher, Albert Camus, author of the Myth of Sisyphus and of The Rebel, made a stirring plea for the world to be guided by universal norms of conduct. In 1942, in the midst of the Second World War, he had written and published The Myth of Sisyphus, which recognized the essence of human dignity and the ongoing challenges of human striving.

In this book I seek to show that, notwithstanding difficulties experienced on the ground, African governments, peoples, and institutions, together, have repeatedly expressed their commitment to the universality of human rights. There is abundant evidence of this, as these pages will show.

Human dignity and rights are inherent in the African philosophy of the Akan in West Africa, of Ubuntu in Southern Africa, and in Sengor's philosophy of negritude. Human dignity and rights are central to the jurisprudence of the South African Constitutional Court, of the African Commission and the African Court on Human and Peoples' Rights.

I have been fortunate to have spent close to four decades in the service of human rights at the United Nations and have had a fair measure of involvement with African issues. I have had assignments in North, South, East, West, Central Africa and in the Horn of Africa. I have been humbled in visiting, on two occasions, the cell that Nelson Mandela occupied on Robben Island for numerous years.

In 1975 I helped organize and participated in a two-week UN conference in Tunis, Tunisia on the human rights of migrant workers. In 1979 I helped organize and participated in another two-week UN conference in Nairobi, Kenya, on issues of equality and non-discrimination in the continent. I helped write the reports and conclusions of these conferences. On both occasions I witnessed the strong African attachment to the universality of human rights.

As Special Assistant to the Director of the UN human rights department, I was at the two-week 1979 UN human rights conference in Monrovia, Liberia, that drafted what became the institutional parts of the African Charter on Human and Peoples' Rights. I repeat, the institutional parts. The normative parts were drafted by Africans, notably from Senegal. I wrote the blueprint that the Seminar discussed and eventually adopted. I have written about this elsewhere. I pay tribute here to Mr Justice Wiredu of the Supreme Court of Ghana, who chaired the drafting group that discussed the institutional blueprint for the African Commission.

In 1991, following Nelson Mandela's release from prison, I observed mass action in the Natal-Kwazulu region of South Africa as part of a UN observer team sent by Secretary-General Boutros Boutros-Ghali at the request of Frederik de Clerk and Nelson Mandela. I had a helicopter at my disposal and for a week I criss-crossed the beautiful Natal-KwaZulu region of South Africa. I could see why Alan Paton had given his book its title: *Cry, the Beloved Country*. I had a historic opportunity to speak with the great Madiba on that occasion.

As a UN representative, I observed the national elections in Ghana in 1992 and was able to see, first hand, the majesty of Ghanaians queuing up in the sun with quiet dignity to cast their votes. On that occasion I had the good fortune of inter-acting with today's President of Ghana, Nana Akufo Addo.

For three years, between 1996 and 1998, I was Director, Africa Division, in the UN Department of Political Affairs, as it was then named. At my request, my Division prepared risk assessments for every African country it covered. I still have those assessments among my papers.

As Director, I chaired a Task Force on the Great Lakes region of Africa that met and reported daily to Secretary-General Kofi Annan. In March, 1997, we recommended to Secretary-General Annan that he address the Summit Meeting of the Central Organ of the OAU Conflict Prevention Mechanism on 26 March, 1997 in the following terms, penned by this author:

> It is precisely one of the lessons to be learned from the current crises in the Great Lakes region that had the mechanisms and the means to detect and head off crises been in operation earlier, it might have been possible to avoid so many deaths, to spare so many people from suffering, and to channel so much resources into building the future rather than picking up the pieces from the ravages of conflict.
>
> There are many deep and troubling issues to be addressed in the future. Inter-group clashes are not new in Rwanda and Burundi. Why then has it not been possible to set in place local monitoring devices that can give the alert to grievances, set in motion corrective mechanisms, spur tolerance, harmony and confidence-building, and allow the society to move forward on a basis of respect for human and minority rights? …
>
> At the centre of these questions are issues of the future African regional political order. The OAU and the United Nations Security Council have clearly laid down the principles that must govern the search for peace in

> the Great Lakes region. These are the principles of respect for the inviolability of internationally recognized borders, the peaceful settlement of disputes, non-acceptance of the seizure of territory through the use of force, respect for the human rights and fundamental freedoms of all, recognition and respect for minority rights, equality of access to resources for all the peoples of a country, and equitable development for all of Africa's peoples. There is also another vital fundamental principle: that those who perpetrate atrocities shall face the sanction of the law.
>
> These principles of African and international public order have influenced the elaboration of African and United Nations policies for dealing with each of the situations occasioning international concern in the Great Lakes region.

One could see in the above, the centrality of respect for human rights in efforts for the prevention of conflicts. One could also see this in other places with deep-seated conflicts, such as Algeria. As Director of the Africa Division, in 1998 I accompanied a high-level mission dispatched by Secretary-General Kofi Annan to Algeria in the midst of the violence in that country. The mission comprised three former Prime Ministers, a Minister of Justice and a former UN Ambassador to the UN. The mission drew up and published a landmark report on the situation in Algeria then.

As Director of the Africa Division, I took a special interest in African Constitutionalism and the Protection of Minority Rights in Africa. I guest-edited an issue of the Review of the International Commission of Jurists devoted to Constitutionalism in Africa and I have written elsewhere on the challenges of protecting minorities in Africa.

As Deputy UN High Commissioner for Human Rights, in the midst of the war then taking place in the country in 2002, I carried out a fact-finding mission to Ivory Coast at the request of Secretary-General Annan. I submitted a report to the then Commission on Human Rights and then presented it to the UN Security Council. I will always remember, when I was in Ivory Coast, how a soldier told me with pride that he had attended courses on international human rights and humanitarian law at the San Remo Institute of Humanitarian Law.

In 2003, I participated in the African Union Ministerial Meeting on human rights, held in Kigali, Rwanda. Also in 2003, I accompanied Secretary-General Annan to the Summit of the African Union held in Mozambique.

Performing the functions of UN High Commissioner for Human Rights, I initiated fact-finding missions into the human rights situations in Liberia and in Darfur. In 2004, I reported to the Security Council on the situation in Darfur. Serving as High Commissioner, I commissioned a legal opinion, and shared it with the Government concerned, that it would be contrary to international human rights law to stone an alleged adulteress to death under Sharia law.

I was a member of the UN Human Rights Council's first-ever fact-finding mission, the "High-Level Panel" on human rights in Darfur, and visited the region with the Panel in 2006. Our report catalogued the atrocities that had taken place in Darfur. Hopefully, it has found its way to the International Criminal Court which has some of the accused in its custody as we write.

I was one of three Commissioners on an ILO Commission of Inquiry into the human and labour rights situations in Zimbabwe and could see the central role that could be played by an independent national human rights institution. We recommended the strengthening of the national commission in the report we submitted.

I participated in an ILO fact-finding mission to look into the conditions of farm workers and vineyard workers in South Africa. I spent a month in Cape Town and the Cape region and in Polokwane and the North-East region of South Africa. I subsequently returned for a visit to the Cape area and visited the Cape of Good Hope, where my grandfather was born on a ship anchored off the Cape, carrying indentured labourers to the then British Guiana. I also visited Cape Agulhas, where the Atlantic and Indian Oceans meet. Not far from there, some of the oldest human bones have been found in a cave. The origins of humanity can be traced in the caves there.

I lectured on international human rights law to an African regional training course on international law organized by the UN Office of Legal Affairs and held in Addis Ababa. I had meaningful interactions with African international lawyers. I have lectured on international human rights law at conferences in Tanzania, Uganda, and Namibia, as well as the Universities of Cape Town and Stellenbosch in South Africa. In Uganda, I visited the Ugandan Commission on Human Rights led by the dynamic Margaret Sekaggiya, and interacted with the UN Human Rights Office in that country.

As someone who had played a part in the holding of the Monrovia conference in 1979 and who had drafted the document considered and adopted by the seminar for the institutional parts of the African Commission on Human and Peoples' Rights, and as a former Director of the Africa Division of the UN Political Department, I have always felt a strong connection with the African Commission on Human and Peoples' Rights and have tried to follow its jurisprudence, as best as I could in a busy career.

As Director in the UN Political Department, I followed closely, and hopefully contributed to, the efforts to establish the early-warning and preventive diplomacy facility in the then OAU, now the African Union, and have visited both Organizations for on-the-spot discussions on preventive diplomacy. In

2019, I was fortunate to have engaged in consultations with the AU Secretariat and with the Secretariat of IGAD on the experiences of their early-warning and preventive diplomacy facilities.

At one stage, former UN Secretary-General Boutros Boutros-Ghali invited me to Cairo to address a conference on human rights in Africa. I also participated in, and addressed, a conference on Women, peace and security, organized in Sharm El Sheik, on the shores of the Red Sea, by former Egyptian First Lady Mme Suzanne Mubarak.

I cite the foregoing simply to demonstrate that I have sought, for some while to be a learner, in the Socratic sense, when it comes to the implementation of human rights in the African continent. I remain a seeker and, hopefully, a learner. This book is part of the seeking and learning effort.

Finally, I may mention that I was born and raised in what is now Guyana, where nearly a half of our population are persons of African descent. We are part of what the current Prime Minister of Barbados, Ms. Mia Motley, has called the Caribbean civilization. Our great historian, the late Walter Rodney wrote a land-mark study on How the West Underdeveloped Africa. He also wrote a history of West Africa, *A History of the Upper Guinea Coast*. It is only natural that I would take an interest in the ancestral country of half of my compatriots.

I dedicate this book to our great historian, the martyred Walter Rodney, and to the late Chief Justice, Taslim Olawale Elias of Nigeria, who pioneered the quest for the rule of law and for respect for human rights in Africa and who made historic contributions on the UN International Law Commission and the International Court of Justice.

Abbreviations

AfComHPR	African Commission on Human and Peoples' Rights.
AfCrtHPR	African Court on Human and Peoples' Rights
AU	African Union
AU PSC	African Union Peace and Security Council
SACC	South African Constitutional Court
EAC	East African Community
EACJ	East African Community Court of Justice
ECCAS	Economic Community of Central African States
ECOWAS	Economic Community of West African States
IGAD	Inter-governmental Authority on Development
ICCPR	International Covenant on Civil and Political Rights
ICESCR	International Covenant on Economic, Social and Cultural Rights
OAU	Organization of African Unity
SADC	Southern African Development Community
SADCT	SADC Tribunal
The Elders	An organization of statespersons founded by Nelson Mandela to work for peace, human rights and development.

CHAPTER 1

Introduction

Abstract

This chapter highlights Africa's contributions to the development of international law. It argues that the African anchors of international law and order can help ground and stabilize the world in a time of Sino-American contestation. The continent that is the cradle of humanity, and which contains a quarter of the Member States of the United Nations, stands geographically at the centre of the American and Eurasian landmasses. Neither the Americas nor Eurasia can decide the content of international law without taking guidance from the cradle of humanity.

1.1 Introduction

One can never step into the same river twice, the ancient Greek Philosopher Heraclitus counselled. The waters commingle, change, and keep on flowing. Each time one steps into the river, one steps into new waters. For the most part, though, the river keeps its course and while the waters may commingle and evolve, the river flows to its destiny. Occasionally it may adapt to changes in the physical environment and change its course. But the great rivers have remained constant to their fate. Constancy and change are their story.

The river of international law is like the river of Heraclitus. It has developed by drawing on inputs from different parts of the world. It absorbs new inputs all the time. And yet, there is a constancy of purpose about it that has never faltered since it first began. As the bell strikes for the first quarter of the twenty-first century, international law remains anchored in its mission of the international rule of law while absorbing the momentous challenges of our times: climate change, environmental degradation, pandemics such as COVID-19, weapons of mass destruction, international terrorism, conflicts – internal and international, pervasive inequalities, and rampant gross violations of human rights and fundamental freedoms world-wide.

In our times there is much discussion of the so-called Thucydides Trap, according to which an emergent China is destined to fight with a hegemonic USA. China challenges many of the rules of international law which, it says, were put into place before it reclaimed its natural place on the world scene. The United States is, to put it charitably, self-serving when it comes to abiding

 | DOI:10.1163/9789004520646_002

by the rules of international law. China, Russia and the United States, the pre-eminent nuclear powers, all treat universal human rights with scant respect. The European Union and India profess adherence to democratic values and universal human rights but are both opportunistic when it comes to the observance of human rights.

The flag of the United Nations languishes at half-mast as countries the world over treat the Charter, the Universal Declaration, and organs such as the Security Council and the International Court of Justice with scant respect. The world is in need of anchors rooted in the UN Charter and the Universal Declaration of Human Rights.

It is our submission in this book that African regional institutions can point us in the direction of those anchors and that it is important to register Africa's contributions to the river of international law. The African anchors of international law and order can help ground and stabilize the world in a time of Sino-American contestation. The continent that is the cradle of humanity, and which contains a quarter of the Member States of the United Nations, stands geographically at the centre of the American and Eurasian land-masses. Neither the Americas nor Eurasia can decide the content of international law without taking guidance from the cradle of humanity.

Africa has taken a firm stance in support of the United Nations Charter, the international rule of law, and universal respect for human rights. While adding African insights to the development of international law and engaging in law-making that takes African needs into account, the African Union and sub-regional African institutions have been firmly in support of the UN Charter, the Universal Declaration of Human Rights and the international rule of law. One sees this in their founding documents and their high-level policy declarations.

In addition to supporting the International Court of Justice with distinguished jurists such as Taslim Olawale Elias, Mohammed Bedjaoui, Keba M'Baye, Abdul Koroma, Abdulqawi Ahmed Yousef and Julia Sebutinde, Africa has the African Court of Justice and Human Rights, the ECOWAS Court of Justice, the East African Court of Justice, the SADC Tribunal (currently in hiatus) and stellar national courts such as the South African Constitutional Court. The jurisprudence of all of these bodies is firmly grounded in the universality of human rights under international law.

The African commitment to democracy is in evidence in the existence of democracy charters of the African Union, ECOWAS, IGAD, other sub-regional institutions. The African Charter on Human and Peoples' Rights is anchored in the Universal Declaration of Human Rights while adding normative provisions reflective of the African experience, such as recognition of peoples' rights to existence, peace, environmental security and development.

Africa as a continent, and African States regionally and sub-regionally, subscribe amply and faithfully to the universality of human rights, as encapsulated in the United Nations Charter and the Universal Declaration of Human Rights. This is evident in the jurisprudence and practice of the African Union, of sub-regional institutions such as ECOWAS, IGAD, and SADC, in the applicable human rights jurisprudence of the United Nations – of which all African States are Members, and of African human rights institutions such as the African Commission and Court on Human and Peoples' Rights, and the ECOWAS Court of Justice. African support for the universality of human rights is pronounced and wide-ranging. This may be seen in the Charter of the African Union, the African Charter on Human and Peoples' Rights, and in Democracy charters adopted by the African Union, ECOWAS. SADC and other institutions.

1.2 Corner Stones

The African Human Rights Commission's affirmation of the universality of human rights is in stellar evidence in its General Comment No. 3 on the Right to Life, adopted in 2015.[1] Key extracts are provided below:

General Comment No. 3 of the African Human Rights Commission

1. The African Commission on Human and Peoples' Rights (the Commission) has described the right to life as the fulcrum of all other rights. It is non-derogable, and applies at all times. In General Comment No. 3, the Commission clarifies the nature of the right to life as recognised in Article 4 of the African Charter ....
2. The Charter imposes on States a responsibility to prevent arbitrary deprivations of life caused by its own agents, and to protect individuals and groups from such deprivations at the hands of others. It also imposes a responsibility to investigate any killings that take place, and to hold the perpetrators accountable. This intersects with the general duty, recognized in the Charter, of all individuals to exercise their rights and freedoms with due regard to the rights of others. Organised crime and terrorism can pose significant threats to the enjoyment of the right to life and require a robust State response, but

1 Adopted by the ACHPR during its 57th Ordinary Session held in Banjul, The Gambia, in November, 2015.

one that at all times takes into account *the requirements of international human rights law.* [Emphasis added]

3. The General Comment proceeds from an understanding that the Charter envisages the protection not only of life in a narrow sense, but of dignified life. This requires a broad interpretation of States' responsibilities to protect life. Such actions extend to preventive steps to preserve and protect the natural environment and humanitarian responses to natural disasters, famines, outbreaks of infectious diseases, or other emergencies. The State also has a responsibility to address more chronic yet pervasive threats to life, for example with respect to preventable maternal mortality, by establishing functioning health systems. Such an approach reflects the Charter's ambition to ensure a better life for all the people and peoples of Africa through its recognition of a wide range of rights, including the right to dignity, economic, social and cultural rights, and peoples' rights such as the right to existence and the right to peace. It is also rooted in widely shared communal values of the continent, according to which the value of one person's life is tied to the value of the lives of others.
4. Article 4 of the Charter enshrines the right to life as follows: 'Human beings are inviolable. Every human being shall be entitled to respect for his life and the integrity of his person. No one may be arbitrarily deprived of this right.' Other African legal instruments protecting the right to life include: Article 4 of the Protocol to the African Charter on Human and Peoples' Rights on the Rights of Women in Africa and Articles 5 and 30 of the African Charter on the Rights and Welfare of the Child.

   A. *The nature of the right and of the obligations of the State in respect of the right to life.*

5. The right to life is universally recognized as a foundational human right. It is guaranteed by Article 4 of the African Charter and all of the other main global and regional human rights instruments. *The right not to be arbitrarily deprived of one's life is recognised as part of customary international law and the general principles of law, and is also recognised as a jus cogens norm, universally binding at all times.* The right to life is contained in the constitutions and other legal provisions of the vast majority of African and other States. All national legal systems criminalise murder, and arbitrary killings committed or tolerated by the State as a matter of the utmost gravity. (Emphasis added).
6. The right to life should not be interpreted narrowly. In order to secure a dignified life for all, the right to life requires the realisation of all

human rights recognised in the Charter, including civil, political, economic, social and cultural rights and peoples' rights, particularly the right to peace.

7. States have a responsibility under the Charter to develop and implement a legal and practical framework to respect, protect, promote and fulfil the right to life. States must take steps both to prevent arbitrary deprivations of life and to conduct prompt, impartial, thorough and transparent investigations into any such deprivations that may have occurred, holding those responsible to account and providing for an effective remedy and reparation for the victim or victims, including where appropriate, their immediate family and dependents. States are responsible for violations of this right by all their organs (executive, legislative and judicial), and other public or governmental authorities, at all levels (national, regional or local). Derogation from the right to life is not permissible in a time of emergency, including a situation of armed conflict, or in response to threats such as terrorism ....

(i) *Interpreting the right to life broadly*

41. The right to life should be interpreted broadly. The State has a positive duty to protect individuals and groups from real and immediate risks to their lives caused either by actions or inactions of third parties. In cases where the risk has not arisen from malicious or other intent then the State's actions may not always be related to criminal justice. Such actions include, *inter alia*, preventive steps to preserve and protect the natural environment and humanitarian responses to natural disasters, famines, outbreaks of infectious diseases, or other emergencies.

42. Attention is required to address more chronic yet pervasive threats to life, for example with respect to preventable maternal mortality, by establishing functioning health systems and eliminating discriminatory laws and practices which impact on individuals' and groups' ability to seek healthcare.

43. Given the role of the State in the enjoyment of a number of other rights which might, collectively, be constitutive of the condition of life, especially a dignified life, its progressive realisation of various economic, social and cultural rights will contribute to securing a full and dignified life. Violations of such rights may in certain circumstances therefore also entail violations of the right to life.

This presentation of the right to life is very much along the lines of the presentations of bodies such as the UN Human Rights Council, the Human Rights Committee (ICCPR), the European Court of Human Rights, the Inter-American Commission and the Inter-American Court of Human Rights. These are all authoritative bodies when it comes to confirming the universality of fundamental human rights.

Seven decades ago, in 1961, jurists from Africa, meeting in Lagos under the inspiration of Taslim Olawale Elias, adopted the Law of Lagos, which situated African human rights and legal philosophy firmly in the international rule of law and universal human rights.

Already in 1961, one could see convincing evidence of Africa's support for the universality of human rights in the concluding declaration of the African Conference on the Rule of Law. That declaration, by decision of the participants of the conference, is known as the Law of Lagos, which we present next.

> *The Law of Lagos*
>
> The African Conference on the Rule of Law consisting of 194 judges, practising lawyers and teachers of law from 23 African nations as well as 9 countries of other continents,
>
> Assembled in Lagos, Nigeria, in January 1961 under the aegis of the International Commission of Jurists,
>
> Having discussed freely and frankly the Rule of Law with particular reference to Africa, and
>
> Having reached conclusions regarding Human Rights in relation to Government security, Human Rights in relation to aspects of criminal and administrative law, and the responsibility of the Judiciary and of the Bar for the protection of the rights of the individual in society,
>
> NOW SOLEMNLY
>
> Recognize that the Rule of Law is a dynamic concept which should be employed to safeguard and advance the will of the people and the political rights of the individual and to establish social, economic, educational, and cultural conditions under which the individual may achieve his dignity and realize his legitimate aspirations in all countries, whether dependent or independent,
>
> Reaffirms the Act of Athens and the Declaration of Delhi with special reference to Africa and
>
> Declares:
>
> 1. That the principles embodied in the Conclusions of this Conference ... should apply to any society whether free or otherwise, but that

the Rule of Law cannot be fully realized unless the legislative bodies have been established in accordance with the will of people who have adopted their Constitution freely;

2. That in order to maintain adequately the Rule of Law all Governments should adhere to the principle of democratic representation in their Legislatures;
3. The fundamental human rights, especially the right to personal liberty, should be written and entrenched in the Constitution of all countries and that such personal liberty should not in peacetime be restricted without trial in a Court of Law;
4. That in order to *give full effect to the Universal Declaration of Human Rights of 1948*, the Conference invites the African Governments to study the possibility of adopting an African Convention on Human Rights, in such a manner that the Conclusions of this Conference will be safeguarded by the creation of a court of appropriate jurisdiction and that recourse thereto be made available for all persons under the jurisdiction of the signatory States; (Emphasis added)
5. That in order to promote the principles and the practical application of the Rule of Law, the judges, practising lawyers and teachers of law in African countries should take steps to establish branches of the International Commission of Jurists.

This Resolution shall be known as the Law of Lagos.

Done at Lagos this 7th day of January, 1961.

Seven years later, Taslim Olawale Elias of Nigeria, one of the leading jurists at the Lagos conference, penned for a special issue of the Journal of the International Commission of Jurists, on the occasion of the International Year for Human Rights in 1968, an article on "Freedom of Assembly and Association", where he wrote the following:

The provisions of Article 20 of the Universal Declaration of Human Rights regarding freedom of assembly and association are … among the most basic to the flowering of democracy in any State. All the newer nations of Africa and Asia that have entrenched a body of fundamental rights in their national constitutions have in respect of these two freedoms followed closely the pattern set by the 1948 Declaration. The older nations, whether or not they have written constitutions, will agree that they have been influenced by the Declaration, if not in the formulation of the specific provisions, at least in the practical application of its legal ideals in the administration of justice.

> The Declaration seeks to guarantee freedom of assembly and association in the manner and within the limits stated in our review of the legal and judicial practices of States … *These freedoms are intended to be universal in their application* … It is by virtue of these freedoms that we have and enjoy our free parliamentary institutions, associations of employers and of employees, trade unions, private clubs and societies of various kinds; and with these go inevitably the right to assemble, to organize group activities and to undertake processions, subject always to the overriding requirement of State security and general public welfare as defined in the relevant municipal laws.[2] (Emphasis added)

Taslim Olawale Elias was an authentic African authority on the universality of fundamental human rights norms. In this book we shall adduce other evidence of this kind to show that African regional and sub-regional institutions are among the leading exponents of the universality of human rights in the world today.

Africa's continuing commitment to universal human rights may be seen in the following *African Union Human Rights Strategy for Africa*:[3]

> 7. The Constitutive Act of the African Union, in its Article 3(h) provides a clear mandate to AU organs and institutions to promote and protect human and peoples' rights on the continent.
> 8. The African Charter on Human and Peoples' Rights commits AU Member States to the adherence of the principles of human and peoples' rights and freedoms contained in the declarations conventions and other instruments adopted by the African Union and the United Nations and their duty to promote and protect human and peoples' rights and all freedoms and taking into account the importance traditionally attached to these rights and freedoms in Africa.
> 9. The Protocol Relating to the Establishment of the Peace and Security Council of the African Union, in its Article 4(c), implores AU Member States to respect the rule of law, fundamental human rights and freedoms, the sanctity of human life and international humanitarian law.
> 10. The Strategic Plan of the African Union Commission (AUC) (2009–2012) gives the AUC the mandate to achieve *good governance,*

2 VIII Journal of the International Commission of Jurists, Special Issue, 1968, International Year of Human Rights, No. 2, pp. 60–73, at pp. 72–73.

3 Issued by the Department of Political Affairs of the African Union Commission. Action Plan 2012–2016.

democracy, human rights, rights-based approaches to development, including social, economic, cultural and environmental rights....[4]

Principles

27. The Strategy is based on principles, standards, norms and instruments that permeate the various policy pronouncements of the AU. The strategy shall be guided in particular by the following principles:
    a. *Respect for human rights and democratic principles;*
    b. *Respect for the rule of law, fundamental human rights and freedoms, the sanctity of human life and international humanitarian law;*
    c. Interdependence between socio-economic development and the security of peoples and States;
    d. *Universality of rights;*[5]
    e. Gender equality;
    f. Effective participation of citizens in governance and development;
    g. Transparency, accountability and fairness;
    h. Non-discrimination on grounds of race, ethnic group, colour, sex, language, religion, political or any other opinion, national and social origin, fortune, birth or other status;
    i. Complementarity and subsidiarity amongst AU organs and institutions, Regional Economic Communities (RECs) and Member States."

1.3 The Peace Architecture of the African Union

While Africa has experienced a large number of conflicts in the post-independence period, due in considerable measure to its colonial legacy, the desire for peace may be seen in the existence of conflict prevention mechanisms in the African Union, ECOWAS, IGAD, SADC and other sub-regional institutions. A culture of conflict prevention has, without doubt, taken roots in the continent, and cooperation with the UN Security Council for the prevention, containment, and resolution of conflicts is a hall-mark of cooperation between Africa and the United Nations.

---

4 Emphasis supplied.

5 Emphasis supplied.

Africa has elaborated normative and policy documents for advancing disarmament, sustainable development, environmental protection, and silencing the guns. To put it in a nutshell, some of the best evidence in support of the international rule of law and the universality of human rights is to be found in the jurisprudence of African regional and sub-regional institutions, which we shall demonstrate in this book.

1.4 Conclusion

This chapter has brought forth convincing evidence of African corner-stones of the international rule of law and the universality of human rights. In the remainder of this book we shall continue to bring forth such evidence of universality. Chapter two offers a discussion of Africans who helped shaped universality. Chapter three reviews Africa, the United Nations, and the universality of human rights. Chapter four discusses the jurisprudence of the African Commission and African Court on Human and Peoples' Rights on the universality of human rights. Chapter five discusses the contributions of the African Union to the universality of human rights, while Chapter six discusses the contributions of sub-regional institutions and courts. Chapter seven discusses the inputs of national human rights institutions and national courts while Chapter eight discusses the contributions of civil society. Chapter nine, the final chapter offers some concluding observations.

CHAPTER 2

Africans Who Shaped Universality

Abstract

This chapter argues that Africans played leading roles in the shaping of universal human rights norms. It highlights the humanistic philosophies of Leopold Sedar Sengor and Nelson Mandela marshalls evidence regarding the drafting of the International Bill of Human Rights, the development of norms concerning the right to development, sovereignty as responsibility, and the rights of disabled persons. It shows the central roles of Africans in the fight for self-determination and justice, and for equality and non-discrimination. It demonstrates that Africans have also led the quest for the universal implementation of human rights, noting the efforts of UN Secretaries-General Boutros Boutros-Ghali and Kofi Annan, among others.

2.1 Introduction

All human beings, the Universal Declaration of Human Rights of 1948 evocatively proclaimed in its very first article, are born free and equal in dignity and rights. They are endowed with reason and conscience and should act towards one another in a spirit of fellowship. Well before 1948, Africans had joined their brethren in Asia, Latin America and the Caribbean, in championing the inherent dignity of each person.

Already in the 1920s, Leopold Sedar Senghor of Senegal, Aime Cesaire of Martinique and Leon Gontran Damas of French Guiana, had articulated the concept of *negritude* as an expression of revolt against colonialism and racism. The proclamation of negritude took shape when the three friends, one African and two Afro-descendants, founded the journal *L'Etudiant noir* in 1934–35.

On the occasion of the publication of an anthology of his poetry, Leon Gontran Damas explained that he had had in view:

> Poverty, illiteracy, exploitation of man by man, social and political racism suffered by the black or the yellow, forced labour, inequalities, lies,

 | DOI:10.1163/9789004520646_003

> resignation, swindles, prejudices, complacencies, cowardice, failures, crimes committed in the name of liberty, of equality, of fraternity …[1]

In a lecture "On Negritude", delivered in Kinshasa, Senghor declared:

> The whole system is founded on the notion of vital force. Pre-existing, anterior to being, it constitutes being. God has given vital force not only to men, but also to animals, vegetables, even minerals. By which they are. But it is the purpose of this force to increase.[2]

This is a philosophy very much applicable to our times, when the earth, its provenance and its inhabitants are in mortal peril.

Speaking at Columbia University in New York on 28 March, 1946, two years before the adoption of the Universal Declaration, the Algerian-born Nobel literature laureate and philosopher Albert Camus, in a speech on "The Human Crisis", made a stirring plea for universal norms to guide humanity as a whole. He argued for a universalism in which all people of goodwill can come together: "The values sustaining this shared consciousness must be rediscovered. The freedom we must finally win is the freedom not to lie. Only then can we discover our reasons for living and for dying."[3] Earlier, in his master-work, The Myth of Sisyphus, published in the 1940s during the Second World War, Camus had probed into the human essence and in the process had placed the spotlight on Sisyphus's quest for human dignity

A belief in universal norms of human rights would come to pervade the ethos of African leaders, philosophers, scholars, lawyers, and human rights campaigners. On the occasion of the fiftieth anniversary of the Universal Declaration of Human Rights in 1998, for example, my good friend Bacre Waly N'diaye, A Senegalese lawyer and Board Member of Amnesty International, then serving as Director of the New York Office of the UN High Commissioner for Human Rights, gave an interview in which he declared:

> For me, human rights work soon became a quest for universality, namely that everyone would share the same basic rights. Human rights is about principles, nothing else. The Universal Declaration of Human Rights

1 See Stanford Encyclopedia of Philosophy, (2018), "Negritude": https://plato.stanford.edu/entries/negritude/, accessed on 10 November, 2021, p. 3.

2 Ibid., p. 5.

3 Albert Camus, "The Human Crisis", 28 March, 1946, Columbia University, New York University.

> states that all people are equal. This means that they must be treated with full respect for their rights even if you don't like them.[4]

He added: "It is very important for people who are living in difficult situations to feel that they are not forgotten and abandoned, that there is humanity, solidarity and hope somewhere else, even if those feelings are lost where they are."[5]

In the same context, Abdullah An'Naim, a Sudanese Law Professor and leading human rights scholar, expressed the following convictions in his interview:

1. All human beings everywhere are *immediately and constantly* vulnerable to the violation of their human rights, whether they live in developed or developing countries. We should therefore all be *conscious of our individual and collective vulnerability.*
2. Actual or potential victims must not only protect their own human rights, but a systematic and collaborated response in this regard is more likely to succeed than isolated disconnected efforts. Accordingly, we must all adopt a *productive approach* to our vulnerability to the violation of human rights.
3. Improving the legitimacy and efficacy of the present international human rights system is our shared *individual and collective responsibility* because we are all benefitting from its effective implementation. That is to say, unless and until an alternative system is developed and implemented, each one of us should act individually and in collaboration with others in resolving whatever problems may exist with the system developed under the auspices of the Universal Declaration instead of passively criticizing it.[6]

Salim Ahmed Salim was President of the 34th session of the UN General Assembly. During his Presidency he made a major address on the centrality of human rights to the achievement of the UN vision of peace, development, and justice.[7] He declared:

> I wish to make three observations. First, the question of human rights and the maintenance of international peace and security are closely linked.

4 See, A Human Rights Message 50. Published by Regeringskansliet, Ministry of Foreign Affairs of Sweden, 1998, p. 117.

5 Ibid, p. 125.

6 Ibid, pp. 16–17. Italics in original.

7 See, Salim A. Salim. (1980) "Human rights and maintenance of peace and security closely linked", UN Chronicle, 17(5), 53–54.

> The enjoyment of human rights is inconceivable in circumstances where peace and security are non-existent. Likewise, peace and security cannot prevail unless there is a guarantee for the enjoyment and protection of human rights. A review of the international situation, and more particularly of the major crisis areas in the world, clearly confirm the linkage between human rights and international peace and security.
>
> Second, a meaningful discussion of the question of human rights must *a priori* entail a proper understanding of the totality of those rights ... Human rights must be seen in their total context encompassing political, civil, economic and social rights.
>
> The third observation which I wish to make is that while all nations profess to respect human rights, no nation can claim perfection in that field. Indeed, one of the anachronisms of our era is the hiatus between rhetoric and performance in that context. For, notwithstanding the fact that all nations publicly declare their commitment to support for human rights, and despite their repeated condemnation of the violations of those rights, human rights violations continue to take place, and in some respects with impunity.[8]

President Salim Salim went on to articulate a lucid balance of the universal and the contextual. He insisted that genuine promotion of human rights presupposed the recognition and observance of the fundamental principles of the right of people to freedom through the exercise of their right to self-determination and independence. This principle embodied the right of all peoples to struggle against colonialism, foreign domination and other forms of oppression and exploitation by every means available for their national liberation. He further argued that human rights had political, economic, social and cultural facets and that the right to development was an essential element of human rights.

He concluded:

- We must insist that the observance of human rights is a fundamental and universal principle which cannot be compromised by a mere resort to the concept of national sovereignty.
- We must strengthen the United Nations machinery for the protection and promotion of human rights and fundamental freedoms.

8 Ibid, p.53.

– We must also support all national, regional and international structures in support of human rights. These include strengthening the regional institutions and, where these do not yet exist, work for their establishment.

Here was a captivating presentation supporting the implementation of universal human rights norms while being mindful of realities on the ground.

Paul Lusaka of Zambia was President of the 39th session of the General Assembly in 1984. He presided over the adoption of the UN Convention against Torture and other Cruel, Inhuman or Degrading Treatment or Punishment. When the Convention was adopted, on 10 December, 1984, he declared:

> The General Assembly has just taken an important decision in adopting this Convention, which crowns the success of seven years of hard work. I wish to congratulate all concerned on the constructive and cooperative spirit in which they approached this task. The Convention represents a major step towards creating a more humane world and I am especially pleased that the Assembly has taken this decision on this day, the thirty-sixth anniversary of the Universal Declaration of Human Rights.[9]

A few years after being President of the General Assembly, on 22 February, 1991 Mr Lusaka made a major address to the University of Dayton, Ohio, on the topic: "The International Protection of Human Rights: An African Perspective". This author was present when he made that address which received a rapturous welcome. Mr Lusaka insisted on global implementation of universal human rights norms, including in Africa. At the same time, he asked for consideration to be given to the historical experiences of Africa with slavery, colonialism, and *apartheid.* This was a subtle balance: we must all implement universal human rights norms, while taking account of the historical experiences of peoples who had been subjected to oppression and injustice.[10]

The next African President of the UN General Assembly, Joseph N. Garba of Nigeria, made a ringing address in Winchester, Massachusetts, on 15 May, 1990 on the topic of the *Human Imperatives of Global Politics on eve of the Twenty-First Century*.[11] Addressing "the third foundation for peace, namely, respect for human rights and fundamental freedoms", President Garba declared:

9 UN General Assembly, Thirty Ninth Session. Official Records. 93rd Plenary Meeting, Monday 10 December, 1984, para. 6.

10 The author was present at the delivery of this speech and recalls the enthusiastic welcome it received.

11 See UN Press Release GA/8036, 15 May, 1990: Address by General Assembly President on Human Imperatives of Global Politics on eve of Twenty-First Century.

> We have indeed come a long way since the Charter, and we now have at our disposal an international code of human rights that is impressive by any standard. A universal culture of human rights is taking root in the world and the foundations have been laid for national and international protecting systems, intended to assure respect for human rights and fundamental freedoms.
>
> And yet, as I am sure you are well aware, violations of human rights are rampant in the world. Notwithstanding the extensive international norms adopted and current efforts to promote and disseminate those norms, the acid test we always have to face is whether human rights and fundamental freedoms are being respected in practice. We are, therefore, in need of enhanced international protection arrangements. Here also, we shall need the resourcefulness of our global community to help us devise better solutions in the future.[12]

Let it be noted that President Garba considered that "*a universal culture of human rights is taking root in the world* ..." Shortly after President Garba spoke, an African Secretary-General took charge of the United Nations, Boutros Boutros-Ghali, who also saw the interconnectedness between peace, development and human rights and would go on to give the world An Agenda for Peace; An Agenda for Development; and An Agenda for Democratization.

His successor, another African Secretary-General, Kofi Annan, would continue the theme of the implementation of universal human rights norms. Addressing the UN General Assembly on decisions to be taken for the implementation of its Millennium Declaration, Secretary-General Kofi Annan told the UN General Assembly on 21 September, 2004:

> Today I will ... seek ... to remind you of the all-important framework in which they should be taken – namely, the rule of law, in each country and in the world.
>
> The vision of 'a government of laws and not of men' is almost as old as civilisation itself. In a hallway not far from this podium is a replica of the code of laws promulgated by Hammurabi more than three thousand years ago, in the land we now call Iraq.
>
> Much of Hammurabi's code now seems impossibly harsh. But etched into its tablets are principles of justice that have been recognized, if seldom fully implemented by almost every human society since his time:

12 Ibid, pp. 6–7.

> – Legal protection for the poor.
> – Restraints on the strong, so they cannot oppress the weak.
> – Laws publicly enacted, and known to all.
>
> That code was a landmark in mankind's struggle to build an order where, instead of might making right, right would make might. Many nations represented in this chamber proudly point to founding documents of their own that embody that simple concept. And this Organization – your United Nations – is founded on the same principle.
>
> … [W]e must start from the principle that no one is above the law, and no one should be denied its protection. Every nation that proclaims the rule of law at home must respect it abroad; and every nation that insists on it abroad must enforce it at home.[13]

These were authentic African voices speaking in support of universal human rights and their implementation.

In exploring, further, the subject of Africa and the universality of human rights, it is important to emphasize that African leaders, diplomats, scholars, experts and thinkers contributed in a major way to the shaping of universality. We will trace this in four notable areas: the development of universal norms of human rights; the struggle for justice and for self-determination; the struggle for equality and non-discrimination; and the quest for the implementation of universal human rights.

In the development of universal norms, during the drafting of the Universal Declaration of Human Rights, Mr Osman Ebeid, Egypt's representative in the General Assembly, made an eloquent plea on the importance of implementing economic, social and cultural rights alongside civil and political rights. George Lamptey of Ghana fought for the provisions of the Convention on Elimination of All Forms of Racism and Racial Discrimination, and may be considered the father of its optional petitions system.

Adamu Mohammed of Nigeria was a dynamic young leader during the drafting of the International Covenants on human rights in the Third Committee. He repeatedly championed the cause of universal human rights. Ms. Halima Embarek Warzazi of Morocco chaired the Third Committee of the General Assembly in 1966 when it adopted the International Covenants on human rights.

Ibrahima Fall of Senegal was Secretary-General of the 1993 Vienna World Conference on Human Rights, which strongly emphasized the universality of

13 Text of statement, as delivered, in the possession of the author.

human rights. Keba M'Baye of Senegal was the father of the idea of the right to development. And Francis Deng of Sudan articulated the concept of sovereignty as responsibility. Justice Mohammed Bedjaoui of Algeria, Judge on the International Court of Justice and, before that, Member of the UN International Law Commission, advocated brilliantly for the rights of humanity.

In the struggle for justice and self-determination, Leopold Senghor, poet, philosopher and statesman, magisterially articulated the inherent dignity and rights of Africans and of all peoples. Kwame N'Krumah of Ghana, Julius Nyerere of Tanzania[14] Kenneth Kaunda of Zambia, and Nelson Mandela of South Africa fought for self-determination, justice and fundamental human rights. Ambassador Salim Salim of Tanzania, Permanent Representative of Tanzania to the United Nations and President of the UN General Assembly, led legendary fights in the UN General Assembly for justice and for human rights. Paul Lusaka of Zambia, Permanent Representative of Zambia and President of the UN General Assembly, was a champion of universal human rights. So was Joseph N. Garba of Nigeria, President of the UN General Assembly.

In the struggle for equality and non-discrimination, Nelson Mandela was a legendary leader agitating for respect for the inherent dignity and human rights of every human being, including for his people in South Africa. James Jonah of Sierra Leone was the Secretary-General of the 1983 World Conference on Racism and Racial Discrimination, which laid down a landmark programme of activities subsequently taken forward in the Durban Declaration and Programme of Action of 2001.

In the quest for the implementation of human rights world-wide, Boutros Boutros-Ghali of Egypt, as the first African Secretary-General, told the world in his Human Rights Day statement on 10 December, 1992, "Human rights abuses flare up in every part of the world ... A crucial test will be our response to massive violations of human rights."[15]

Kofi Annan as the second African UN Secretary-General made the implementation of universal human one of his central policy objectives during his ten-years as Secretary-General. Ellen Johnson Sirleaf of Libera, as Assistant Administrator of UNDP in charge of African affairs, led a programme on the strengthening of governance in Africa. As President of Liberia and in other capacities, she championed the rights of women. She received the Nobel Peace Prize for her leadership.

14 See, Julius K. Nyerere, Uhuru Na Uhaama. Freedom and Socialism. Oxford, Oxford University Press, 1968; Julius K. Nyerere, Freedom and Development. Uhuru Na Maendeleo, Oxford, Oxford University Press, 1974.

15 UN Press Release SG/SM/1380; HRD/52, 30 November, 1992.

Pierre Sanon of Burkina Fasso, formerly Upper Volta, championed universal human rights when he was Deputy Director of the UN Division of Human Rights, as did Kwado Faka Nyamekye of Ghana, who succeeded him as Deputy Director. Bacre Waly N'Diaye, cited at the beginning of this chapter, distinguished himself on the Board of Amnesty International, as UN Special Rapporteur on arbitrary, summary and extra-judicial executions and as the Director of the New York Office of UN High Commissioner for Human Rights. Pierre Sane of Senegal championed universal human rights as Secretary-General of Amnesty International and as UN Special Rapporteur against racism and racial discrimination. Margaret Sekkaggya of Uganda was a brilliant champion of universal rights as the Chairperson of the Uganda Human Rights Commission and as the UN Special Rapporteur on human rights defenders. She prepared and launched a Guide on the rights of human rights defenders as provided for in the UN Declaration on this topic. At the launch of the Guide, she stated: "Despite the efforts to implement the declaration, human rights defenders continue to face numerous violations … I hope that this essential guide will contribute to the development of a safer and more conducive environment for defenders to be able to carry out their work."[16]

We discuss further below such African contributions to the universality of human rights.

2.2 The Development of Universal Norms

During the consideration of the draft universal declaration of human rights in the Third Committee of the UN General Assembly, the Egyptian representative, Osman Obeid, made the following stirring plea for justice for the peoples of the world: "The principles of human rights should be set forth in clear terms. The peoples of the world would greet with enthusiasm the first action taken by the United Nations to enforce redressment of wrongs."

George Lamptey of Ghana is the father of the concept of a petitions system in UN human rights treaties. It was he who pioneered the proposal that was subsequently adopted as Article 14 of the International Convention on The Elimination of All Forms of Racial Discrimination. Petitions systems would be implemented in subsequent UN human rights treaties, such as the International

16 See," Margaret Sekaggya, an Independent UN expert, launches guide on rights of human rights defenders". http://www.fundsforngos.org/guides/margaret-sakkaggya-independent-expert-launches-guide-human-rights-defenders/ accessed on 7 November, 2021.

Covenant on Civil and Political Rights and the International Convention on the Elimination of All Forms of Discrimination Against Women.

The draft convention on the elimination of racial discrimination that had been drawn up in the then Sub-Commission on Prevention of Discrimination and Protection of Minorities, the Commission on Human Rights and the Economic and Social Council, and transmitted to the Third Committee of the General Assembly, did not contain an article dealing with communications or petitions by individuals. A draft for what would eventually become Article 14 of the Convention was introduced for the first time on the floor of the Third Committee. It took the form of a three-power proposal sponsored by Ghana, Mauritania and the Philippines.[17] It was discussed at the 1361–1363rd meeting of the Third Committee in 1965.

Introducing the three-power proposal, Mr Lamptey said that the new article had been drafted after much thought as it was recognized that it would be controversial. It had been necessary to take into account the sincere wish of many delegations to use the right of petition and communication as an effective weapon against racial discrimination, whilst not losing sight of the fact that many States were jealous of their sovereignty and were reluctant to acknowledge that right.[18]

A perusal of the Summary Records of the Third Committee of the UN General Assembly for 1965, when the convention against racial discrimination was adopted, would show Lamptey introducing the proposal for an optional petitions system and defending it against strong opposition from the then communist Eastern-European countries as well as from their supporters in other parts of the world. Lamptey was resolute and prevailed in the end.

The Summary Record of the 1355th meeting of the Third Committee, on 26 November 1965, shows Lamptey piloting the proposal:

> 38. Mr Lamptey (Ghana) said that the new article ... had been drafted after much thought as it was one of those most likely to lead to controversy.
>
> 39. It had been necessary to take into account the sincere wish of many delegations to use the right of petition and communications as an effective weapon against discrimination. It was also essential not to lose sight of the fact that many States were jealous of their sovereignty and were reluctant to acknowledge that right. The only way

17 A/C.3/L.1291/Add 1.

18 A/C.3/SR.1355, p. 384, paras. 38–39.

to reconcile those opposite points of view was to make optional any measures intended to provide an effective guarantee of that right.

40. ... [H]e pointed out that the draft offered as much choice as it possibly could, since it provided that a State Party to the Convention could at any time declare that it recognized the committee's competence to receive and consider communications from individuals. That paragraph was based on a provision of the Statute of the International Court of Justice ...[19]

The Article, as eventually adopted, Article 14 in the Convention, provided that:

1. A State Party may at any time declare that it recognizes the competence of the Committee [on the Elimination of Racial Discrimination] to receive and consider communications from individuals or groups of individuals within its jurisdiction claiming to be victims of a violation by that State Party of any of the rights set forth in this Convention. No such communication shall be received if it concerns a State Party which has not made such a declaration.

But for George Lamptey of Ghana, this optional petitions system, the first of its kind in a UN human rights treaty, would, purely and simply, not have been adopted.

The Chairperson of the Third Committee of the UN General Assembly which finalised the drafting of the two Covenants on human rights and the Optional Protocol to the civil and political Covenant was a dynamic young representative of Morocco, Ms Halima Embarek Warzazi, then in her twenties. After the Covenants and the Optional Protocol were formally adopted by the General Assembly on 16 December, 1966, she addressed the General Assembly as follows:

I ... must pay a tribute to the spirit which has at all times prevailed in our debates ...

We have had long weeks of discussion and, as a witness who has tried to remain impartial throughout our debates, I am happy to be able to say that the members of the Third Committee have indeed made one of the greatest efforts that could be made in the field of human rights, finally culminating this year in the adoption of the covenants. Although

19 Official Records of the General Assembly, Twentieth Session. Third Committee. Social, Humanitarian and Cultural Questions. Summary Records of Meetings, p. 384.

our discussions have at times been protracted and difficult, they have always been imbued with that spirit of conciliation and friendship which is typical of the Third Committee. We were able to work in that excellent atmosphere because all the members of the Committee, without exception, have proved once again this year, but perhaps even more specifically, how the faith of our delegations prompts them to cooperate in the human cause.

After the unanimous adoption of these two covenants, I do not think I need to say that, despite the differences among our countries, our civilizations, our thinking and our ways of life, we have nevertheless succeeded in proving that, when we are all motivated by the desire to do well, to understand one another and to put ourselves in the position of others whenever necessary, we can accomplish a great task in accordance with the wishes of mankind in all its diversity."[20]

The Nigerian representative on the Third Committee, Adamu Mohammed, was one of the strongest advocates supporting the draft Covenants on human rights that had been prepared by the Commission on Human Rights. His legendary contributions to the debates are recorded for history in the official proceedings of the Third Committee of the General Assembly. When the Covenants were adopted in the Plenary of the General Assembly on 16 December, 1966, he addressed the Assembly in the following terms:

> We believe that in these Covenants lie all the aspirations, the hopes and the protection of the human person. All people the world over, I am sure, will now congratulate the United Nations on this singular and most important achievement since the adoption of the Universal Declaration of Human Rights in 1948.
>
> ...
>
> We consider the Covenants, both in relation to ourselves and to the rest of the world, as a guiding line for this and many future generations.
>
> It is important to have a document such as this in existence. If we are to avoid the conditions which force the human being into rebellion and terrorisms because his rights are not recognized or protected, if we are to live together to achieve the common aims of progress for the human being – whether it be social, economic or political – it is most necessary

20 Official Records of the General Assembly. Twenty First Session. Plenary Meetings. Verbatim Records of Meetings, 1966, Vol. III, 1496 meeting, 16 December, 1966, paras. 78–79.

> that we should understand each other and respect each other. This is one of the many points on which the Covenants we have just adopted seek to give us guidance. It is our hope that before long all States Members of the United Nations will adopt and implement these Covenants with respect to their own countries and peoples.[21]

Underlining the importance of individual petitions for the correction of wrongs, Mr Mohammed concluded his address to the General Assembly as follows:

> There is one vital element regarding the implementation of these Covenants as far as the individual human being is concerned. This vital element is embodied in a separate Protocol to the Covenant on Civil and Political Rights. It is one element which seeks to revolutionize the status of the individual in the achievement of his own rights. This Protocol seeks to give him, although on an extremely limited basis, the right to submit communications when his rights are violated under the Covenant. We believe in this, looking to the future when, it is our hope, the faithful compliance with the provisions of these Covenants will lead to greater understanding between peoples, when it will become necessary for the human being to emerge in the light of what he is and what he should be. The idea of petitions is not new. What is new in the Protocol – which is in fact the right to submit communications – is that it deals with the idea of the submission of communications by an individual to an international body with very limited powers. That is a long leap forward, if we take into consideration the fact that there are countries in Africa today where the people are not even allowed the right of petition within the domestic legal systems of their own countries. We are therefore grateful to see that both Covenants have been adopted unanimously and that the Optional Protocol has been adopted by a majority vote of this Assembly.[22]

The representative of Liberia, Mrs Stevenson, speaking at the same meeting, remarked that the adoption of the International Covenants on Human Rights constituted an extremely valuable contribution to the promotion of respect for human rights and fundamental freedoms. She added:

---

21 Ibid, paras. 117–120.

22 Ibid, para. 122.

> In an era of increasing tension and grave political, economic and social problems, the necessity of defending and confirming at every opportunity the values of the human person cannot be overemphasized. It is an undeniable fact that gross violations of human rights still persist in many parts of the world in the form of racial discrimination, *apartheid* and other forms of human deviation.[23]

There could be no doubt that Africa had played a central part in the shaping of the International Covenants on Human Rights and the Optional Protocol

It was an African eminent jurist, Keba M'Baye, then Chief Justice of Senegal, Member and Chairperson of the UN Commission on Human Rights, who first launched the idea of a right to development. M'baye was so moved by the plight of his ancestors and the impact of slavery on his continent that, in an address at the International Institute of Human Rights in Strasbourg in 1972, he articulated, for the first time, the concept of the right to development.[24]

Nicodeme Ruhashyankiko of Rwanda authored the first global study on the crime of genocide as Special Rapporteur of the former UN Sub-Commission on the Prevention of Discrimination and the Protection of Minorities[25]. C.L.C. Mubanga Chipoya of Zambia, as Special Rapporteur of the same Sub-Commission, did the first global study on the right to leave and return to one's country.[26]

The Secretary-General of the International Year for Disabled Persons was UN Assistant Secretary-General Ms Zala N'Kanza of the then Zaire, now Democratic Republic of the Congo. Ms N'Kanza helped to pioneer the adoption of international norms for the protection of the rights of disabled persons. A major outcome of the International Year of Disabled Persons was the

---

23 Ibid, para. 17.

24 See Keba M'Baye, "Le droit au developpement comme un droit de l'homme » (The right to development as a human rights), Inaugural lecture at the International Institute of Human Rights, Strasburg, France, 1972. See also, Keba M'Baye, "Emergence of the Right to Development as a Human Rights in the Context of the New International Economic Order". Address to a meeting of experts on human rights, human needs, and the establishment of a new international economic order, 16 July, 1979. SS-78/CONF.630/8.

25 Study on the question of the prevention and punishment of the crime of genocide, prepared by Mr Nicodeme Ruhashyankiko, Special Rapporteur appointed by the Sub-Commission at its twenty-fourth session, in 1971 (resolution 7(XXIV), UN Doc. E/EN,4/ Sub.2/ 416).

26 UN doc. E/CN.4/Sub.2/1988/35 and Add.1 and Add 1/Corr.1: "Analysis of current trends and developments regarding the right to leave any country, including one's own, and to return to one's own country", prepared by Mr C.L.C. Mubanga-Chipoya, Special Rapporteur appointed by the Sub-Commission at its thirty-fifth session in 1982 (resolution 1982/23).

formulation of the World Programme of Action concerning Disabled Persons, adopted by the General Assembly on 3 December, 1982. Equalization of opportunities was a central theme of the World Programme of Action and its guiding philosophy for the achievement of full participation of persons with disabilities in all aspects of social and economic life. An important principle underlying this theme was that issues concerning persons with disabilities should not be treated in isolation, but within the context of normal community services.

This author had occasion to discuss with Ms N'Kanza the human rights principles that should be enshrined in the World Programme of Action. Following these discussions, Ms N'Kanza pushed for the inclusion in the World Programme of Action of notable human rights principles such as the following:

> Persons with permanent disabilities who are in need of community support services, aids and equipment to enable them to live as normally as possible both at home and in the community should have access to such services. Those who live with such disabled persons and help them in their daily activities should themselves receive support to enable them to have adequate rest and relaxation and an opportunity to take care of their own needs.
>
> The principle of equal rights for the disabled and non-disabled implies that the needs of each and every individual are of equal importance, that these needs must be made the basis for the planning of societies, and that all resources must be employed in such a way as to ensure, for every individual, equal opportunity for participation. Disability policies should ensure the access of the disabled to all community services.[27]

Francis Deng, one of the first African staff members of the UN Division of Human Rights, was a strong advocate of the idea that the sovereignty of Governments entailed their responsibility to uphold and protect universal human rights. In a publication, *Sovereignty as Responsibility: Conflict Management in Africa*, he and his co-authors asserted that sovereignty could no longer be seen as a protection against interference, but as a charge of responsibility where the state is accountable to both domestic and external constituencies. Sovereignty as Responsibility presented a framework to guide both national governments and the international community in discharging their respective responsibilities. Approaching conflict management from the perspective of the responsibilities

27 World Programe of Action Concerning Disabled Persons, adopted by the General Assembly on 3 December, 1982 by its resolution 37/52, Chapter on "Equalization of opportunities."

of sovereignty provided a framework for evaluating government accountability. It provided standards to guide performance and sharpen tools of conflict prevention.[28]

Francis Deng also led the process that produced the internationally acclaimed *Guiding Principles on Internal Displacement*. Deng steered the adoption of the Guiding Principles in his capacity as Special Representative of the Secretary-General on Internally Displaced Persons.[29] In an Introductory Note to the UN publication of the Guiding Principles, Dr Deng wrote:

> The international community is confronted with the monumental task of ensuring protection for persons forcibly uprooted from their homes by violent conflicts, gross violations of human rights and other traumatic events, but who remain within the borders of their own countries. Nearly always they suffer from severe deprivation, hardship and discrimination. It is to meet this challenge that the Guiding Principles on Internal Displacement were developed.
>
> The Principles identify the rights and guarantees relevant to protection of the internally displaced in all phases of displacement. They provide protection against arbitrary displacement, offer a basis for protection and assistance during displacement, and set forth guarantees for safe return, resettlement and reintegration, Although they do not constitute a binding instrument, these Principles reflect and are consistent with international human rights and humanitarian law and analogous refugee law.[30]

2.3 Self-Determination and the Quest for Justice

African freedom fighters such as Kwame N'Krumah, Julius Nyerere, Kenneth Kaunda and Nelson Mandela fought valiantly to end colonialism and injustice and to enshrine the principle of self-determination, celebrated in the opening articles of the two international covenants on human rights: "All peoples have the right of self-determination. By virtue of that right they freely determine their political status and freely pursue their economic, social and cultural development."

---

28 See Francis M. Deng, et. al,1996. Sovereignty as Responsibility. Conflict Management in Africa. The Brookings Institution, Washington. D.C.

29 See, UN Office for the Coordination of Humanitarian Affairs (OCHA), Guiding Principles on Internal Displcement. OCHA/IDP/2004/01; UN Publication, E/CN.4/1998/53/Add2.

30 Ibid.

The human rights philosophy of Nelson Mandela is a fitting way of elucidating the African quest for Justice. A 1997 publication of key pronouncements of Nelson Mandela[31] revealed the following insights into his philosophy:

On Humanity: To deny any person their human rights is to challenge their very humanity.[32]

On Freedom: No power on earth can stop an oppressed people determined to win their freedom.[33]

On Democracy: Democracy and Human Rights are inseparable.[34]

On Oppression: To overthrow oppression has been sanctioned by humanity and is the highest aspiration of every free man.[35]

On Liberation: The People are their own liberators.[36]

On The South African Freedom Charter: The Freedom Charter is a political programme born of our struggle and rooted in South African realities. It has received international acclaim as an outstanding human rights document.[37]

On the South African Constitution: Respect for human life, liberty and well-being must be enshrined as rights beyond the power of any force to diminish.

The key to the protection of any minority is to put core civil and political rights beyond the reach of temporary majorities by guaranteeing them as fundamental human rights, enshrined in a democratic constitution.[38]

On a Bill of Rights: A Bill of Rights is an important statement about the nature of power relations in any society.[39]

On Government: That the will of the people is the basis of the authority of government is a principle universally acknowledged as sacred throughout the civilized world, and constitutes the basic foundations of freedom and justice.[40]

On Society: The great lesson of our time is that no regime can survive if it acts above the heads of the ordinary citizens of the country.[41]

---

31 Source: *In the Words of Nelson Mandela. A Little Pocketbook*. Edited by Jennifer Crwys-Williams. Penguin 1997.

32 Ibid., p.39.

33 Ibid., p. 26.

34 Ibid., p. 19.

35 Ibid., p. 51.

36 Ibid., p. 44.

37 Ibid., p. 28.

38 Ibid., p. 18.

39 Ibid., p. 8.

40 Ibid., p. 29.

41 Ibid., p. 74.

On Politics: Political division, based on colour, is entirely artificial and, when it disappears, so will the domination of one colour group by another.[42]

On Virtue: Virtue and generosity will be rewarded in ways that one cannot know.[43] .

On Ubuntu: The spirit of *Ubuntu* – that profound African sense that we are human only through the humanity of other beings – is not a parochial phenomenon, but has added globally to our common search for a better world..[44]

On Self-Respect: If you are in harmony with yourself, you may meet a lion without fear, because he respects anyone with self-confidence.[45]

On Poverty and the dignity of the individual: It should never be that the anger of the poor should be the finger of accusation pointed at all of us because we failed to respond to the cries of the people for food, for shelter, for the dignity of the individual.[46]

2.4 Equality and Non-discrimination

A historic breakthrough in UN activities against racism and racial discrimination was the 1983 World Conference against Racism and Racial Discrimination. The conference's adoption of its Declaration and Programme of Action owed much to the efforts of its Secretary-General, UN Assistant-Secretary-General James Jonah of Sierra Leone. The Programme of Action adopted by the Conference focused on:

- Action to combat *apartheid.*
- Education, teaching and training to create an atmosphere for the eradication of racism and racial discrimination.
- Measures for the promotion and protection of persons belonging to minority groups, indigenous population and people and migrant workers who were subjected to racial discrimination.
- Recourse procedures for victims of racial discrimination.
- Implementation of the International Convention on the Elimination of All Forms of Racial Discrimination and other related international instruments.
- National legislation and institutions.

42 Ibid., p. 61.
43 Ibid., p. 86.
44 Ibid., p. 82.
45 Ibid., p. 74.
46 Ibid., p. 62.

- Seminars and studies.
- Action by non-governmental organizations.
- International cooperation.

Addressing the opening of the conference as its Secretary-General, James Jonah told it:

> During the past year, I have visited all regions comprising the membership of the Organization and I have been able to learn first-hand the hopes and aspirations of Member States regarding the outcome of the present Conference ….
>
> In my contacts with Governments, I discern a broad agreement that racism and racial discrimination constitute global phenomena warranting urgent and appropriate international action. On the national level, a number of Governments have enacted legislation to eradicate the evils of racism and racial discrimination. Nevertheless, it remains true that the virulence of racial discrimination is on the increase, particularly in countries that have very high unemployment."[47]

Two decades later, speaking at the opening of a follow-up conference in Durban, South Africa, UN Secretary-General Kofi Annan declared:

> Let us remember that no one is born a racist. Children learn racism as they grow up, from the society around them – and too often the stereotypes are reinforced, deliberately or inadvertently, by the mass media. We must not sacrifice freedom of the press, but we must actively refute pseudo-scientific arguments and oppose negative images with positive ones – teaching our children and our fellow-citizens not to fear diversity, but to cherish it.[48]

2.5 Universal Implementation of Human Rights

On the eve of the Vienna World Conference on Human Rights of 1993, Boutros Boutros-Ghali, the first African Secretary-General told the world on the occasion of Human Rights Day 1992 that the adoption of the Universal Declaration

---

47 See, Report of the Second World Conference to Combat Racism and Racial Discrimination. UN Doc. A/CONF.119/26. United Nations, New York, 1983, pp.41–42.

48 Report of the World Conference against Racism, Racial Discrimination, Xenophobia and Related Intolerance, UN doc. A/CONF.189/12, 2001, p 133.

had profoundly affected human history. The Declaration had become the cornerstone of the international system. Despite this achievement, human rights abuses were flaring up in every part of the globe. "A crucial test will be our response to massive violations on human rights."

Another test, he added, "lies in our understanding of the relationship between development and human rights. Full human dignity means not only freedom from torture, but also freedom from starvation. It means freedom to vote as it means the right to education. It means freedom of belief as it means the right to health. It means the right to enjoy all rights without discrimination. And true development requires a solid basis of democracy and popular participation."[49]

In his Human Rights Day statement the following year, Secretary-General Boutros-Ghali called for an urgent strengthening of worldwide efforts to protect basic human rights worldwide in an effort to halt abuses of economic, social, cultural, political and civil rights which were occurring "with frightening regularity". Human rights, Boutros-Ghali added, "reflect our common humanity." But there was "far to go".[50] "Attaining the goals of the Vienna Declaration will be a major undertaking for the United Nations. It will not be easy to achieve. A positive attitude among all parties involved will be indispensable. The task before us is monumental, but it also is possible to achieve."[51]

My friend, Assistant Secretary-General for Human Rights Ibrahima Fall of Senegal, who had steered the Vienna World Conference on Human Rights as its Secretary-General, issued a five-point call for action to begin realizing the mandate of the World Conference on Human Rights. He stressed the following minimum necessary steps:

- Universal ratification of the core human rights conventions should be pursued with renewed vigour. These included the Convention on the Rights of the Child, and its full integration into national action plans by 1995; the Convention on the Elimination of all Forms of Discrimination against Women by the year 2000; the two Covenants on civil and political rights and on economic, social and cultural rights; and the Convention against Torture by the year 2000.
- Balancing the implementation of human rights, integrating economic, social and cultural rights with civil and political rights.

49 UN Press Release SG/SM/1380; HRD/52, 30 November, 1992.
50 UN Press Release HR/3606, 8 December, 1993, p. 1.
51 Ibid.

- Strengthening the efficiency of implementing human rights through the United Nations Commission on Human Rights, human rights treaties, monitoring bodies of various covenants, preventive diplomacy, and the participation of non-governmental organizations. This included better coordination within the United Nations system regarding the implementation of human rights, especially in the context of linking human rights and peace-keeping and human rights and development.
- Putting the rights of women in the mainstream of all human rights.
- Strengthening the United Nations Centre for Human Rights.

Human rights, Mr Fall continued, "are the substance of human life."[52]

2.6 Conclusion

The foregoing is only a selection of the numerous African contributions to the shaping of universal human rights norms. They could be expanded upon considerably, and the contributions of many more African personalities could be documented. But what has been presented above suffices to demonstrate not only Africans' commitment to universal human rights, but their contributions to shaping the content of universality. Africans placed their stamp on the drafting of the International Convention on the Elimination of All Forms of Racial Discrimination, the International Covenants on Human Rights and the Optional Protocol to the civil and political covenant. Africans gave the world the concept of the right to development, and the concept of sovereignty as responsibility. Boutros-Boutros Ghali and Kofi Annan championed the universal implementation of human rights as did James O.C. Jonah, Ibrahima Fall and Bacre Wale N'Diaye.

52 UN Press Release HR/3606, 8 December, 1993, p. 3.

CHAPTER 3

Africa, the United Nations and the Universality of Human Rights

Abstract

This chapter argues that as Member States in the world community, all African Governments are bound by international customary law, by treaties to which they have subscribed, and by general principles of law. As Member States of the United Nations, they are also bound by the rules of international law developed by the world body, as well as by the jurisprudence of its International Court of Justice and as those of treaty-monitoring bodies such as the UN Human Rights Committee. It also examines the concept of universality and its bases.

3.1 Introduction

There are fifty-four African States among the 193 Members of the United Nations, a full quarter of the membership. Like all Member States they have binding obligations under the Charter, as elaborated upon by the Universal Declaration of Human Rights, to uphold human rights in their own countries and in the world at large. There are thirteen African States out of the forty-seven that comprise the membership of the UN Human Rights Council and their charge, as Members of the Council, is to uphold universal human rights. All African States participate in the Universal Periodic Review of the Human Rights Council, and in their participation in the system they all profess adherence to the universality of human rights.

Many African States are States Parties to United Nations human rights treaties such as the Convention on the Rights of the Child, and cooperate with the supervision of the monitoring organs established by those treaties. They engage in an ongoing process of international cooperation for the implementation of treaties such as the International Covenants on human rights which, in large measure contain universal human rights norms, such as equality of treatment and the prohibition of torture.

Many African States have also subscribed to Optional petitions procedures, cooperate in the processing of individual petitions, and cooperate in the implementation of decisions handed down by the supervisory treaty organs. Among

 | DOI:10.1163/9789004520646_004

such decisions are spectacular cases affirming the universality of human rights, such as the principle of equality in the case of Shirin Aumeeruddy-Cziffra and 19 Other Mauritian Women v. Mauritius, a case involving gender equality in Mauritius.[1]

In this chapter we shall look at these different dimensions of universality in Africa's participation at the UN. We begin with the obligations of States Members under international law, the Charter of the United Nations, and the Universal Declaration of Human Rights.

3.2 Obligations under International Law, the Charter and the Universal Declaration

Article 38 of the Statute of the International Court of Justice is an authoritative statement of the sources of international law, binding on every and all States. This article enumerates three main sources of international law: treaties agreed to by a State, international customary law, and general principles of law in the major legal systems of the world. In addition to these law-creating sources of international law, there are two, subsidiary, law-determining ones: judicial decisions and opinions of highly qualified international lawyers.

The Charter of the United Nations, which is binding on all Member States of the Organization, contains universal human rights norms, such as the equal dignity and rights of every human being, and the prohibition of discrimination on grounds of race, religion or gender. A treaty such as the Convention on the Rights of the Child, which has been accepted as binding by every Member State of the United Nations, bar one, contains universal norms of human rights. The Convention on the Prevention and Punishment of Genocide also contains universal human rights norms.

On the occasion of the twenty-fifth anniversary of the United Nations the UN General Assembly, based on the deliberations of eminent lawyers on a Special Committee it had established on this topic, adopted the Declaration on Principles of International Law concerning Friendly Relations and Cooperation among States in accordance with the Charter of the United Nations.[2] This Declaration is widely considered a codification of the key principles of international law in the UN Charter.

1 CCPR/C/12/D/35/1978.

2 GA resolution 2625 (XXV), adopted on 24 October, 1970.

In elaborating on the duty of States to cooperate with one another in accordance with the Charter, the General Assembly affirmed that States have the duty to cooperate with one another in accordance with the Charter. To this end, "States shall cooperate in the promotion of universal respect for, and observance of, human rights and fundamental freedoms for all, and in the elimination of all forms of racial discrimination and all forms of religious intolerance."

Through practice over time, all States of the world have come to be bound by the norms of international customary law. In the field of human rights these would include universal human rights norms such as the prohibition of genocide, slavery, torture, and racial discrimination. Among the general principles of law that may be distilled from the various legal systems of the world one could include the principle of the inherent dignity and equality of all human beings.[3]

All States of the world are bound by what are technically known as norms of *jus cogens*. A manual of international law published in South Africa describes such norms neatly:

> *jus cogens* denotes the peremptory nature of certain norms. According to Brownlie, the least controversial examples of such norms are the prohibition of the use of force in international relations, the law of genocide and crimes against humanity, the principle on racial discrimination, and the rules prohibiting piracy and the trade in slaves.[4]

Article 53 of the Vienna Convention on the Law of Treaties famously stated that a treaty will be void if, at the time of its conclusion, it conflicts with a peremptory norm of general international law. Such a norm is one that is "accepted and recognized by the international community of States as a whole as a norm from which no derogation is permitted and which can be modified only by a subsequent norm of general international law having the same character".[5]

There are also norms of international law that are known as norms 'erga omnes'. Erga omnes obligations have been defined by the International Court of Justice as obligations a state owes 'towards the international community as a whole', as opposed to obligations that arise vis-à-vis another state. In contemporary international law, such obligations arise, according to the Court, from

3 See on this, Drucilla Cornell and others, The Dignity Jurisprudence of the Constitutional Court of South Africa. 2 volumes. New York, Fordham University Press, 2013.

4 LoSA, Constitutional Law of South Africa, Chapter 30 on International Law by Hennie Styrdom and Kevin Hopkins, accessed on the internet on 26 July, 2020, #30 (3).

5 Ibid.

the "outlawing of acts of aggression and of genocide, as also from the principles and rules concerning the basic rights of the human person, including protection from slavery and racial discrimination."[6]

In *Prosecutor v. Furundzija*, the International Criminal Tribunal for the former Yugoslavia (ICTY) clarified the distinction between *erga omnes* and *jus cogens*. In ruling that the prohibition of torture had acquired the status of *jus cogens*, the ICTY took the view that when it came to international enforcement:

> the violation of such an [*erga omnes*] obligation [to enforce the prohibition of torture] simultaneously constituted a breach of the correlative right of all members of the international community and gives rise to a claim for compliance accruing to each and every member, which then has the right to insist on fulfilment of the obligation or in any case to call for the breach to be discontinued.[7]

At the Vienna World Conference on Human Rights, held in 1993, the Conference declared that "The universal nature of these rights and freedoms is beyond question."[8] Seventeen years later, in the Millennium Declaration, world leaders gathered at the United Nations declared: "We resolve . . . to respect fully and uphold the Universal Declaration of Human Rights; to strive for the full protection and promotion in all our countries of civil, political, economic, social and cultural rights for all."[9]

The UN Summit of World Leaders in 2005 reaffirmed the centrality of human rights in the UN's work and endorsed the responsibility to protect.[21] The world leaders declared their readiness to refer genocide, ethnic cleansing, crimes against humanity, and war crimes to the UN Security Council.

During his tenure, Secretary-General Kofi Annan had to deal with numerous crises, conflicts, and governance problems in Africa. He had to contend with assertions by some African leaders that international human rights norms were foreign impositions and did not correspond to African culture and realities. He met these challenges head on in an address to the OAU summit in Harare on 2 June 1997. He declared:

---

6 Ibid.

7 Ibid. 121 International law Reports (2002), p. 213, at p. 260.

8 Vienna Declaration, paragraph 1.

9 Millennium Declaration, paragraph 25.

> [L]et us dedicate ourselves to a new doctrine for African politics: where democracy has been usurped let us do whatever is in our power to restore it to its rightful owners, the people.
>
> Verbal condemnation, though necessary and desirable, is not sufficient. We must also ostracize and isolate putschists.
>
> The success of Africa's third wave depends equally on respect for fundamental human rights. The conflicts which have disfigured our continent have, all too often, been accompanied by massive human rights violations.
>
> Africa can no longer tolerate and accept as *faits accomplis,* coups against elected governments, and the illegal seizure of power by military cliques. I am aware of the fact that some view this concern as a luxury of the rich countries for which Africa is not ready. I know that others treat it as an imposition, if not a plot, by the industrialized west. I find these thoughts truly demeaning, demeaning of the yearning for human dignity that resides in every African heart.
>
> Do not African mothers weep when their sons or daughters are killed or maimed by agents of repressive rule? Are not African fathers saddened when their children are unjustly jailed or tortured? Is not Africa as a whole impoverished when even one of its brilliant voices is silenced?
>
> We cannot afford to lose one life, spare one idea, relinquish one hope, if we are to succeed on our chosen course. So, I say this to you, my brothers and sisters, that *human rights are African rights, and I call upon you to ensure that all Africans are able fully to enjoy them.*[10]
>
> Let us work together and with the United Nations to develop good governance and respect for the rule of law. When we succeed, Africa will have taken a great step forward."[11]

The Summit of World Leaders in 2005 reaffirmed the centrality of human rights in the UN's work and endorsed the responsibility to protect. The world leaders declared their readiness to refer genocide, ethnic cleansing, crimes against humanity, and war crimes to the UN Security Council.

The universality of human rights must be vigorously upheld. It rests on the idea that there is a minimum body of basic human rights that belongs to every human being regardless of his or her country of origin or philosophical,

---

10 Emphasis supplied.

11 Text in the possession of the author.

religious, or other beliefs. Regional or national charters may add to the universal body of human rights but may not detract from them.

The validity of the universality of human rights is not lessened by the fact that, in practice, human rights are violated in many parts of the world. Rights exist even if they are breached, and the challenge is to work for their implementation and protection. We discuss briefly next universality as an idea, a goal, a normative concept, its democratic test, the basis of universality, and problems of implementation.

3.3 Universality as an Idea, a Goal, and a Normative Concept

The concept of human rights has developed over the centuries and has roots in all of the major world religions. In turn, these principles have been codified in international legal instruments, namely the Universal Declaration of Human Rights (UDHR). Since its proclamation in 1948, the UDHR has been re-endorsed in international and regional treaties and in authoritative policy pronouncements by governments and people in Africa, the Americas, Asia, and Europe. This certainly underscores the universality of human rights.

Some years ago, the late Senator José Diokno of the Philippines summarily dispatched spurious arguments about cultural diversity that diminished universality:

> Two justifications for authoritarianism in Asian developing countries are currently fashionable . . . One is that Asian societies are authoritarian and paternalistic and so need governments that are also authoritarian and paternalistic; that Asia's hungry masses are too concerned with filling their stomachs to concern themselves with civil liberties and political freedoms; that the Asian conception of freedom differs from that of the West; that, in short, Asians are not fit for human rights.
>
> Another is that developing countries must sacrifice freedom temporarily to achieve the rapid economic development that their exploding populations and rising expectations demand; in short, that governments must be authoritarian to promote development.
>
> Well, the first justification is racist nonsense. And I will say no more than that. The second is a lie: authoritarianism is not needed for development; what it is needed for is to maintain the status quo.
>
> Regardless . . . of what dictators and social scientists may say, we Asians know that the loss of freedom does not lead to a better life. On

the contrary, we know that life cannot become better – it cannot even be good – unless people are free.[3]

3.3.1 *Universality as a Goal*

If human beings have so many things in common, is it strange to want to preserve these common characteristics and to reach out in mutual support and cooperation? Can we protect the environment or keep the air clean unless we do so together? Is it wrong to say that every human being should have an equal opportunity to develop his or her potential? Is universality then not valid as a goal for common aspirations?

The idea that all human beings in the first quarter of the twenty-first century possess, as part of their birth-right, a core of inalienable rights is not disputed. What is sometimes debated is the content of particular rights and the need for change. This is a legitimate debate. The international human rights treaties inspired by the UDHR contain amendment procedures that could deal with claims for modernization or updating. The UDHR, however, stands on its own as a historic, inspirational document. The universality of core human rights is quite compatible with cultural diversity, and the argument of cultural diversity should not challenge the core universal human rights but, rather, might influence the mode and manner of their application in particular societies. One can, for example, proclaim freedom of religion or belief, while leaving it to each person to choose a religion or belief. The notion of good faith in applying universal human rights norms comes into the picture here.

The existence of duties does not negate the universality of human rights. Rather, as is explicitly recognized in article 29 of the UDHR, everyone has duties to his or her community. That same article further states that one may be subject only to such limitations as determined by law in the exercise of rights and freedoms. Such limitations may only be for the purpose of securing due recognition and respect for the rights and freedoms of others and of meeting the requirements of morality, public order, and general welfare.

3.3.2 *Universality as a Normative Concept*

In the history of the international community, has it not been found necessary to postulate universal norms? And have the norms not been useful? Is not the very notion of international law grounded in the concept of a law applicable to all communities – at least in respect of imperative norms of public policy (*jus cogens*) and international customary law? Would order be possible in the international community without a system of norms of universal applicability and validity? The answer can only be in the negative. That being the case, is it not entirely natural and proper that the stock of norms of international law would also include norms of universal human rights?

By the very act of joining the organization, all UN member states commit to the principle of universality contained in the Charter and the UDHR. The commitment to universality is itself universal. When the Commission on Human Rights began drafting the UDHR in 1947, Charles Malik of Lebanon urged that the commission base itself on the following four principles: (a) the human person is more important than the racial, national, or other group to which he may belong; (b) the human person's most sacred and inviolable possessions are in his or her mind and conscience, enabling the person to perceive the truth, choose freely, and to exist; (c) any social pressure on the part of the state, religion, or race involving the automatic consent of the human person is reprehensible; (d) the social group to which the individual belongs may, like the human person himself or herself, be wrong or right. The person alone is the judge.

The spirit animating the UDHR drafting committee members is inspiring to read, even decades years later. At an early drafting session, Rene Cassin proposed that two or three fundamental principles be incorporated in the outline: a) the unity of the human race or family; (b) the idea that every human being has a right to be treated like every other human being; (c) the concept of solidarity and fraternity among men.

Hernán Santa Cruz of Chile opined that the drafting committee must draw up a charter of human rights, giving it not only legal but real human content. He further suggested that this charter should be a spiritual guide for humanity, enumerating the rights that must be respected everywhere.

The UDHR's opening article was significantly influenced by Asia. During the second session of the drafting committee, on 5 December 1947, Carlos Romulo of the Philippines proposed to redraft article 1 as discussed in the first session in June 1947 on the basis of Cassin's draft proposal. In response, the chairman invited the French and Philippine representatives to submit a new text of the article. At the ninth meeting of the drafting committee, on 10 December 1947, Romulo proposed the following text: "All men are brothers. Being endowed by nature with reason and conscience, they are born free and possess equal dignity and rights."

After further discussion, the following text proposed by the Philippines and France was adopted: "All men are born free and equal in dignity and rights. They are endowed with reason and conscience and should act towards one another like brothers." With some subsequent polishing, the following is what was adopted as the UDHR's opening article: "All human beings are born free and equal in dignity and rights. They are endowed with reason and conscience and should act towards one another in a spirit of brotherhood."

The Egyptian representative, Osman Obeid, made a case for including a mention of individuals' duties as a corollary to his or her rights. He made the following stirring plea for justice for the peoples of the world: "The principles of human rights should be set forth in clear terms. The peoples of the world would greet with enthusiasm the first action taken by the United Nations to enforce redressment of wrongs."

Representatives from Africa, Asia, the Americas, and Europe thus influenced the drafting of the UDHR. In the drafting process, detailed draft declarations were submitted by Chile, Cuba, and Panama. In compiling materials from all over the globe to aid in drafting the declaration, the secretariat drew on the constitutions and legislation of 55 countries from Africa, Asia, Latin America, and Eastern Europe. Only 14 were from Western countries.

Developing countries also were actively involved. The Philippines proposed an article stating that everyone had the right to participate in their government, both directly or indirectly, through elections that are periodic, free, and conducted by secret ballot. The Panamanian representative proposed an article declaring that the state has a duty to maintain comprehensive arrangements to promote health, prevent sickness and accident, and provide medical care and compensation for the loss of livelihood.

Charles Malik of Lebabon argued that social and economic rights and the problem of discrimination were very important and should form part of the instrument. P C. Chang of China called for a document that would accord with the spirit and atmosphere of the post-war era and argued that the document should reflect freedom from want. India tabled a draft declaration that included the following statement: "Every human being has the right of equality, without distinction of race, sex, language, religion, nationality or political belief."

This is a mere sampling of the defining contributions of the representatives from Africa, Asia, and Latin America in drafting the UDHR. At the World Conference on Human Rights in 1993, the representatives, assembled from around the world, reaffirmed the universality of human rights in the most emphatic terms.

The UDHR has inspired regional instruments to protect human rights throughout the globe, all of which have reaffirmed its precepts. This may be seen in the constitution of the OAU (now the African Union), the African Charter on Human and People's Rights, the Arab Charter on Human Rights, the Cairo Islamic Declaration on Human Rights, the LAWASIA Statement of Basic Principles of Human Rights, the American Convention on Human Rights, the

ASEAN Charter on Human Rights, and the European Convention on Human Rights. These endorsements of the UDHR bear witness to its universal status.

There is an irrefutable democratic test that confirms the concept of the universality of rights. It is a simple matter. Just ask any human being: Would you like to live or be killed arbitrarily? Would you like to be tortured or enslaved? Would you like to live free or be in prison? Would you like to be in bondage? Would you like to have a say in how you are governed? The democratic test of universality is the basis for its strongest affirmation.

3.4 The Bases of Universality

The bases of the universality of human rights are: (1) all human beings claim their inherent human rights; (2) the common humanity of all human beings and the inherency of rights; (3) the formal affirmation and reaffirmation of human rights in consensual processes of authoritative decision-making bodies such as the GA and world conferences on human rights.

There may, indeed, be discussion about whether every internationally proclaimed human right is universal or if global consensus is lacking regarding a particular asserted right. There was, at one stage, for example, a lively debate about the right to change one's religion or belief. This right was included in the UDHR but not in the International Covenant on Civil and Political Rights and was finessed in the 1992 Declaration on Freedom of Religion or Belief. Where a particular human right is contested by one or more government or group, the matter must be assessed by referring to the tests of inherency and consensus.

When a right is contested, recourse may be had to the principle of inherency, namely that one should enjoy certain rights from the very nature of one's common humanity. The example of the right to change one's religion or belief may be cited. One can understand religions or laws prohibiting religious proselytizing or forbidding campaigns to convince people to change religions. But if an individual decides to change her or his religion or belief, how can this be forbidden by any religion or law? The universality of the right to change one's religion or belief would therefore rest in the principle of inherency.

There are repeated instances of the reaffirmation of consensus over the universality of human rights in authoritative fora of the international community such as the Vienna World Conference on Human Rights, the Millennium Declaration, and the outcome document of the Summit of World Leaders in 2005.

The Vienna conference reaffirmed all states' solemn commitment to fulfil their obligations to promote universal respect for, observance of, and protection of all human rights and fundamental freedoms in accordance with the UN Charter, other instruments relating to human rights, and international law. In ringing terms, it proclaimed that: "The universal nature of these rights and freedoms is beyond question."

The Millennium Declaration reaffirmed the UN's commitment to the Charter's Purposes and Principles, "which have proved timeless and universal. Indeed, their relevance and capacity to inspire have increased, as nations and peoples have become increasingly interconnected and interdependent." It pledged: "We resolve . . . to respect fully and uphold the Universal Declaration of Human Rights; to strive for the full protection and promotion in all our countries of civil, political, economic, social and cultural rights for all."[19]

The GA considered certain fundamental values essential to international relations in the twenty-first century. These included: freedom, equality, solidarity, tolerance, respect for nature, and shared responsibility.

It has been argued that the universality of human rights is belied by the fact that these rights are not respected in practice or are grossly violated in many parts of the world. Lack of implementation is certainly a feature of our contemporary world. So are gross violations of human rights. But this is not an argument against universality. In national legal systems, the validity of laws is not belied by the fact that many are breached. This is an issue of law and order and protection.

An individual's rights are not taken away because they are not respected or are violated. This is a challenge of universal implementation and protection that the entire international human rights movement is striving to address.

3.4.1 *African States' Participation in UN Organs, such as the Human Rights Council and Its Universal Periodic Review*

As Members of the United Nations, indeed more than a full quarter of its membership, African States participate integrally and have a strong impact in the UN General Assembly, the Security Council and in organs like the Human Rights Council. African Governments thus help draft new global human rights norms, participate in monitoring their implementation, and participate in their enforcement through the Security Council. All of this may be summarised in a single sentence: Africa partakes integrally in the universality of human rights at the United Nations.

African States hold thirteen seats on the 47-member Human Rights Council and exercise a pronounced influence on the actions of the Council. By its very terms of reference, the Human Rights Council is pledged to uphold the universality of human rights and their protection through cooperative endeavours.

Africa thus partakes integrally of the universality of human rights at the United Nations.

Every African State has participated in the Universal Periodic Review system operated by the Human Rights Council and every African State has formally confirmed to the Council that it subscribes to the universality of human rights. Africa thus partakes integrally in the universality of UN human rights norms.

In Africa itself there is the African Peer Review Mechanism in which African governments strive to uphold universal and African norms of human rights. The universality of human rights is thus part of the law and governing philosophy of Africa.[12]

The UN in general, and African States in particular, recognize that the concept of a national protection system is one of the most strategic for the universal realization of human rights. The protection of human rights should take place in one's country, where one lives and comes face to face with authority or power. Every country should have in place an adequate and effective national protection system. This is a basic duty of governments, which exist to advance and protect the dignity and rights of their people. It was in this sense that Article 21 of the Universal Declaration of Human Rights affirmed that the will of the people shall be the basis of the authority of government. This will, shall be expressed in periodic and genuine elections which shall be by universal and equal suffrage and shall be held by secret vote or by equivalent free voting procedures. Article 25 of the International Covenant on Civil and Political Rights states that everyone shall have the right and the opportunity, without any of the distinctions mentioned in article 2 and without unreasonable restrictions (a) to take part in the conduct of public affairs, directly or through freely chosen representatives; (b) to vote and to be elected at genuine periodic elections which shall be by universal and equal suffrage and shall be held by secret ballot, guaranteeing the free expression of the will of the electors; (c) to have access, on general terms of equality, to public service in his or her country.

Even before the adoption of the Universal Declaration of Human Rights, the Economic and Social Council, in 1946, had recognized that national implementation arrangements and human rights information and education would be essential to take forward the task of implementing the provisions of the Charter and the eventual declaration universally. The Council invited Member States to consider the desirability of establishing information groups or local human rights committees to collaborate with them in furthering the work of

12 See, further, Bertrand Ramcharan, The UN Human Rights Council. Law, Policy, Politics, Leiden, Brill Nijhoff, 2015. Eric Tistounet, The UN Human Rights Council. A Practical Anatomy. London, Routledge, 2020.

the Commission on Human Rights. The former Commission on Human Rights, early on, highlighted these two aspects and decided to give them particular attention.

The attention given to both subjects, however, would be spasmodic in subsequent years. The Commission did call for reports from the Secretariat on the topic and also mandated the organization of world-wide seminars on the role of national institutions in the promotion and protection of human rights. A UN Seminar on National Institutions for the Promotion and Protection of Human Rights, held in 1978, put forward a set of helpful guidelines for the functioning of national human rights institutions. Those guidelines were further built upon in the Principles relating to the Status of National Institutions (The Paris Principles), which were endorsed by the General Assembly in its resolution 48/134 of 20 December, 1993.

The Paris Principles called for national institutions to have responsibilities such as: submitting recommendations, proposals and reports on matters relating to human rights to the Government, Parliament, or other competent bodies; promoting conformity of national laws and practices with international human rights standards; encouraging ratification and implementation of international standards; contributing to the reporting procedures under international instruments; assisting in formulating and executing human rights teaching and research programmes and increasing public awareness of human rights through information and education; and cooperating with the United Nations, regional institutions and national institutions of other countries.

In 2003, the then High Commissioner for Human Rights wrote to all Governments inviting them to provide concise summaries of their national protection systems under the following headings: 1. In what ways are the provisions of the principal human rights instruments and treaties reflected in the constitution of the country? 2. Is there an oversight process on the reflection of international human rights norms in national legislation? 3. What is the experience of the judiciary in drawing upon the provisions of international human rights norms when considering cases before them? 4. Are there any specific arrangements to promote human rights education in the country? 5. What specialized national human rights institutions are in existence and which of their good practices can be highlighted? 6. Are there arrangements to detect and anticipate threats to human rights of groups at risk?

A report that the Office of High Commissioner submitted to the Commission in 2004 summarized the replies of some three dozen countries. It showed that each country had positive experiences to report but that few of them had previously thought methodically about the six questions in their policy and governmental frameworks. The aim of the exercise was precisely to encourage each country to consider the six questions as a policy framework and, eventually, to publish a world report on the national protection systems of all countries of the world.[13]

As part of his reform programme, and as suggested by the Office of High Commissioner, Secretary-General Kofi Annan had called on the different parts of the United Nations system to concert their efforts to support the endeavours of Governments to develop, or enhance, their national protection systems. Pursuant to this decision, a programme of cooperation was worked out, which is still continuing, to help support the enhancement of national protection systems. The aim of the process was two-fold: to respond positively to requests by Governments for support in strengthening their national protection systems; and to follow the recommendations of the human rights treaty bodies and the human rights special procedures and to see discreetly in what areas a government might be in need of assistance. A national protection system, as advanced by the Office of High Commissioner and by the Secretary-General, has the following key dimensions that we shall discuss below: constitutional, legislative, judicial, institutional, educational, and preventive. In addition, it requires an independent and efficient judiciary and law enforcement systems, and human rights education. National human rights plans of action can also help reinforce a national protection system.

3.4.2 *Constitutional Dimension*

The constitutional structure of a country is a matter for the sovereign choice of its people. However, three issues require particular attention and scrutiny from the perspectives of international human rights law: first its fundamental human rights guarantees; second, its judicial institutions; and third, its national institutions for the protection of human rights.

Fundamental human rights guarantees in the constitution or the bill of rights, if there is one, should not be less but may be more than what is provided for in international human rights law. Each country should be able to show that it has done two things: first, that it has methodically made a comparison between the provisions of its fundamental human rights guarantees and those in the principal international human rights instruments; second that rights guaranteed in international customary law, particularly norms of *jus cogens*, are among its constitutional human rights guarantees.

The Third Restatement of the Foreign Relations Laws of the USA provides a good summary of rights that are guaranteed in international law:

---

13 UN doc. E/CN.4/2004/12 and Addenda.

A state is obliged to respect the human rights of persons subject to its jurisdiction that it has (a) undertaken to respect by international agreements; (b) that states generally are bound to respect as a matter of customary international law; and (c) that it is required to respect under general principles of law common to the major legal systems of the world[14]

A state violates international customary law if, as a matter of state policy, it practices, encourages, or condones:

(a) Genocide.
(b) slavery or slave trade.
(c) the murder or causing the disappearance of individuals
(d) torture or other cruel, inhuman or degrading treatment or punishment.
(e) prolonged arbitrary detention
(f) systematic racial discrimination, or
(g) a consistent pattern of gross violations of internationally recognized human rights."[15]

3.4.3 *Legislative Dimension*

International law gives a discretion to States whether they would make treaties they have accepted directly applicable in their legal systems or whether they would reflect the provisions of those treaties in national legislation. Whichever route a country chooses, there is an obligation to make sure that its national laws correspond to its legal commitments under international human rights law or international human rights treaties. National parliaments should exercise oversight over whether this obligation has been met and, where action is required, see to it that legislative changes or enactments are done. The human rights treaty bodies operating under particular international conventions often make suggestions for legislative updating and national parliaments should require regular reports from the Executive about the recommendations of the human rights treaty bodies. There is a role for parliamentary oversight over Governmental compliance with international human rights obligations each parliament should ideally establish a human rights committee to perform this role.

14 Article 701.
15 Article 702.

3.4.4 *Judicial Dimension*

The judicial dimension requires that courts be independent and effective. There are United Nations declarations and statements on the meaning of judicial independence and effectiveness. As already indicated, international law leaves it to the choice of a Government whether it makes a treaty directly applicable in its legal system or whether it enacts legislation incorporating the obligations under the treaty. It would be our submission, however, that international human rights norms of *jus cogens* status, and human rights norms that have the status of international customary law should be directly applicable in national courts.

International law makes it obligatory that each State provide adequate guarantees for human rights violations. This responsibility falls, in the first place, primarily upon the national judiciary. In the event that there is a failure to protect, there may be remedies under international law. The Third American Restatement, which we cited earlier, summarized these remedies as follows:

> (1) A state party to an international human rights agreement has, as against any other state party violating the agreement, the remedies generally available for violation of an international agreement, as well as any special remedies provided by the agreement;
> (2) Any state may pursue international remedies against any other state for a violation of the customary international law of human rights.
> (3) An individual victim of a violation of human rights agreement may pursue any remedy provided by that agreement or by other applicable international agreements.[16]

It is of great importance that judges and legal practitioners be provided with access to the key decisions of international human rights bodies in local languages so that they may be aware of them and may draw upon them. This is a task with which international human rights organizations and NGOs may assist. But it would be important also that national ministries of justice, or their equivalent, pay attention to this matter so that judges may have access to the latest human rights precedents and reasoning.

3.4.5 *Institutional Dimension*

Experience has shown that, in addition to the courts, institutions such as national human rights commissions, national human rights commissioners or ombudspersons can be quite helpful in advancing and protecting human

16 Article 703.

rights.[17] International law does not make such institutions mandatory but, as a matter of policy, a country should periodically assess its institutional arrangements, or lack thereof to see whether the establishment of national human rights bodies could be helpful for the protection of human rights.

The Paris Principles provided that national human rights institutions could perform, among others, key tasks such as: seeking an amicable settlement of human rights grievances through conciliation, binding decision or other means; informing the complainant of his or her rights and of available means of redress, and promoting access to such redress; hearing complaints or referring them to a competent authority; and making recommendations to the competent authorities, including proposals for amendment of laws, regulations, or administrative practices that obstruct the free exercise of rights.

3.4.5.1 Monitoring Dimension

The responsibility to protect and to prevent demands that every country monitor itself to detect situations of distress and to address them well before they erupt into violations of human rights or conflict.[18] This calls for independent bodies that will systematically watch out for such distress situations and draw attention to them. A national human rights commission could be given the mandate to do this. In multi-ethnic countries special arrangements may need to be devised. But the concept of self-monitoring is a vital part of a national protection system.

A national protection system should provide for adequate and effective remedies to prevent violations of human rights and to provide redress in cases of breach. The absence of a remedy available to test an arguable claim for breach amounts to a violation of human rights[19] The right to an effective remedy may, in certain circumstances, require Governments to provide for, and implement, provisional or interim measures to avoid continuing violations and to endeavour to repair at the earliest possible opportunity any harm that may have been done.[20]

A national protection system should be particularly attentive to the risks of genocide, ethnic cleansing, crimes against humanity and war crimes and

17 See, generally, B.G. Ramcharan (Ed.), The Protection Roles of National Human Rights Institutions. Martinus Nijhoff, 2005. J.A. Mertus, Human Rights Matters. Local Politics and National Human Rights Institutions. Stanford, Stanford University Press, 2009.

18 See, generally, B.G. Ramcharan, Preventive Human Rights Strategies in a World of New Threats and Challenges. London, Routledge, 2009.

19 See the Annual Report of the Human Rights Committee, 2001, Faure v. Australia.

20 See General Comment 31 of the Human Rights Committee.

should provide effective guarantees against them. As the Human Rights Committee stated in its General Comment 6/16 of 27 July, 1982, States have the supreme duty to prevent wars, acts of genocide, and other acts of mass violence causing arbitrary loss of life. A national protection system should provide for a system of regular visits by national, regional or international bodies to all places of detention.

In the event of a violation of human rights, the national protection system must provide for measures, beyond a victim-specific remedy, to be taken to avoid recurrence of the type of violation in question. Such measures may require changes in the State's laws or practices.[21]

A national protection system should provide for investigations of gross violations of human rights and for justice to the victims. A national protection system should provide for safeguards against deportation or extradition to a state where the deportee/extraditee may face serious risks of torture or arbitrary execution. A national protection system should be particularly protective of human rights defenders.

National human rights institutions are an essential component of a national protection system. Each National Commission could map and analyse the human rights history of the country and the contemporary and future challenges of protection. Each National Commission could do a study on the state of implementation of economic, social and cultural rights and identify issues and situations of concern. National Commissions could do a study of situations where there is evidence of a consistent pattern of gross violations of human rights. National Commissions could do a study of population groups at risk. National Commissions could offer policy recommendations for the advancement of women's rights. National Commissions could maintain, as a principal focus, policies and strategies for the prevention of gross violations of human rights. National Commissions could encourage and support the work of judges in the protection of human rights. National Commissions could disseminate the core international human rights norms and jurisprudence to judges and magistrates. National Commissions could develop a policy for the spread of human rights education in schools and higher institutions of learning. National Commissions could enhance their cooperation with protection partners.

Human rights education in primary and secondary schools, in universities and other higher institutions of learning, and in professional education of law enforcement personnel can help instil respect for a culture of human rights

21 See General Comment 31 of the Human Rights Committee.

in each country and lay the foundations for societies aspiring to, and living up to international, regional, and national human rights norms. While there are courses on human rights in some law schools and other university departments, there is still a sad lack of human rights education in most countries. It is vital to remedy this situation.

3.4.6 *Cooperation under UN Human Rights Treaties*

As Member States of the United Nations, African States have participated in the development of various human rights treaties most of which they have then gone on to accept as binding legal obligations. The UN Convention on the Rights of the Child, for example, is the most widely ratified UN human rights treaty and the whole of Africa has undertaken to be bound by its provisions. There can be no doubt that through their participation in the various UN human rights treaties African States have voluntarily agreed to be bound by various universal norms of human rights.

African Governments regularly submit reports on the measures they are pursuing to implement the human rights treaty provisions in their countries. Like other States parties, they engage in ongoing dialogues with monitoring organs established under the various treaties. They pay attention to concluding observations of those monitoring organs. They also pay attention to general comments adopted by the monitoring organs, such general comments being interpretative statements on the meanings of various treaty provisions or offering advice on their implementation drawn from the experience of States Parties as a whole.[22]

UN human rights treaty organs also provide important clarifications of the content of the legal obligations of Governments, including those of African States parties, when they consider petitions from people complaining that their human rights have been violated. The United Nations human rights jurisprudence so elaborated is, as we shall see next, an integral part of the human rights jurisprudence of Africa.

General Comment No. 31 adopted by the Human Rights Committee on 26 May 2004 is a superb statement of the nature of human rights treaty obligations. A State Party, the Committee declared, must respect and ensure the rights in the Covenant to anyone within its power or effective control. The obligations in the Covenant in general and under Article 2 in particular are binding

22 See on this, Bertrand G. Ramcharan, The Fundamentals of International Human Rights Treaty Law. Leiden, Martinus Nijhoff, 2011.

on every State Party as a whole. All branches of government (executive, legislative and judicial), and other public or governmental authorities, at whatever level – national, regional or local – are in a position to engage the responsibility of the State Party.

States Parties must adopt legislative, judicial, administrative, educative and other appropriate measures in order to fulfil their legal obligations. It is important to raise levels of awareness about the Covenant not only among public officials and state agents but also among the population at large.

The positive obligations on States Parties to ensure Covenant rights will only be discharged if individuals are protected by the state not just against violations of Covenant rights by its agents, but also against acts committed by private persons or entities that would impair the enjoyment of Covenant rights in so far as they are amenable to application between private persons or entities. There may be circumstances in which a failure to ensure Covenant rights as required by article 2 would give rise to violations by States Parties of those rights as a result of States Parties' permitting or failing to take appropriate measures or to exercise due diligence to prevent, punish, investigate or redress the harm caused by such acts by private persons or entities. States parties have a duty to address the activities of private persons or entities such as the duty to ensure that private persons or entities do not inflict torture.

States parties are required to respect and to ensure the Covenant rights to all persons who may be within their territory and to all persons subject to their jurisdiction. This means that a State Party must respect and ensure the rights laid down in the Covenant to anyone within the power or effective control of that State Party, even if not situated within the territory of the State Party. The enjoyment of Covenant rights is not limited to citizens of States Parties, but must also be available to all individuals, regardless of nationality or statelessness, such as asylum seekers, refugees, migrant workers and other persons who may find themselves in the territory or subject to the jurisdiction of the State Party. This principle also applies to those within the power or effective control of the forces of a State Party acting outside its territory, regardless of the circumstances in which such power or effective control was obtained, such as forces constituting a national contingent of a State Party assigned to an international peace-keeping or peace-enforcement operation.

The Covenant applies also in situations of armed conflict to which the rules of international humanitarian law are applicable. While, in respect of certain Covenant rights, more specific rules of international humanitarian law may be especially relevant for the purposes of the interpretation of Covenant rights, both spheres of law are complementary, not mutually exclusive.

Article 2, paragraph 2 of the Covenant requires that States Parties take the necessary steps to give effect to the Covenant rights in the domestic order. It follows that, unless the Covenant's rights are already protected by their domestic law or practices, States Parties are required on ratification to make such changes to domestic laws and practices as are necessary to ensure their conformity with the Covenant. Where there are inconsistencies between domestic law and the Covenant, article 2 requires that the domestic law or practice be changed to meet the standards required by the Covenant's substantive guarantees.

Article 2 allows a State Party to pursue this in accordance with its own domestic constitutional structure and accordingly does not require that the Covenant be directly applicable in the courts by incorporation of the Covenant into national laws. The Committee takes the view, however, that Covenant guarantees may receive enhanced protection in those states where the Covenant is automatically or through specific incorporation part of the domestic legal order. The Committee invited those States Parties in which the Covenant did not form part of the domestic legal order to consider incorporation of the Covenant to render it part of domestic law to facilitate full realization of Covenant rights as required by article 2.

The requirement under Article 2, paragraph 2, to take steps to give effect to the Covenant rights is unqualified and of immediate effect. A failure to comply with this obligation cannot be justified by reference to political, social, cultural or economic considerations within the state.

Article 2, paragraph 3, requires that in addition to effective protection of Covenant rights States Parties must ensure that individuals also have accessible and effective remedies to vindicate those rights. Such remedies should be appropriately adapted so as to take account of the special vulnerability of certain categories of person, including in particular children. The Committee attaches importance to States Parties establishing appropriate judicial and administrative mechanisms for addressing claims of rights violations under domestic law.

Article 2, paragraph 3 of the Covenant requires that States Parties make reparation to individuals whose Covenant rights have been violated. Without reparation to individuals whose Covenant rights have been violated, the obligation to provide an effective remedy, which is central to the efficacy of Article 2, paragraph 3, is not discharged. In addition to the explicit reparation required by articles 9, paragraph 5, and Article 14, paragraph 6, the Committee considers that the Covenant generally, entails appropriate compensation. The Committee noted that, where appropriate, reparation can involve restitution, rehabilitation and measures of satisfaction, such as public apologies, public memorials, guarantees of non-repetition and changes in relevant laws and practices, as well as bringing to justice the perpetrators of human rights violations.

In general, the purposes of the Covenant would be defeated without an obligation integral to article 2 to take measures to prevent the recurrence of a violation of the Covenant. Accordingly, it has been a frequent practice of the Committee, in its consideration of individual petitions under the Optional Protocol, to include in its Views the need for measures, beyond a victim-specific remedy, to be taken to avoid recurrence of the type of violation in question. Such measures may require changes in the State Party's laws or practices.

Where investigations reveal violations of certain Covenant rights, States Parties must ensure that those responsible are brought to justice. As with failure to investigate, failure to bring to justice perpetrators of such violations could in and of itself give rise to a separate breach of the Covenant. These obligations arise notably in respect of those violations recognized as criminal under either domestic or international law, such as torture and similar cruel, inhuman and degrading treatment (article 7), summary and arbitrary killing (article 6) and enforced disappearance (articles 7 and 9 and frequently 6). Indeed, the problem of impunity for these violations, a matter of sustained concern by the Committee, might well be an important contributing element in the recurrence of the violations. When committed as part of a widespread or systematic attack on a civilian population, these violations of the Covenant are crimes against humanity (Rome Statute of the ICC, Article 7).

Accordingly, where public officials or state agents have committed violations of the Covenant rights, the States Parties concerned may not relieve perpetrators from personal responsibility. Furthermore, no official status justifies persons who may be accused of responsibility for such violations being held immune from legal responsibility. Other impediments to the establishment of legal responsibility should also be removed, such as the defence of obedience to superior orders or unreasonably short periods of statutory limitation in cases where such limitations are applicable. States Parties should also assist each other to bring to justice persons suspected of having committed acts in violation of the Covenant that are punishable under domestic or international law.

The Committee further took the view that the right to an effective remedy may in certain circumstances require States Parties to provide for and implement provisional or interim measures to avoid continuing violations and to endeavour to repair at the earliest possible opportunity any harm that may have been caused by such violations.

General Comment 31 is a solid reflection of the legal obligations of States under the Covenant and under international human rights treaties generally.

Superimposed on all of this is the United Nations Charter, which has concrete legal obligations on every Member State to uphold universal human rights.

3.5 The Jurisprudence of the International Court of Justice Applicable to all Countries, Including in Africa

The International Court of Justice has made a significant contribution to the development of international human rights law through its clarification of the legal foundations of the international public order. The official Handbook of the ICJ has an illuminating section with the title, "The Court contributes to the development of the international law which it applies". The Handbook highlights judgments and advisory opinions since the establishment of the Court that have broken new ground in the clarification or development of the law. These include the following: the UN Charter considered in the light of the principles of International law; the prohibition of the use of force; the law of the sea; the principles and rules of international law which apply to maritime expanses under State jurisdiction; territorial sovereignty; decolonization; the law of treaties; State responsibility; genocide; asylum; consular relations; *jus cogens;* human rights; and environmental law.[23] In this section we shall highlight some of these skeletally.

3.5.1 *Obligations Erga Omnes*

In the *Barcelona Traction Case*, the ICJ drew attention to the existence of obligations 'towards the international community as a whole' deriving in contemporary international law, *inter alia*, from the principles and rules concerning the basic rights of the human person, including protection from slavery and racial discrimination. 'Some of the corresponding rights of *protection*,' it affirmed, 'have entered into the body of general international law'.[24]

3.5.2 *Jus Cogens*

Following the recommendation of the International Law Commission[25] Article 53 of the Vienna Convention on the Law of Treaties, of 1969, had consolidated the position of norms of *jus cogens* in international law as follows:

23 The International Court of Justice Handbook. UN publication, Sales No.1162, 2019.

24 Emphasis added. *Barcelona Traction Light and Power Co. Ltd*, Judgement of the I.C.J., 5 February 1970, *I.C.J. Reports*, 1970, 1 at 32.

25 See, generally, Bertrand G. Ramcharan, The International Law Commission. The Hague, Martinus Nijhoff, 1977.

> A treaty is void if, at the time of its conclusion, it conflicts with a peremptory norm of general international law. For the purposes of the present Convention, a peremptory norm of general international law is a norm from which no derogation is permitted and which can be modified only by a subsequent norm of general international law having the same character.

The issue of *jus cogens* came up in the Military Activities against Nicaragua case (Nicaragua v. United States), decided in 1986. In dealing with the principle of the prohibition of the use of force in Article 2(4) of the UN Charter, the Court noted that the rule is frequently referred to in statements by State representatives as being not only a principle of customary international law but also a fundamental or cardinal principle of such law. The Court then quoted the International Law Commission, which had stated that the rule had the character of *jus cogens*.[26]

Frowein has commented: "Although the Court does not formally confirm this character it seems difficult not to conclude that the Court indirectly, by quoting the ILC and both parties, expressed its agreement with this qualification."[27]

More recently, as the ICJ Handbook noted,[28] the Court has recognized the peremptory (*jus cogens*) character of fundamental importance for the international community as a whole, and from which derogation is never permitted, of the prohibition of genocide[29] and the prohibition torture.[30]

3.5.3 *Protection of the Right to Life*

In the case concerning the legality of nuclear weapons, the Court affirmed that the protection of the right to life in the International Covenant on Civil and Political Rights does not cease in times of war, except by operation of Article 4 of the Covenant whereby certain provisions may be derogated from in time of national emergency. Respect for the right to life is not, however, such a provision. In principle, the right not to be deprived of one's life arbitrarily applies also in hostilities. The test of what is an arbitrary deprivation of life, however, then falls to be determined by the applicable *lex specialis*, namely, the

---

26 ICJ Reports 1986, pp. 100–101.

27 Jochen Abr. Frowein,"Jus Cogens", in R. Bernhardt (Ed.), Encyclopaedia of Public International Law. Vol. III, Amsterdam, Elsevier, 1997, p.65 at p. 68.

28 Op. cit., pp. 99–107.

29 Armed Activities on the Territory of the Congo (New Application: 2002 (Democratic Republic of Congo v. Rwanda) 2006).

30 Questions relating to the Obligation to Prosecute or Extradite (Belgium v. Senegal) 2012.

law applicable in armed conflict which is designed to regulate the conduct of hostilities. Thus, whether a particular loss of life, through the use of a certain weapon in warfare, is to be considered an arbitrary deprivation of life contrary to Article 6 of the Covenant, can only be decided by reference to the law applicable in armed conflict and not deduced from the terms of the Covenant itself.[31]

3.5.4 *Protection of the Environment*

Also in the Legality case. the Court affirmed that States must take environmental considerations into account when assessing what is necessary and proportionate in the pursuit of legitimate military objectives.[32] The Court found that while the existing international law relating to the protection and safeguarding of the environment did not specifically prohibit the use of nuclear weapons, there are important environmental factors that are properly to be taken into account in the context of the implementation of the principles and rules of the law applicable in armed conflict.[33]

The Court stated:

> The environment is not an abstraction but represents the living space, the quality of life and the very health of human beings, including generations unborn. The existence of the general obligation of States to ensure that activities within their jurisdiction and control respect the environment of other States or of areas beyond national control is now part of the corpus of international law relating to the environment.[34]

A year later, citing the above passage, the Court reaffirmed "the great significance that it attaches to respect for the environment, not only for States but also for the whole of mankind", adding the following:

> [I]n the field of environmental protection, vigilance and prevention are required on account of the often-irreversible character of damage to the environment and of the limitations inherent in the very mechanism of reparation of this type of damage.
>
> Throughout the ages, mankind has, for economic and other reasons, constantly interfered with nature. In the past, this was often done

31 Legality, para. 25.
32 Legality, para. 30.
33 Legality, para. 33.
34 Legality, para 35; ICJ Handbook, Op. cit., p. 106.

without consideration of the effects on the environment. Owing to new scientific insights and to a growing awareness of the risks for mankind – for present and future generations – of pursuit of such interventions at an unconsidered and unabated pace, new norms and standards have been developed, set forth in a great number of instruments during the last two decades. Such new norms have to be taken into consideration, and such new standards given proper weight, not only when States contemplate new activities but also when continuing with activities begun in the past. This need to reconsider economic development with protection of the environment is aptly expressed in the concept of sustainable development.[35]

3.5.5 *The Legality of Nuclear Weapons*

In the Legality case, the Court held that In view of the present state of international law viewed as a whole, as examined by the Court, and of the elements of fact at its disposal, the Court could not reach a definitive conclusion as to the legality or illegality of the use of nuclear weapons by a State in an extreme circumstance of self-defence, in which its very survival would be at stake.[36] The Court said it could not lose sight of the fundamental right of every State to survival, and thus its right to resort to self-defence, in accordance with Article 51 of the Charter, when its survival is at stake.[37]

The Court went on to take the following decisions:[38]

> Unanimously: There is in neither customary nor conventional international law any specific authorization of the threat or use of nuclear weapons.
>
> By eleven votes to three: There is in neither customary nor conventional international law any comprehensive and universal prohibition of the threat or use of nuclear weapons as such.
>
> Unanimously: A threat or use of force by means of nuclear weapons that is contrary to Article 2, paragraph 4, of the United Nations Charter and that fails to meet all the requirements of Article 51, is unlawful.

35 Gabcikovo-Nagymaros Project; ICJ Handbook, op. cit, p. 106.
36 Legality, 97.
37 Legality, 96.
38 Legality, 105.

> Unanimously, A threat or use of nuclear weapons should also be compatible with the requirements of international law applicable in armed conflict, particularly those of the principles and rules of international humanitarian law, as well as with specific obligations under treaties and other undertakings which expressly deal with nuclear weapons.
>
> By seven votes to seven, by the President's casting vote: It follows from the abovementioned requirements that the threat or use of nuclear weapons would generally be contrary to the rules of international law applicable in armed conflict, and in particular the principles and rules of humanitarian law;
>
> However, in view of the current state of international law, and of the elements of fact at its disposal, the Court cannot conclude definitively whether the threat or use of nuclear weapons would be lawful or unlawful in an extreme circumstance of self-defence, in which the very survival of a State would be at stake.
>
> Unanimously: There exists an obligation to pursue in good faith and bring to a conclusion negotiations leading to nuclear disarmament in all its aspects under strict and effective international control.[39]

3.5.6 *The Principle of the Non-use of Force*

The ICJ Handbook attaches high importance to the jurisprudence of the Court on the non-use of force:

> The contributions made by the Court's jurisprudence with regard to the prohibition on the use of force and to self-defence are particularly significant. In its very first contentious case, the Court affirmed that a policy of force 'such as has in the past given rise to most serious abuses ... cannot, whatever be the present defects in international organizations, find a place in international law.' (*Corfu Channel*). In its 1986 Judgment in the case concerning *Military and Paramilitary Activities in and against Nicaragua*, the Court had the opportunity to examine in detail the

39 See, generally, Roger S. Clark and Madeleine Sann (Eds.), The Case Against the Bomb. Marshall Islands, Samoa and Solomon Islands before the International Court of Justice in Advisory Proceedings on the Legality of the Threat or Use of Nuclear Weapons. Camden, New Jersey, Rutgers University School of Law, 1996. Georg Schwarzenberger, The Legality of Nuclear Weapons. London, Stevens, 1956.

> international rules on the subject, confirming that they were customary in nature and explaining the conditions for the exercise of self-defence. It confirmed those rules ten years later in the context of its Advisory Opinion on the *Legality of the Use of Nuclear Weapons*. This issue remains at the heart of the Court's concerns.[40]

The Handbook went on to cite subsequent Judgments in which the Court had highlighted that the prohibition of the use of force was a "corner-stone of the UN Charter and recognized the customary character of the relevant provisions of the Declaration on Principles of International law concerning Friendly Relations and Cooperation among States in accordance with the Charter of the United Nations (resolution 2625 (XXV) adopted by the General Assembly on 24 October 1970).[41]

3.5.7 *Self-Determination*

As the ICJ Handbook noted, in the area of decolonization, the Court has had occasion to stress the primordial role of the principle of self-determination viewed as an ongoing process, for example in the advisory proceedings in the case concerning the *Legal Consequences for States of the Continued Presence of South Africa in Namibia*, and in the *Western Sahara* case. In the case concerning *East Timor* (*Portugal v. Australia*), the Court recognized that "the right of peoples to self-determination, as it has evolved from the Charter and from United Nations practice, has an *erga omnes* character" and that the corresponding principle is "one of the essential principles of contemporary international law. The Court also cited its Advisory Opinion on the *Legal Consequences of the Construction of a Wall in the Occupied Palestinian Territory*.[42]

In regard more generally to territorial integrity, the ICJ Handbook notes that the Court has enshrined the principle of the intangibility of frontiers inherited from the decolonization process, as well as that of *uti possidetis juris*, whereby the legal title enjoys priority over effective possession as the basis of sovereignty, possession being decisive only in the absence of such title. (*Frontier Dispute* (*Burkina Faso/Mali*); *Land and Maritime Boundary between Cameroon and Nigeria; Sovereignty over Palau Ligitan and Palau Sipadan: Territorial and Maritime Dispute*)[43]

40 ICJ Handbook, op. cit., p. 100.
41 Ibid, p. 100.
42 Ibid, p. 102.
43 ICJ Handbook, op. cit., p. 102.

3.5.8 *Prevention of Genocide*

In 2007, the ICJ considered the question of State responsibility in respect of genocide in the case, *Application of the Convention on the Prevention and Punishment of the Crime of Genocide* (*Bosnia and Herzegovina v. Serbia and Montenegro*). The Court stated that "if an organ of the State or a person or group whose acts are legally attributable to the State, commits any of the acts proscribed in Article III of the [Genocide] Convention, the international responsibility of that State is incurred."

The Court found that genocide had been committed in Srebrenica in July, 1995, but that proof had not been shown to the Court that legal responsibility was directly attributable to the Respondent. However, it did conclude that the Respondent State had violated its obligations under the Convention to prevent the genocide at Srebrenica and to transfer to the International Criminal Tribunal for the former Yugoslavia for trial any individuals finding themselves in its territory and indicted for genocide by that Tribunal in relation to the Srebrenica massacres.[44]

3.5.9 *International Human Rights Law*

Through its clarification of the content of international human rights law, the ICJ has made an important contribution to the promotion and protection of human rights.[45] The Court has done this in Advisory Opinions as well as in decisions in contentious cases. It has notably spelled out the obligations of Governments to prevent genocide, clarified the relationship between international human rights law and international humanitarian law, pronounced on the obligations of governments not to engage in discriminatory laws or practices, has clarified the duties of Governments to ensure that detained foreign nationals are able to have access to the consulates of their countries if they so wish, has commented on the legality of the use of nuclear weapons, has spelled

44 Ibid., p. 104.

45 See on this ICJ Handbook, op. cit., p. 105: "[In] its Advisory Opinion on the *Legal Consequences of the Construction of a Wall in the Occupied Palestinian Territory*, the Court recalled the importance of respecting the rules of international humanitarian law. In particular, it emphasized that the rules in question incorporate obligations which are essentially of an *erga omnes* character, given the character and importance of the rights and obligations involved [deriving from the Geneva Conventions], and that all States are under an obligation nor to recognize the illegal situation resulting from their violation.". In the Case concerning *Armed Activities on the Territory of the Congo* (*Democratic Republic of the Congo v. Uganda*), The Court found that, as a result of killings, torture and other forms of inhumane treatment committed by Ugandan armed forces against the Congolese civilian population, the Republic of Uganda had violated its obligations under international human rights law and international humanitarian law.

out the duties of an Occupying Power under international humanitarian law, and has pronounced on the principle of self-determination in contemporary international law.

In the Corfu Channel Case, 1949, the ICJ based itself on 'general and well-recognized principles' namely, 'elementary considerations of humanity, even more exacting in peace than in war'. In the *Barcelona Traction Case*, the ICJ drew attention to the existence of obligations 'towards the international community as a whole' deriving in contemporary international law, *inter alia*, from the principles and rules concerning the basic rights of the human person, including protection from slavery and racial discrimination. 'Some of the corresponding rights of *protection*,' it affirmed, 'have entered into the body of general international law'.[46]

On the individual and joint human rights responsibilities of Member States under the UN Charter, the ICJ advised in the 2004 *Wall opinion* that all States are under an obligation: (1) not to recognize the illegal situation resulting from the construction of the wall. (2) not to render aid or assistance in maintaining the situation created by such construction.[47] More specifically, "...all States parties to the Fourth Geneva Convention relative to the Protection of Civilian Persons in Time of War of 12 August 1949 have in addition the obligation, while respecting the United Nations Charter and international law, to ensure compliance by Israel with international humanitarian law as embodied in that Convention."[48]

On the existence of non-derogable rights, the ICJ, as we saw earlier, affirmed in the Nuclear Weapons case that "...the protection of the International Covenant on Civil and Political Rights does not cease in times of war, except by operation of Article 4 of the Covenant whereby certain provisions may be derogated from in a time of national emergency. Respect for the right to life is not, however, such a provision. In principle, the right not to arbitrarily be deprived of one's life applies also in hostilities. The test of what is an arbitrary deprivation of life, however, then falls to be determined by the applicable *lex specialis*, namely, the law applicable in armed conflict which is designed to regulate the conduct of hostilities."[49]

---

46 Emphasis added. *Barcelona Traction Light and Power Co. Ltd*, Judgement of the I.C.J., 5 February 1970, *I.C.J. Reports*, 1970, 1 at 32.

47 Advisory Opinion of 9 July 2004 in the case concerning the Legal Consequences of the Construction of a Wall in the Occupied Palestinian Territory, *ICJ Reports* 2004, para. 163.

48 Ibid.

49 Advisory Opinion of 8 July 1996 on the Legality of the Threat or Use of Nuclear Weapons, *ICJ Reports* 1996, p. 240, para. 25.

The ICJ, in the *Hostages advisory opinion*, recognized the principles of the Universal Declaration of Human Rights: "Wrongfully to deprive human beings of their freedom and to subject them to physical constraint in conditions of hardship is in itself manifestly incompatible with the principles of the Charter of the United Nations, as well as with the fundamental principles enunciated in the Universal Declaration of Human Rights."[50]

In its Advisory Opinion Namibia, 1971, the ICJ held that to establish and to enforce distinctions, exclusions, restrictions and limitations exclusively based on grounds of race, colour, descent or national or ethnic origin which constitute a denial of fundamental human rights is a flagrant violation of the purposes and principles of the Charter.[51] The ICJ has held the rules of Common Article 3 of the four Geneva Conventions of 12 August, 1949 to be a 'minimum yardstick' of treatment in all international and non-international armed conflicts.[52] In the Nuclear Weapons case, the Court stated that in principle human rights obligations do not cease in times of armed conflict (unless derogations are permitted by the relevant treaty), but that international humanitarian law may operate as a *lex specialis* excluding more general human rights standards. In other contexts, for example belligerent occupation, it may even be that international human rights law constitutes the more specialized standard.

On the relationship between international human rights law and international humanitarian law in situations of armed conflict, the ICJ, in its Advisory Opinion in the Wall case, noted that there might be three situations: 1) some rights may be exclusively mattes of international humanitarian law, 2) others may be exclusively matters of human rights law, and 3) yet others may be matters of both these branches of law.[53]

In its Advisory Opinion Concerning Reservations to the Convention on the Prevention and Punishment of Genocide, the International Court of Justice (ICJ) provided important insights into the nature of international human rights treaty obligations that would be applicable to most of the human rights treaties in existence today. The ICJ, advancing the doctrine of the common interest of all humanity in the observance of international human rights treaty provisions, affirmed:

50 Case Concerning United States Diplomatic and Consular Staff in Tehran, *ICJ Reports* (1980), p. 30, para. 62.

51 Ibid, p. 57.

52 ICJ Reports, Nicaragua Case, 1986, p. 14, 114.

53 *ICJ Reports* (2004), p. 178, para. 106.

> The origins of the Convention show that it was the intention of the United Nations to condemn and punish genocide as a 'crime under international law' involving a denial of the right of existence of entire human groups, a denial which shocks the conscience of mankind and results in great losses to humanity, and which is contrary to moral law and to the spirit and aims of the United Nations. The first consequence arising from this conception is that the principles underlying the Convention are principles which are recognized by civilized nations as binding on States, even without any conventional obligation. A second consequence is the universal character both of the condemnation of genocide and of the cooperation required 'in order to liberate mankind from such an odious scourge' (Preamble of the Convention). The Genocide convention was therefore intended by the General Assembly and by the Contracting Parties to be definitely universal in scope. It was in fact approved on December 9th, 1948 by a resolution which was unanimously adopted by fifty-six States. The objects of such a Convention must also be considered. The Convention was manifestly adopted for a purely humanitarian and civilizing purpose. It is indeed difficult to imagine a Convention that might have this dual character to a greater degree, since its object on the one hand is to safeguard the very existence of certain human groups, and on the other to confirm and endorse the most elementary principles of morality. In such a Convention the contracting States do not have any interests of their own; they merely have, one and all, a common interest, namely the accomplishment of those high purposes which are the *raison d'etre* of the Convention. Consequently, in a convention of this type, one cannot speak of individual advantages or disadvantages to States, or of the maintenance of a perfect contractual balance between rights and duties. The high ideals which inspired the Convention provide, by virtue of the common will of the parties, the foundation and measure of all its provisions.[54]

The International Criminal Tribunal for the Former Yugoslavia (ICTY) in the case of *Kupreskic and others* expressed similar views:

> The absolute nature of most obligations imposed by rules of international humanitarian law reflects the progressive trend towards the so-called

54 ICJ, Reservations to the Convention on Genocide, Advisory Opinion, 28 May, 1951, *ICJ Reports* (1951), p. 15.

> 'humanisation' of international legal obligations, which refers to the general erosion of the role of reciprocity in the application of international humanitarian law over the last century. After the First World War, the application of the laws of war moved away from a reliance on reciprocity between belligerents, with the consequence that, in general, rules came to be increasingly applied by each belligerent despite their possible disregard by the enemy. The underpinning of this shift was that it became clear to States that norms of international humanitarian law were not intended to protect State interests; they were primarily designed to benefit individuals *qua* human beings. Unlike other international norms, such as those of commercial treaties which can legitimately be based on the protection of reciprocal interests of States, compliance with humanitarian rules could not be made dependent on a reciprocal or corresponding performance of these obligations by other States. This trend marks the translation into legal norms of the 'categorical imperative' formulated by Kant in the field of morals: one ought to fulfil an obligation regardless of whether others comply with it or disregard it.[55]

The Inter-American Court of Human Rights, in the case of *Villagran Morales* and others, of 19 November, 1999, declared in respect of the right to life:

> The right to life is a fundamental human right, and the exercise of this right is essential for the exercise of all other human rights. If it is not respected, all rights lack meaning. Owing to the fundamental nature of the right to life, restrictive approaches to it are inadmissible. In essence, the fundamental right to life includes not only the right of every human being not to be deprived of his life arbitrarily, but also the right that he will not be prevented from having access to the conditions that guarantee a dignified existence. States have the obligation to guarantee the creation of the conditions required in order that violations of this basic right do not occur and, in particular, the duty to prevent its agents from violating it.[56]

55 International Tribunal for the Prosecution of Persons Responsible for Serious Violations of International Humanitarian Law Committed in the Territory of the former Yugoslavia since 1991, *Kupreskic et al.* Case No. IT-95-16-T of 14 January, 2000, p. 201.

56 Inter-American Court of Human Rights, *Villagran Morales et. al.* Case (the 'Street Children' case), Judgment, 19 November, 1999.

In the 1971 Namibia advisory opinion, the ICJ declared: "Under the Charter of the United Nations, the former mandatory had pledged itself to observe and respect, in a territory having an international status, human rights and fundamental freedoms for all without distinction as to race. To establish instead, and to enforce, distinctions, exclusions, restrictions and limitations exclusively based on grounds of race, colour, descent or national or ethnic origin which constitute a denial of fundamental human rights is a flagrant violation of the purposes and principles of the Charter."[57]

Furthermore, "…no factual evidence is needed for the purpose of determining whether the policy of *apartheid* as applied by South Africa in Namibia is in conformity with the international obligations assumed by South Africa under the Charter of the United Nations. In order to determine whether the laws and decrees applied by South Africa in Namibia, which are a matter of public record, constitute a violation of the purposes and principles of the Charter of the United Nations, the question of intent or governmental discretion is not relevant; nor is it necessary to investigate or determine the effects of those measures upon the welfare of the inhabitants."[58]

On the content of individual and joint responsibilities, the ICJ advised in the 2004 *Wall case* that all States are under an obligation: (1) not to recognize the illegal situation resulting from the construction of the wall. (2) not to render aid or assistance in maintaining the situation created by such construction.[59] More specifically,

> … all States parties to the Fourth Geneva Convention relative to the Protection of Civilian Persons in Time of War of 12 August 1949 have in addition the obligation, while respecting the United Nations Charter and international law, to ensure compliance by Israel with international humanitarian law as embodied in that Convention.[60]
>
> On the existence of *jus cogens* rights, Judge *ad hoc* Lauterpacht noted that "… the prohibition of genocide has generally been accepted as having the status not of an ordinary rule of international law but of *jus*

57 Ibid, p. 57.

58 *ICJ Reports*, 1971, p. 57.

59 Advisory Opinion of 9 July 2004 in the case concerning the Legal Consequences of the Construction of a Wall in the Occupied Palestinian Territory, *ICJ Reports* 2004, para. 163.

60 Ibid.

> *cogens*. Indeed, prohibition of genocide has long been regarded as one of the few undoubted examples of *jus cogens*[61]

On the existence of obligations *erga omnes*, the ICJ held in the *Barcelona Traction case* that "...an essential distinction should be drawn between the obligations of a State towards the international community as a whole, and those arising *vis-à-vis* another State in the field of diplomatic protection. By their very nature the former are the concern of all States. In view of the importance of the rights involved, all States can be held to have a legal interest in their protection: they are obligations *erga omnes*"[62]

On the emergence of international customary law, Judge Guillaume, then President of the ICJ, told the Legal Committee of the UN General Assembly in 2002, "...the Court, by characterizing certain conventional obligations as customary ones and then treating such obligations as obligations *erga omnes*, has sought to impose on all States minimum norms deriving from the elementary considerations of humanity already invoked by the Court in the Corfu Channel case. It has thus given those considerations a specific content. In doing so, it has laid the foundations for a universal customary law which, without challenging conventional law, is binding."[63]

The ICJ, in the *Hostages advisory opinion*, recognized the principles of the Universal Declaration of Human Rights: "Wrongfully to deprive human beings of their freedom and to subject them to physical constraint in conditions of hardship is in itself manifestly incompatible with the principles of the Charter of the United Nations, as well as with the fundamental principles enunciated in the Universal Declaration of Human Rights."[64]

In its Advisory Opinion Namibia, 1971, the ICJ held that to establish and to enforce distinctions, exclusions, restrictions and limitations exclusively based on grounds of race, colour, descent or national or ethnic origin which

---

61 Judge *ad hoc* E. Lauterpacht, Application of the Convention on the Prevention and Punishment of the Crime of Genocide (*Bosnia and Herzegovina v. Yugoslavia*), *ICJ Reports*, 1993, p. 440.

62 Barcelona Traction case, *ICJ Reports*, 1970, p. 51.

63 Address of Judge Glibert Guillame, President of the International Court of Justice to the Sixth Committee of the UN General Assembly on 30 October 2002, cited in S.R.S. Bedi, *The Development of Human Rights Law by the Judges of the International Court of Justice* (Hart Publishing, 2007) p. 368.

64 Case Concerning United States Diplomatic and Consular Staff in Tehran, *ICJ Reports* (1980), p. 30, para. 62.

constitute a denial of fundamental human rights is a flagrant violation of the purposes and principles of the Charter.[65]

The International Court has held the rules of Common Article 3 of the four Geneva Conventions of 12 August, 1949 to be a 'minimum yardstick' of treatment in al international and non-international armed conflicts. Nicaragua, ICJ Reports, 1986, p. 14, 114. In Nuclear Weapons, the Court stated that in principle human rights obligations do not cease in times of armed conflict (unless derogations are permitted by the relevant treaty), but that international humanitarian law may operate as a l;ex specialis excluding more general human rights standards. In other contexts, for example belligerent occupation, it may even be that international human rights law constitutes the more specialized standard.

> On the relationship between international human rights law and international humanitarian law in situations of armed conflict, the ICJ, in its Advisory Opinion in the Wall case, noted that there might be three situations: 1) some rights may be exclusively mattes of international humanitarian law, 2) others may be exclusively matters of human rights law, and 3) yet others may be matters of both these branches of law.[66]

In 1979, the UN General Assembly "conscious of the responsibility of the United Nations ... in dealing with situations of mass and flagrant violations of human rights", reaffirmed "that mass and flagrant violations of human rights are of special concern to the United Nations" and urged "the appropriate United Nations bodies, within their mandates, particularly the Commission on Human Rights [now the Human Rights Council], to take timely and effective action in existing and future cases of mass and flagrant violations of human rights." The Assembly stressed "the important role that the Secretary-General can play in situations of mass and flagrant violations of human rights."[67]

3.5.10 *The Jurisprudence of UN Human Rights Treaty Bodies*

The jurisprudence of UN human rights treaty organs are replete with principles of international human rights law applicable to all countries. In this section we shall take as an example one of the leading bodies, the United Nations Human Rights Committee, which functions under the International Covenant

65 Ibid, p. 57.

66 *ICJ Reports* (2004), p. 178, para. 106.

67 GA resolution 34/175.

on Civil and Political Rights (ICCPR). The Human Rights Committee has contributed solidly in shaping the human rights jurisprudence of the world and it is helping to help build a world of human dignity and progress based on respect for human rights. The Committee monitors the implementation of the International Covenant on Civil and Political Rights (1966). The first thing that stands out from the case law is that the Human Rights Committee is in the process of clarifying the constitutional or public order of the world and its corresponding legal norms. The Human Rights Committee is articulating the principle of international supervision of human rights, namely that what is legal or illegal is determined, in the final instance, by a UN Human Rights body. 111 States are at present bound by the petitions procedure operated by the Committee and, undoubtedly, the remaining States will do so when they see the light – as eventually they must if they are to do justice to their own citizens.

The second thing that stands out is that the Human Rights Committee is in the process of humanising sovereignty. The Committee insists that governments are not at liberty to act as they see fit but must conform to international human rights standards. Of equal significance, third, the Human Rights Committee has just held in a landmark case that the foremost United Nations organ, the Security Council, must comply with international human rights norms when its actions affect individuals. This is a breath-taking decision of the Human Rights Committee in the case of Sayadi and others v. Belgium (2008). In that case, Belgium argued that it was shielded from scrutiny because it was acting to implement a Security Council resolution. 'No', the Committee replied; Belgium must comply with its human rights obligations, which took precedence. The Security Council cannot act in breach of human rights.

Fourth, the Human Rights Committee has insisted that even in times of public emergency there can be no excuses for violating fundamental rights such as the right to life or not to be tortured. In a time when human rights are being flouted in the name of acting against terrorism, the Human Rights Committee holds aloft the banner of international human rights law and insists that no Government is above the law.

Fifth, among the legal precepts developed by the Human Rights Committee are the following:

- Governments are legally bound to take reasonable and appropriate measures to protect people within their jurisdiction or control.
- The law must strictly control and limit the circumstances in which a person may be deprived of his or her life by the authorities of the State.
- A State, by invoking the existence of exceptional circumstances, cannot evade the obligations it has undertaken under international human rights law by ratifying the Covenant.

- A situation in which the functions and competences of the judiciary and the executive are not clearly distinguishable or where the executive is able to control of direct the judiciary is incompatible with the notion of an independent and impartial judiciary.
- Governments are under a legal obligation to ensure that remedies for violations are effective. Expedition and effectiveness are particularly important in the adjudication of cases involving torture.
- Where violations have taken place Governments must take measures to ensure that similar violations do not take place in the future.
- Governments should take specific and effective measures to prevent the disappearance of individuals and establish effective facilities and procedures to investigate thoroughly by an appropriate and impartial body, cases of missing and disappeared persons.
- Being subjected to incommunicado detention in an unknown location constitutes cruel and inhuman treatment.
- Women and men are entitled to equal treatment in the application of laws.[68]

United Nations human rights jurisprudence is an integral part of African human rights jurisprudence. African institutions, including the African Commission and Court on Human and Peoples' Rights regularly invoke the General Comments and jurisprudence of UN treaty organs. Most important of all, African civil society invariably rallies behind UN human rights jurisprudence. Even where the decision of a human rights treaty body, such as the Human Rights Committee operating under the ICCPR is not immediately implemented by the Government in power in a State party, African civil society invoke and agitate for changes within the country in line with the United Nations human rights jurisprudence, for example, for a change from one-party to democratic governance. In discussing United Nations human rights jurisprudence applicable to Africa we shall use as an example the case law of the Human Rights Committee operating under the ICCPR and its Optional Protocol.

In their monumental book on the case law of the Human Rights Committee during the period 1977–2008, Jakob Th. Moller and Alfred de Zayas discuss cases brought against the following African countries: Algeria, Angola, Burkina Faso, Cameroon, Central African Republic, Democratic Republic of the Congo, Equatorial Guinea, Libya, Madagascar, Mauritius, Senegal, Sierra Leone, Togo,

68 See, further, J. Moller and A. de Zayas, The Case Law of the UN Human Rights Committee 1977–2008. Engel Publishers, 2009.

Zaire, and Zambia.[69] The case law of the Human Rights Committee includes pronouncements on core universal principles of human rights of great value including: recognition as a person before the law, equality, democratic rule and the right to participate in the governance of one's country, protection from torture, enforced disappearance and arbitrary deprivation of liberty, the right to a fair trial, and the right to redress for violations of human rights. In pronouncing on particular petitions, the Human Rights Committee has helped in the interpretation of particular rights and in the development of standards for assessing the conduct of governments. Put simply, African governments and institutions, like governments and institutions the world over, need to implement basic human rights in accordance with the interpretations and standards of the Human Rights Committee.

In case No 1328/2004, (*Messaoudi Kimouche, nee Cheraitia, et al v. Algeria*), the Human Rights Committe found a violation of the right to recognition as a person before the law under article 16 of the Covenant, as well as violation of article 7 and 9 in a case involving enforced and involuntary disappearance. The Committee laid down detailed remedies required of the Algeria: the State party was under an obligation to provide the authors with an effective remedy, including a thorough and effective investigation into the disappearance and the fate of their son, his immediate release if he was s ill alive, and providing the petitioner with the appropriate information emerging from its investigation. The State party was also under obligation to ensure that the petitioners and the family receive adequate reparation, including in the form of compensation.[70]

In case No. 49/179 (*Dave Marais v. Madagascar*), the Human Rights Committee addressed the issue that fundamental rights cannot be suspended in any circumstance In this case, the Human Rights Committee took note of the State party's submission referring to a state of emergency in force in Madagascar. The Committee repeatedly requested the State party to clarify, pursuant to article 4 (3) of the Covenant, whether the right of derogation had been applied and, if so, whether any derogation had in any way affected the alleged victim. It received no reply from the State party and the Committee accordingly, ignored the State party's reference to a 'state of emergency' in its examination of the case and proceeded to find violations of several provisions of the Covenant.[71]

---

69 Jakob Th. Moller and Alfred de Zayas, United Nations Human Rights Committee. Case Law 1977–2008. N.P. Engel Publisher, Kehl am Rhein, Germany, 2009.

70 Ibid, pp. 497–498.

71 Ibid, p. 137.

In Case No. 90/1981, (*Luyeye Magana v. Zaire*), the Human Rights Committee held that article 9 of the Covenant had been breached with respect to a victim who had been arrested on 24 March 1977 and detained until 9 January 1978 (I.e. over nine months) without having been brought before a judge.[72]

In case No. 542/1993 (*Tshishimbi v. Zaire*), the victim had disappeared. The Human Rights Committee recalled that article 9, paragraph 1 of the Covenant may be invoked outside the context of arrest and detention, and that an interpretation which would allow States parties to tolerate, condone or ignore threats made by persons in authority to the personal liberty and security of non-detained individuals within the State party's jurisdiction would render ineffective the guarantee of the Covenant. The Committee concluded that article 9, paragraph 1 had been violated.[73]

In case No. 16/1977 (*D. Monguya Mbengue et al v.* Zaire), the Human Rights Committee found that Abraham Oyabi had been arrested on 1 September 1977 in order to force him to disclose the whereabouts of Simon Biyanga and that he was not released from detention until late in 1978 or early in 1979. The State party did not claim that there was a criminal charge against him. In the view of the Human Rights Committee, therefore, he had been subjected to arbitrary arrest and detention contrary to article 9 of the Covenant.[74]

In case No.49/1979 (*Dave Marais v. Madagascar*), where the victim had been held incommunicado for several years in a cell measuring 1 meter by 2 meters in the basement of the political police prison at Ambohibao, the Human Rights Committee found a violation of article 7 of the Covenant together with article 10. It made a similar finding in case No. 115/1982 (*John Wight v. Madagascar*), where the victim had been kept in a solitary room at the political police prison at Ambohibao, chained to a bed spring on the floor, with minimal clothing and a severe rationing of food, and because during hospitalization he was chained to the floor and held totally incommunicado.[75]

The case of *Shirin Aumeruddy-Cziffra and 19 Other Mauritian Women v. Mauritius*, decided on 23 March, 1981 and accepted and implemented by the State Party, is a superb example of the application of universal human rights norms, in this instance the right to gender equality. In this case, the authors of the petition were 20 Mauritian women who claimed that Mauritius' enactment of the Immigration (Amendment) Act 1977, and the Deportation (Amendment) Act, 1977 constituted discrimination based on sex against

72 Ibid, p. 195.

73 Ibid, p. 183.

74 Ibid., p. 193.

75 Ibid, p. 165.

Mauritian women, violation of the right to found a family and home, and removal of the protection of the courts of law, in breach of articles 2, 3, 4, 17, 23, 25 and 26 of the International Covenant on Civil and Political Rights. The authors stated that prior to the enactment of the laws in question, alien men and women married to Mauritian nationals enjoyed the same residence status, that is to say, by virtue of their marriage, foreign spouses of both sexes had the right, protected by law, to reside in the country with their Mauritian husbands or wives.

The authors of the communications complained that, under the new laws, alien husbands of Mauritian women lost their residence status in Mauritius and had to apply for a 'residence permit' which might be refused or removed at any time by the Minister of Interior. The new laws, however, did not affect the status of alien women married to Mauritian husbands, who retained their legal right to residence in the country. The authors further contended that under the new laws alien husbands of Mauritian women might be deported under a ministerial order that was not subject to judicial review.

Seventeen of the co-authors of the communication were unmarried. Three of the co-authors were married to foreign husbands when, owing to the coming into force of the Immigration (Amendment) Act, 1977, their husbands lost the residency status in Mauritius that they had enjoyed before. Their further residence together with their spouses in Mauritius was based under the statute on a limited, temporary residence permit issued in accordance with section 9 of the Immigration (Amendment) Act, 1977. This residence permit was subject to specified conditions that might at any time be varied or cancelled by a decision of the Minister of the Interior, against which no remedy was available. In addition, the Deportation (Amendment) Act, 1977, subjected foreign husbands to a permanent risk of being deported from Mauritius.

In the case of Mrs Aumeruddy-Cziffra, one of the three married co-authors, more than three years had elapsed since her husband had applied to the Mauritian authorities for a residence permit, but no formal decision had been taken. If her husband's application were to receive a negative decision, she would be obliged to choose between either living with her husband abroad and giving up her political career, or living separated from her husband in Mauritius and there continuing to participate in the conduct of public affairs of that country.

In coming to a decision in the case, the Human Rights Committee made a distinction between the different groups of the authors of the communication. A person, it held, could only claim to be a victim in the sense of Article 1 of the Optional Protocol to the Covenant [which provided for the submission of individual petitions] if he or she was actually affected. It held that no individual could in the abstract, by way of an *actio popularis*, challenge a law or practice claimed to be contrary to the Covenant. If the law or practice had not already been concretely applied to the detriment of that individual, it must in any event be applicable in such a way that the alleged victim's risk of being affected was more than a theoretical possibility.

In this respect, the Committee noted that in the case of the 17 unmarried co-authors there was no question of actual interference with, or failure to ensure equal protection by the law to any family. Furthermore, there was no evidence that any of them was actually facing a personal risk of being thus affected in the enjoyment of this or any other rights set forth in the Covenant by the laws complained against.

On the substance of the case as it affected the three married petitioners, the Human Rights Committee took the view that the common residence of husband and wife had to be considered as the normal behaviour of a family. Hence, and as the State Party had admitted, the exclusion of a person f rom a country where close members of his family are living can amount to an interference within the meaning of article 17 of the Covenant. In principle, article 17 (1) applies also when one of the spouses is an alien. Whether the existence and application of immigration laws affecting the residence of a family member was compatible with the Covenant depended on whether such interference was either 'arbitrary or unlawful' as stated in article 17 (1), or conflicted in any other way with the State party's obligation under the Covenant.

In the present case, not only the future possibility of deportation, but the precarious residence situation of foreign husbands in Mauritius represented, in the opinion of the opinion of the Committee, an interference by the authorities of the State party with the family life of the Mauritian wives and their husbands. The Statutes in question had rendered it uncertain for the families concerned whether and for how long it would be possible for them to continue their family life by residing together in Mauritius. Moreover, in one of the cases, even the delay for years, and the absence of a positive decision granting a residence permit, must be seen as a considerable inconvenience, among other reasons because the granting of a work permit, and hence the possibility of the husband to contribute to supporting the family, depended on the residence permit, and because deportation without judicial review was possible at any time.

The Human Rights Committee noted that it was an obligation of the States parties to the Covenant under article 2 (1) generally to respect and ensure the rights of the Covenant "without distinction of any kind, such as ... (inter alia) sex.", and more particularly under article 3 "to ensure the equal right of men and women to the enjoyment" of all these rights, as well as under article 26 to provide "without discrimination" for "the equal protection of the law."

The Committee found that the authors who were married to foreign nationals were suffering from the adverse consequences of the statutes referred to above only because they were women. The precarious residence status of their husbands, affecting their family life, resulted from the 1977 laws which did not apply the same measures of control to foreign wives. The Committee held that whenever restrictions are placed on a right guaranteed by the Covenant, this had to be done without discrimination on the ground of sex. In the present case, an adverse distinction based on sex had been made, affecting the alleged victims in their enjoyment of one of their rights. No sufficient justification for this difference had been given. The Committee therefore found that there had been a violation of articles 2 (1) and 3 of the Covenant, in conjunction with article 17 (1).

At the same time, each of the coupled concerned in this case constituted also a family within the meaning of article 23 (1) of the Covenant, in one case at least also with a child. They were therefore as such "entitled to protection by society and the State" as required by that article. The principle of equal treatment of the sexes applied by virtue of articles 2 (1), 3 and 26, of which the latter was also relevant because it referred particularly to the "equal protection of the law". Where the Covenant required a substantial protection as in article 23, it followed from those provisions that such protection must be equal, that is to say not discriminatory, for example on the basis of sex. The protection of a family cannot vary with the sex of one or the other spouse. The Committee was of the view that the legislation, which only subjected foreign spouses of Mauritian women to those restrictions, but not foreign spouses of Mauritian men, was discriminatory with respect to Mauritian women and could not be justified by security requirements. The Committee therefore found that there was also a violation of articles 2 (1), 3 and 26 of the Covenant in conjunction with the right of the three married co-authors under article 23 (1).

The Human Rights Committee expressed the view that the State Party should adjust the provisions of the Immigration (Amendment) Act, 1977 and of the Deportation (Amendment) Act 1977 in order to implement its obligations under the Covenant and should provide immediate remedies for the victims of the violations found above.

The Government of Mauritius accepted the findings of the Human Rights Committee and amended the laws in question accordingly. This case is a notable example of an African State's acceptance and implementation of universal human rights norms regarding the prohibition of discrimination on grounds of sex and also the protection of family life.[76]

The case of *Chiiko Bwalya v. Zambia*[77] is instructive for its influence on the march to democracy in Zambia. Zambia is today a democratic country but it was not thus hitherto. The author of the petition, Peter Chiiko Bwalya, a Zambian citizen and then chairman of the People's Redemption Organization, a political party in Zambia, claimed to be a victim of violations of the ICCPR by Zambia. In 1983, at the age of 22, he had sought to run for a parliamentary seat in the Constituency of Chifubu, Zambia. He complained that the authorities prevented him from properly preparing his candidacy and from participating in the electoral campaign. The author alleged that by September, 1988 he had been detained for 31 months on charges of belonging to the People's Redemption Organization, an association considered illegal under the terms of the country's one-party Constitution, and for having conspired to overthrow the Government of the then President Kenneth Kaunda. He subsequently alleged continuing oppressive measures against him by Governmental authorities.

In considering the complaint, the Human Rights Committee noted with concern that, with the exception of a brief note informing the Committee of the author's release, the State Party had failed to cooperate in the case. In respect of issues under article 19 of the Covenant, the Committee held that the uncontested response of the authorities to the attempts of the author to express his opinions freely and to disseminate the political tenets of his party constituted a violation of his rights under article 19 of the Covenant.

The Committee noted that when the petition was placed before it for consideration, Mr Bwalya had been detained for a total of 31 months, a claim that had not been contested by the State party. It noted that the author was held solely on charges of belonging to a political party considered illegal under the country's then one-party constitution and that on the basis of the information before the Committee, Mr Bwalya had not been brought promptly before a judge or other officer authorized by law to exercise judicial power to determine the lawfulness of his detention. This, in the Committee's opinion, constituted a violation of the author's right under article 9, paragraph 3 of the Covenant.

76 See, Human Rights Committee, Twelfth Session, 1981: Shirin Aumeeruddy-Cziffra and 19 Other Mauritian Women v. Mauritius. Views. Communication No. 35/1978; UN Doc. CCPR/C/12/D/35/1978.

77 Human Rights Committee, Forty-Eighth Session, Views, Communication No. 314/1988: Chiko Bwalys v. Zambia. Communication No. 314/1998, UN Doc. CCPR/C/48/D314/1988 (1993).

In the circumstances of the case, the Human Rights Committee further concluded that Zambia had violated Mr Bwalya's right to security of person under article 9, paragraph 1 of the Covenant. Furthermore, Zambia had not denied that the author continued to suffer restrictions on his freedom of movement, and that the authorities had refused to issue a passport to him,. This, in the Committee's view, amounted to a violation of article 12, paragraph 1 of the Covenant.

As to the alleged violation of article 25 of the Covenant, the Committee noted that the author, a leading figure of a political party in opposition to the former President, had been prevented from participating in a general election campaign as well as from preparing his candidacy for this party. This amounted to an unreasonable restriction on the author's right to "take part in the conduct of public affairs" which the State party had failed to explain or justify. In particular, it had failed to explain the requisite conditions for participation in the elections. Accordingly, it must be assumed that Mr Bwalya had been detained and denied the right to run for a parliamentary seat in the Constituency of Chifuba merely on account of his membership in a political party other than that officially recognized. In this context, the Committee observed that restrictions on political activity outside the only recognized political party amounted to an unreasonable restriction of the right to participate in the conduct of public affairs.

Finally, on the basis of the information before it, the Human Rights Committee concluded that the author had been discriminated against in his employment because of his political opinions, contrary to article 26 of the Covenant.

Pursuant to article 2 of the Covenant, the Human Rights Committee held that Zambia was under an obligation to provide Mr Bwalya with an appropriate remedy. The Committee urged Zambia to grant appropriate compensation to Mr Bwalya. Zambia, the Committee added, was also under an obligation to ensure that similar violations did not occur in the future. The Committee expressed its wish to receive information, within 90 days, on any relevant measures taken by the Zambian Government to follow up on the decisions of the Committee.

At the time, the Zambian one-party government paid scant attention to the decisions of the Human Rights Committee. However the findings and views of the Committee helped inform and inspire the debate for the restoration of multi-party democracy in Zambia, something that now obtains in the country. The significance of the Human Rights Committee's views in this case is that they are now also part of the jurisprudence of Zambia when it comes to the exercise of democratic rights in the country. The right to democracy is undoubtedly a fundamental universal human right.

In case No. 138/1983 (*Ngalula et al v. Zaire*), the authors were twelve former parliamentarians and a Zairean businessman who had been detained at various prisons throughout Zaire, and who, upon release, were subjected to an administrative banning measure and deported along with their families to different parts of the country. The banned family members included children still of elementary school age, adolescent boys and girls and married brothers who were heads of families and whose wives had been left in Kinshasa alone with small children and without any means of support. The Human Rights Committee found a violation of article 12 (1) of the Covenant "because they were deprived of their freedom of movement during long periods of administrative banishment.".[78]

In case No. 157/1983, (*Mkapa-Nsusu v. Zaire*), the author, a former presidential candidate, had been subjected to detention without trial. Following his release, he was not allowed to remain in the capital but was subjected to banishment. He subsequently fled the country and was living in exile at the time of the submission of his petition. The Human Rights Committee found a violation of article 12 (1) "because he was banished to his village or origin for an indefinite period."[79]

In case No. 505/1992, (*Ackla v. Togo*), the Committee found a violation of article 12 (1) because the petitioner had been prohibited from entering the district in which his native village was located and the State party had failed to provide any explanations justifying this restriction of his freedom of movement.[80]

In joint views that it adopted in November 1989 in cases Nos. 241 and 242/1987, (*Birindwa and Tshisekedi v. Zaire*), the Human Rights Committee found a violation of article 10 (1) of the Covenant because Mr Tshisekedi "was not treated with humanity during his detention ..." and of article 7 because "he was subjected to inhuman treatment, in that he was deprived of food and drink for four days after his arrest and was subsequently kept interned under unacceptable sanitary conditions."[81]

In case No. 386/1989 (*Kone v. Senegal*), the petitioner had been arrested on 15 January 1982 and released on 9 May 1986. During this time no trial date was set. The Human Rights Committee concluded that the author's detention of

78 Ibid, p. 230.
79 Ibid, p, 230.
80 Ibid., pp. 230–231.
81 Ibid, p. 209.

four years and four months was incompatible with the provisions of article 9 (3) of the Covenant.[82]

In case No. 390/1990 (*Luboto v. Zambia*), the petitioner had been convicted and sentenced to death for aggravated robbery with the use of firearms. The Committee, considering that in the particular case no one had been killed or wounded and that the court under the applicable law could not take these elements into account when sentencing, was of the view that the mandatory imposition of the death penalty in those circumstances was in violation of article 6, paragraph 2 of the Covenant. The Committee observed:

> The issue that must accordingly be decided is whether the sentence in the instant case is compatible with article 6, paragraph 2 of the Covenant, which allows for the imposition of the death penalty only 'for the most serious crimes'. Considering that in this case use of firearms did not produce the death or wounding of any person and that the court could not under the law take these elements into account in imposing sentence, the Committee is of the view that the mandatory imposition of the death sentence under these circumstances violates article 6, paragraph 2 of the Covenant;[83]

In case No. 458/1991 (*Albert Wumah Mukang v Cameroon*), the petitioner claimed that the State party had imposed unreasonable restrictions on his freedom of expression by, inter alia, banning one of his publications and detaining him. Finding a violation of article 19 of the ICCPR, the Committee observed as follows:

> The State party has indirectly justified its actions on grounds of national security ... by arguing that the author's right to freedom of expression was exercised without regard to the country's political context and continued struggle for unity. While the State party has indicated that the restrictions on the author's freedom of expression were provided for by law, it must still be determined whether the measures taken against the author were necessary for the safeguard of national security and/or public order ... It further considers that the legitimate objective of safeguarding and indeed strengthening national unity under difficult circumstances cannot be achieved by attempting to muzzle advocacy of multi-party

82 Ibid, p. 197.

83 Ibid, p. 155.

> democracy, democratic tenets and human rights; in this regard, the question of deciding which measures might meet the 'necessity' test in such situations does not arise.[84]

In case No.414/1990 (*Primo J. Essona Mike Miha v. Equatorial Guinea*), the Human Rights Committee held that article 19 of the ICCPR had been violated and observed:

> the State party has not refuted the author's claim that he was arrested and detained solely or primarily because of his membership in, and activities for a political party in opposition to the regime of President Obiang Nguema.[85]

In case No. 428/1990, (*Francois Bozize v the Central African Republic*), the Human Rights Committee found a violation of article 14 (3) © of the ICCPR because Mr Bozize, a political opponent of the Government, still had not been tried at the first instance after four years of detention.[86]

In case No. 542/1993 (*Tshishimbi v. Żaire*), the Human Rights Committee noted that Mr Tshishimbi had been abducted under circumstances that had not been clarified and had no contact with his family or with the outside world since his abduction. The State party consistently ignored the Committee's requests for information regarding Mr Tshishimbi's abduction and whereabouts. In the circumstances, the Committee concluded that the removal of the victim and the prevention of contact with his family and with the outside world constituted cruel and inhuman treatment, in violation of article 7 of the ICCPR.[87]

In case No. 1134/2002, (*Gorji-Dinka v. Cameroon*), the petitioner claimed that the removal of his name from the voters' register violated his rights under article 25 (b) of the ICCPR. The Human Rights Committee observed that the exercise of the right to vote and to be elected may not be suspended or excluded on grounds established by law that were objective and reasonable, and reiterated that persons who were deprived of liberty but who had not been convicted should not be excluded from exercising the right to vote. The Committee also recalled that persons who were otherwise eligible to stand for election should not be excluded by reason of political affiliation. In the absence of any

84 Ibid, p. 356.
85 Ibid, p. 356.
86 Ibid, p. 281.
87 Ibid, p. 168.

objective and reasonable grounds to justify the author's deprivation of his right to vote and to be elected, the Committee concluded that article 25 (b) of the ICCPR had been violated.[88]

In case No. 1107/2002 (*El Ghar v. The Libyan Arab Jamahiriya*), the Libyan Consulate in Casablanca had refused to issue a passport to the petitioner, a Libyan citizen, and thereby prevented her from travelling to study abroad. The Human Rights Committee recalled that in the case of a national living abroad, the State of nationality was still bound by article 12 (2) of the ICCPR. While there may be circumstances in which a State may refuse to issue a passport to one of its citizens, in this case the State had not put forward any such argument but had assured the Committee that it had issued instructions to ensure that the author's passport application was duly processed. The Human Rights Committee found a violation of article 12 (2) "insofar as the author was denied a passport without any valid justification and subjected to unreasonable delay, and as a result was prevented from traveling abroad to continue her studies."[89]

In case No. 1128/2002 (*Marques de Morais v. Angola*), the Human Rights Committee examined whether the author's arrest and subsequent detention were arbitrary. The Committee recalled its jurisprudence, according to which the notion of "arbitrariness" is not to be equated with "against the law", but has to be interpreted more broadly to include elements of inappropriateness, injustice, lack of predictability and due process of law. This meant that remand in custody had to be not only lawful but also reasonable and necessary in all the circumstances, for example to prevent flight, interference with evidence or the recurrence of crime. No such element had been invoked in the Marques de Morais case. Irrespective of the applicable rules of criminal procedure, the Committee observed that the author was arrested on charges of defamation which, although qualifying as a crime under Angolan law, did not justify his arrest at gunpoint by 20 armed policemen, nor the length of his detention of 40 days, including 10 days in incommunicado detention. The Committee concluded that, in the circumstances, the author's arrest and detention were neither reasonable nor necessary but were, at least in part, of a punitive character and thus arbitrary in violation of article 9 (1) of the ICCPR. The Committee reached a similar conclusion in case No 1134/2002 (*Gorji-Dinka v. Cameroon*), where it also recalled that article 9 (1) applied to all forms of deprivation of liberty including house arrest.[90]

88 Ibid, p. 401.
89 Ibid, p. 232.
90 Ibid, p. 187.

In case No. 1132/2002 (*Chisanga v. Zambia*) concerning a death row prisoner awaiting execution by hanging, the Human Rights Committee found violations of various articles of the ICCPR, including article 14 (5) on the right to appeal. The Committee held that the commutation of the author's death sentences was a "necessary prerequisite" for providing him with a remedy to which he was entitled.[91]

During February and March 2002, over 150 government opponents in Equatorial Guinea had been arbitrarily arrested, tortured and subjected to an unfair trial, in violation of articles 7, 9 and 14 (1) and (3) (a), (b), (d) and (g) of the Covenant. The six victims in communications Nos. 1152 and 1190/2002 (*Ndong bee et. Al. and Mico Abogo v. Equatorial Guinea*) were among the 150 government opponents so treated. The Human Rights Committee found violations and stated that the State party was required to provide an effective remedy, including immediate release and adequate compensation, not only to the six victims in the communication, but also to all the other detained and convicted prisoners that had suffered the same fame.[92]

In cases No. 992/2001 (*Bousroual v. Algeria*) and 1196/2003 (*Boucherf v. Algeria*), the Human Rights Committee recalled the definition of enforced disappearance contained in article 7, paragraph 2 (i) of the Rome Statute of the International Criminal Court and stated that any act of such disappearance constitutes a violation of many of the rights enshrined in the ICCPR, including the right to liberty and security of the person (art. 9), the right not to be subjected to torture or to cruel, inhuman or degrading treatment or punishment (art. 7), and the right of all persons deprived of their liberty to be treated with humanity and with respect for the inherent dignity of the human person (art. 10). It also violates or constitutes a grave threat to the right to life (art. 6).[93]

In case No. 641/1995 (*The Gedumbe v. The Democratic Republic of the Congo*), the Human Rights Committee found a violation of the ICCPR and observed:

> that the author has made specific allegations relating, on the one hand, to his suspension in complete disregard of the legal procedure and, in particular, in violation of the Zairian regulations governing State employees, and, on the other hand, to the failure to reinstate him in his post, in contravention of decisions of the Ministry of Primary and Secondary Education. In this connection the Committee noted also that the non-payment of the author's salary, notwithstanding the instructions by

91 Ibid, p. 495.

92 Ibid, p. 495.

93 Ibid, p. 189.

> the Ministry of Foreign Affairs, was the direct consequence of the failure to implement the above-mentioned decisions by the authorities. In the absence of a response by the State party, the Committee found that the facts in the case showed that the decisions by the authorities in the author's favour had not been acted upon and could not be regarded as an effective remedy for violations of article 25 © of the ICCPR read in conjunction with article 2 of the same covenant.[94]

In case No. 933/2000 (*Adrien Mundya Busyo, Thomas Osthudi Wongodi, Rene Sibu Matubuka et al. v. The Democratic Republic of the Congo*), the Human Rights Committee recalled that the principle of access to public service on general terms of equality implied that the State had a duty to ensure that it did not discriminate against anyone and that this was all the more applicable to persons employed in the public service and to those who had been dismissed. In finding a violation of article 25 © of the ICCPR, the Committee observed:

> that the authors have made specific and detailed allegations relating to their dismissal, which was not in conformity with the established legal procedures and safeguards. The Committee notes in this regard that the Minister of Justice, in his statement of June 1999, … and the Attorney-General of the Republic, in the report by the Public Prosecutor's Office of 19 September, 2000 …, recognize that the established procedures and safeguards for dismissal were not respected. Furthermore, the Committee considers that the circumstances referred to in Presidential Decree No. 144 could not be accepted by it in this specific case as grounds justifying the fact that the dismissal measures were in conformity with the law and, in particular, with article 4 of the Covenant ….[95]

3.6 Conclusion

This chapter has defined the universality of human rights to mean the legal human rights obligations of all Governments, including African governments under the UN Charter, combined with the Universal Declaration of Human Rights, international customary law and international treaty law, norms of *jus cogens*, and obligations *erga omnes*. African States make up a full quarter of

94 Ibid, p. 403.
95 Ibid, p. 403.

the Membership of the United Nations and participate fully in its organs such as the General Assembly, the Security Council, and the Human Rights Council. The universality of human rights is an article of faith in the mandate of the Human Rights Council and its Universal Periodic Review. All African States have participated in the Universal Periodic Review and have declared their commitment to the universality of human rights.

African Governments submit reports required under UN human rights treaties, engage in on-going dialogue with the monitoring organs established by these treaties, and benefit from the concluding observations and general comments of the treaty bodies. The United Nations human rights jurisprudence elaborated by treaty organs such as the Human Rights Committee, which we reviewed above in some detail, are integral parts of the human rights jurisprudence of African Governments and African institutions.

It may therefore be fairly concluded that through their participation in United Nations organs, African Governments are integral participants in the universality of human rights as elaborated by the United Nations. In some instances, such as in the African Charter on Human and Peoples' Rights, African Governments have recognized rights going beyond those in UN human rights instruments. What this means is that, for African Governments, the point of departure is the foundation of UN universal human rights norms supplemented by African regional instruments. In this way, Africa builds upon, and enriches the universality of human rights across the world.

CHAPTER 4

The African Commission and Court on Human and Peoples' Rights

Abstract

The jurisprudence of the African Commission and the African Court on Human and Peoples' Rights have consistently upheld the applicability in Africa of international human rights law, and the universality of human rights. While enforcing the African Convention on Human and Peoples' Rights the Commission and the Court have interpreted its provisions in the light of international human rights law.

4.1 Introduction

The idea of an African Commission on Human Rights goes back to the 1960s and Taslim Olawale Elias of Nigeria was one of its leading promoters. Seminars organized by the International Commission of Jurists on the Rule of Law in Africa sought to advance the idea. The United Nations Division of Human Rights took up the idea and organized two seminars in the 1960s to help take the idea forward but it did not develop traction. Theo van Boven, when he became Director of human rights, took the initiative to organize a third seminar in Monrovia, Liberia, and this turned out to be a decisive initiative, leading directly to the establishment of today's African Commission on Human and Peoples' Rights.

As part of the process of promoting regional cooperation for the promotion and protection of human rights, the Division of Human Rights cooperated closely with the International Commission of Jurists which, under its distinguished Secretary-General Niall MacDermot, was also pushing regional strategies for the promotion and protection of human rights.

The seminar was held in Monrovia in 1979. Van Boven and I took with us a draft convention which envisaged the adoption of a resolution by the Assembly of the Organization of African Unity establishing an African Commission, as the General Assembly of the OAS had done for the Americas.

At the opening of the Monrovia Seminar, van Boven delivered an opening address in which he stated the following:

 | DOI:10.1163/9789004520646_005

> The idea of the seminar is to work along with the aspirations and energies of African Governments and peoples and to provide them with an opportunity of discussing these matters with a view to deciding for themselves whether any further institutions in the field of human rights are necessary on the African continent, and if so, what form it should take.
>
> ...
>
> This seminar, while mindful of the experience of other regions, will be focusing on the needs of Africa. ... In discussing this matter the seminar may wish to be flexible. Thus, it could well be that, as occurred in the Inter-American region, while work is underway for the preparation of the draft Charter of Human Rights recently requested by the OAU Heads of State and Government, and for the establishment of African human rights organs under that Charter, measures could be taken in the meantime to establish arrangements which could function pending the entry into force of the Charter, and even to prepare the ground so that when, eventually, any organ established by the future African Charter begins to function, they will have had the experience of any such earlier arrangements.[1]

When van Boven went to Liberia he found significant opposition on the part of some participants. Morocco was then smarting from the OAU's recognition of the Polisario Liberation Front (Western Sahara) and was obstructive. The legal adviser of the OAU, a Nigerian, was unfriendly to the idea. The other participants were sitting on the fence in the first two days of the seminar. One of the NGO participants was Mr Eya Nchama of Equatorial Guinea, who was a respected representative of an anti-discrimination NGO in Geneva.

After we saw that the seminar was making no headway we had a strategy session with him and he agreed, the next day, to make a strong appeal for progress. He is a powerful speaker and commanded the audience the next day. Following his speech, the seminar accepted a proposal we had arranged for him to make, suggesting the establishment of a drafting committee to prepare the text of an African Commission.

There were views, which would subsequently prevail in the African Charter, that the establishment of an African Commission should go in tandem with the adoption of African norms of human rights. We were pushing for the model of the OAS in which the establishment of a convention by resolution

1 People Matter, pp. 167–169.

had preceded the adoption of a convention. The work of the drafting group went along with our line of reasoning.

The Chairman of the drafting group was Mr Justice Wiredu of Ghana. Without him the process would not have advanced. He believed in the idea of an African Commission and he was a strong chair. He faced down filibusterers. He subsequently became Chief Justice of Ghana. The institutional parts of the African Charter on Human and Peoples' Rights are basically as drafted in Monrovia.

There is one point about the deliberations of the drafting committee that might be remarked upon. In our draft we had, following the Statute of the International Court of Justice, put in that the African Commission could apply African regional customary law. The Senegalese participant, Mr Justice M'Backe, stoutly resisted this. He did not wish Africa to be imprisoned in retrograde customs. We therefore inserted in the text that the African Commission could draw upon African customs to the extent that they were consistent with international human rights standards. It was thus that the international standard prevailed in the Monrovia draft. One could say that this was the M'Backe standard!

4.2 The African Human Rights Commission and the Universality of Human Rights

The functions of the Commission, under Article 45 (1)(c) of the African Charter, are to cooperate with other African and international institutions concerned with the promotion and protection of human and peoples' rights. The African Commission on Human and Peoples' Rights has distinctly affirmed the universality of human rights. This can be seen in the following statement in the decision it adopted in the 1990s in a case on freedom of opinion and expression in Nigeria:

> Governments should avoid restricting rights, and have special care with regard to those rights protected by constitutional or *international human rights law*. No situation justifies the wholesale violation of human rights. In fact, general restrictions on rights diminish public confidence in the rule of law and are often counter-productive.
>
> ... According to Article 9(2) of the Charter, dissemination of opinions may be restricted by law. This does not mean that national law can set aside the right to express and disseminate one's opinions; this would make the protection of the right to express and disseminate one's

> opinions ineffective. To allow national law to have precedence over the international law of the Charter would defeat the purpose of the rights and freedoms enshrined in the Charter. *International human rights standards must always prevail over contradictory national law.* Any limitation on the rights of the Charter must be in conformity with the provisions of the Charter.
>
> ... In contrast to other international human rights instruments, the African Charter does not contain a derogation clause. Therefore, limitations on the rights and freedoms enshrined in the Charter cannot be justified by emergencies or special circumstances.
>
> ... The only legitimate reasons for limitations to the rights and freedoms of the African Charter are found in Article 27(2), that is that the rights of the Charter 'shall be exercised with due regard to the rights of others, collective security, morality and common interest.'
>
> ... The reasons for possible limitations must be founded in a legitimate state interest and the evils of limitations of rights must be strictly proportionate with and absolutely necessary for the advantages which are to be obtained.
>
> ... Even more important, a limitation may never have as a consequence that the right itself becomes illusory.[2]

We shall look further into its jurisprudence on universality later in this chapter. Before doing so, however, it would be helpful to take note at this point of the African Charter on Democracy, Elections and Governance adopted by the African Union on 30 January, 2007. This Charter blends seamlessly with the African Charter on Human and Peoples' Rights and together they confirm that African regional human rights law is grounded in universal, democratic values. We discuss the African Charter on Democracy in the next chapter, below.

The universality of human rights leaps out from the jurisprudence of the African Commission when considering petitions brought before it under the African Charter. The decisions of the African Commission invoke standards of justice quite well-known in United Nations human rights treaty bodies, the European Court of Human Rights, the Inter-American Commission, and Court of Human Rights. They also invoke universal norms such as the UN Basic Principles and Guidelines on the Right to a Remedy and Reparation for Victims of Gross Violations of International Human Rights Law and Serious Violations

---

2 Communications 105/93, 128/94, 130/94 and 152/96: Media Rights Agenda and Constitutional Rights Project v. Nigeria, Twelfth Activity Report 1998–1999, Annex V, pp. 725–726, paras. 65–70. Emphasis supplied.

of International Humanitarian Law. A sample of the decisions of the African Commission is provided below.

4.2.1 *Protection of the Right to Life: Noah Kazingachire, John Chitsenga, Elias Chemvura and Batanai Hadzisi v. Zimbabwe*[3]

These cases involved four men killed by law-enforcement officers. The African Commission found that Zimbabwe had violated articles 1 and 4 (right to life) of the African Charter. While the right to life is not absolute, law enforcement officers are only permitted to kill in self-defence or in defence of others against the imminent threat of death or serious injury. Use of deadly force must be a last resort. In all four deaths in question the deceased posed no serious risk to anyone. In none of the cases were the officers acting in self-defence. Therefore, the use of deadly force was not justified and the killings violated the victims' right to life.

The African Commission held that Lameck Chemvura's death was not directly attributable to the State because the army officers involved were not acting on official orders but rather were acting in their personal capacities. However, an act that violates human rights laws, even if it is not directly imputable to a State, can lead to international responsibility of the State if the State fails to exercise due diligence by failing to provide an adequate wrongful death remedy. The army officers' violations were imputable to the State. The other homicides were directly attributable to the State. There was therefore a violation of article 1.

The African Commission invoked the UN Basic Principles and Guidelines on the Right to a Remedy and Reparation for Victims of Gross Violations of International Human Rights Law and Serious Violations of International Humanitarian Law, which provides that victims have a right to reparation for harm suffered as a result of a gross violation of human rights law. Adequate reparation included damages for emotional harms as well as physical harms; thus, a suit for bereavement damages must be available to the families of people wrongfully killed by the State.

There was no tort action under the then Zimbabwe law to recover bereavement damages for a wrongful death. A cause of action only existed for loss of support or actual damages (medical, hospital, and funeral costs). The African Commission therefore recommended that Zimbabwe establish a wrongful death suit to provide bereavement damages.[4]

---

3 ACHPR, 295/04, 51st Ordinary Session, April, 2012.

4 See Case Digest, Decisions of the African Commission on Human and Peoples' Rights 2010 – 2014, published by the Open Society Justice Initiative, September, 2015, pp. 19–20.

4.2.2 *Freedom from Torture: Gabriel Shumba v. Zimbabwe*[5]

Personnel from the Central Intelligence Organization had arrested the complainant, a citizen of Zimbabwe and a human rights lawyer, as well as confiscated his belongings, and beat him up. He was then detained without charge or access to counsel and denied food and water. The day after his arrest, he was driven to an unknown location, where he was tortured until the third day of his arrest, when his lawyers were able to reach him. He was charged with organizing, planning and conspiring to overthrow the government. He subsequently fled to South Africa for fear of his life.

The African Commission found that the state was in violation of the victim's rights under article 5 not to be tortured and ill-treated. The victim had provided evidence (including medical and psychological reports) to support his claims that he had been beaten and subjected to prolonged electrocution, and the state had taken no steps to investigate or address these detailed allegations. The African Commission recommended that the state pay compensation to the victim for this trauma and carry out an inquiry to bring the officials who perpetrated the crime to justice.[6]

4.2.3 *The Right to Liberty and Freedom from Torture: Abdel Hadi, Ali Radi and Others v. Republic of Sudan*[7]

In this case, the victims were some ninety victims, Sudanese nationals who had fled Darfur due to the war in the region in 2005. They had settled in a refugee camp outside of Khartoum. Police officers arrested them and held them for over twelve months without providing a reason for their arrest. The officers denied the victims any access to lawyers, family members, and medical care. It was also alleged that all the complainants had been tortured. Following a court order, all the complainants were released a little over a year from their first arrest.

The African Commission found that sustained beatings, whippings, falaga, food deprivation, death threats, and the other forms of ill-treatment along with the physical and psychological effects, clearly constituted torture. The incommunicado detention, lack of medical access, lack of toilet facilities, and death threats also qualified as inhuman and degrading treatment. The African Commission held that the actions of the government, in imprisoning the people without legal justification and keeping them in detention for 12 months

5 ACPHR, 288/04, 51st Ordinary Session, April 2012.

6 See Case Digest, op. cit., p. 17.

7 ACHPR, 368/09, 54th Ordinary Session, November, 2013.

without charge, breached article 6. The Commission also held that that the one-year period that had elapsed before the victims appeared before a judge was too long. The victims were not told why they were arrested and they weren't allowed access to a lawyer for 9 months, which constituted violations of article 7(1) (c)and (d). Furthermore, the Commission found a violation of article 1 of the Charter on account of the respondent State's failure to investigate allegations of wrongdoings by its agents, provide adequate remedies to the victims, and put in place adequate legislative frameworks to protect the physical integrity of individuals.[8]

4.2.4 *The Right to a Fair Trial: Hargewoin Gabre-Selassie and* IHRDA *(on Behalf of Former Derge Officials v. Ethiopia)*[9]

This case involved former Derge Officials kept in detention for years before being tried. In finding the communication admissible, the African Commission held that a communication need not cite the particular articles of the African Charter that were allegedly violated, and that a communication may be valid even if it is in the form of a letter to its Special Rapporteur on Prisons and Conditions of Detention. Ethiopia had failed to respond to the complainant's allegations on these counts, creating a presumption against the State.

The African Commission held that Ethiopia had violated articles 1, 2 (equal protection), 7(1)(b) (right to be presumed innocent until proven guilty) and 7(1)(d) (right to be tried within a reasonable time by an impartial tribunal). The Commission held that the establishment of the special prosecutor's office had violated the presumption of innocence because it had been established with the stated purpose of recording the 'brutal offenses' committed against the Ethiopian people and otherwise presupposed the guilt of the Dergue regime. Government officials had also made public statements while the trials were ongoing that stated or presupposed the defendants' guilt. Furthermore, the extreme length of the defendants' pre-trial detention constituted *de facto* punishment for the alleged crimes before guilt had been proven. The Commission discussed a number of causes for the delay, but noted that none were attributable to the defendants and that, as a result, fell within the scope of responsibility of the state. The Commission found that Ethiopia had violated articles 1 and 2 by virtue of their violations of article 7.[10]

8 Case Digest, op. cit., p. 22.

9 ACHPR, 301/05, 50th Ordinary Session, October 2011.

10 Case Digest, op. cit., p. 19.

4.2.5 *The Independence of the Judiciary: Tsatsu Tsikata v. Republic of Ghana*[11]

The petitioner alleged that the respondent State was trying him retroactively for an act that did not constitute an offence at the time of its commission. He was arraigned before a 'Fast Track Court' after being summoned to appear 'in the name of the President'. The African Commission found a violation of article 26 of the African Charter due to a series of concerted actions taken by the executive directed towards a desired outcome on the review by the Supreme Court's decision on the constitutionality of the Fast Track Court. It held that those actions, including what appeared to be a 'targeted appointment of a Justice of Appeal and a strategic reconstitution of the Supreme Court', amounted to a 'tacit escalated interference with the independence' of that court.[12]

4.2.6 *The Right to Property: Dino Noca v. Democratic Republic of the Congo*[13]

Mr Noca was an Italian who lived in the DRC and owned a building there. On 2 July, 1974, the DRC passed a law under which abandoned or undeveloped properties would be ceded to the State and then given to Congolese nationals without intervention by the Courts. When Mr Noca left the country, he arranged for the State-Owned National Insurance Company (SONAS) to manage his building, which should have been sufficient to avoid application of the law. Nevertheless, the property was declared abandoned. SONAS appealed and won, voiding the declaration of abandonment. However, despite being told of this verdict and while awaiting verification by SONAS, the head of the lands department had granted the land to a third party. The verdict was later confirmed but the grant was not rescinded.

The African Commission found that the State had violated articles 3 (equal protection), 14 (right to property), and 7(1)(c) (right to have one's cause heard). The Commission found a violation of article 14 because Mr Noca was deprived of his property even though he complied with all requirements of DRC law: his land was under the control of SONAS and was not abandoned, but the head of the lands department nonetheless granted it to a third party. Furthermore, the department had demonstrated a lack of due diligence and goodwill by insufficiently investigating the legal status of the land prior to giving it to the third party. Article 1 created a duty in the State to investigate and remedy violations of the other articles. Thus, the failings of the State employees were imputed

---

11 ACHPR, 322/06, 55th Ordinary Session, April-May, 2014.

12 Case Digest, op. ci., pp. 24–25.

13 ACHPR, 286/04, 52nd Ordinary Session, October 2012.

to the State. The Commission further held that article 3 and 7(1)(c) had been violated because Mr Noca's heir had been called by the Supreme Court to continue his father's case but had not been given a chance to present his defence. This had violated the heir's right to be heard. Furthermore, since the Supreme Court had heard the other side's arguments but not the heir's, his right to equal treatment before the law had been violated.

In a notable pronouncement on the implementation of economic, social and cultural rights, the African Commission has stated the following:

> The African Commission would ... like to state that it is aware that millions of people in Africa are not enjoying the right to health maximally because African countries are generally faced with the problem of poverty which renders them incapable to provide the necessary amenities, infrastructure and resources that facilitate the full enjoyment of this right. Therefore, having due regard to this depressing but real state of affairs, the African Commission would like to read into Article 16 [of the ACHPR] the obligation on part of States ... to take concrete and targeted steps, while taking full advantage of its available resources, to ensure that the right to health is fully realised in all its aspects without discrimination of any kind.[14]

4.3 The African Human Rights Court and the Universality of Human Rights

In its very first judgment on the merits, Tanganyika Law Society and another v. Tanzania, delivered on 14 June, 2013, the African Court on Human and Peoples' Rights vigorously upheld universal precepts of international human rights law as contained in the African Charter on Human and Peoples' Rights. The Applicants in the case contended that the Respondent, Tanzania, was in violation of article 13(1) of the African Charter on Human and Peoples' Rights and that the violations were still continuing as it pertained to constitutional and statutory provisions still in force. The Applicants also relied on Articles 3 and 25 of the International Covenant on Civil and Political Rights and Article 21 (1) of the Universal Declaration of Human Rights.[15]

---

14 Communication 155/96, Purohit and Moore v. The Gambia, Sixteenth Activity Report 2002–2003, Annex VII, para. 84.

15 The judgment of the African Court is reproduced in Human Rights Law Journal, Vol. 33 No. 1–6, 30 August,2013, p. 18: African Court on Human and Peoples' Rights, Judgment of

In summary, they contended that the judgment of the Tanzanian Court of Appeal, Articles 39, 47, 67 and 77 of the Constitution of the United Republic of Tanzania 1977, and the Local Authorities (Elections) Act No. 7 of 2002, which collectively required that candidates for Presidential, Parliamentary and Local Government elections must be members of, and be sponsored by, a political party, constituted a violation of Articles 2, 10, and 13 of the African Charter and Articles 3 and 25 of the ICCPR.

The Respondent, for its part, submitted that the decision on whether or not to introduce independent candidatures in Tanzania was dependent on the social needs of the country, based on its historical reality. The Respondent further argued that the issue of independent candidatures was political and not legal. This argument was in line with the decision of the Tanzanian Court of Appeal.

The Respondent contended, in addition, that the restriction on independent candidatures was a means for avoiding absolute and uncontrolled liberty "whole and free from restraint which would lead to anarchy." The Respondent, moreover, pointed out that the Applicant involved in the case had formed his own political party and, effectively, had not been prevented from participating in politics.

Article 13 (1) of the African Charter on Human and Peoples' Rights provides that "1. Every citizen shall have the right to participate freely in the government of his country, either directly or through freely chosen representatives in accordance with the provisions of the law." The African Court commented on this provision:

> It is imperative to state here that the rights guaranteed under the Charter as stated in Article 13(1) are individual rights. They are not meant to be enjoyed only in association with some other individuals or group of individuals such as political parties. Therefore, in an application such as the instant one, what is of paramount significance is whether or not an individual right has been placed in jeopardy., or otherwise violated, not whether or not groups may enjoy the particular right.[16]

---

14 June 2013 – Consolidated matter – Application No. 009/2011 – Tanganyika Law Society and the Legal and Human Rights Centre v. The United Republic of Tanzania; Application No. 011/2011 – Reverend Christopher R. Mtikila v. The United Republic of Tanzania. Court's first judgment on the merits ...

16 Judgment, para. 98.

The Court continued:

> In view of the patently clear terms of Article 13 (1) of the Charter, which gives to the citizen the option of participating in the governance of her country directly or through representatives, a requirement that a candidate must belong to a political party before she is enabled to participate in the governance of Tanzania surely derogates from the rights enshrined in Article 13 (1) of the Charter.[17]

After reviewing the submissions of the Respondent on the issue of restrictions on rights, the Court went on to hold as follows:

> Jurisprudence regarding the restrictions on the exercise of rights has developed the principle that the restrictions must be necessary in a democratic society; they must be reasonably proportionate to the legitimate aim pursued.[18]

The Court proceeded to review relevant jurisprudence of the Inter-American Court of Human Rights, the European Court of Human Rights, and the UN Human Rights Committee. In paragraph 107.4 of its Judgment, the Court stated the following:

> The United Nations Human Rights Committee's General Comment No. 25 on the right to participate in public affairs, voting rights and the right of equal access to public service (Art. 25), at paragraph 17 thereof, provides that 'The right of persons to stand for election should not be limited unreasonably by requiring candidates to be members of political parties or of specific parties. If a candidate is required to have a minimum number of supporters for nomination this requirement should be reasonable and not act as a barrier to candidacy. Without prejudice to paragraph (1) of Article 5 of the Covenant, political opinion may not be used as a ground to deprive any person of the right to stand for election.' The Court agrees with this General Comment, as it is an authoritative statement of interpretation of Article 25 of the ICCPR, which reflects the spirit of Article 13 of the Charter and which, in accordance with Article 60 of the Charter, is an 'instrument adopted by the United Nations on human and

17 Ibid, para. 99.

18 Ibid, para. 106.1.

peoples' rights' that the Court can 'draw inspiration from' in its interpretation of the Charter.

108. Furthermore, it is the view of the Court that the limitation imposed by the Respondent ought to be in consonance with international standards, to which the Respondent is expected to adhere. This is in line with the principle set out in Article 27 of the Vienna Convention on the Law of Treaties which provides that: 'A party may not invoke the provisions of its internal law as justification for its failure to perform a treaty.' ... Additionally, Article 32 of the International Law Commission Articles on State Responsibility, 2001 provides that 'the Responsible State may not rely on the provisions of its internal law as justification for failure to comply with its obligations.[19]

The African Court went on to hold, in paragraph 113 of its Judgment:

> It is the view of the Court that freedom of association is negated if an individual is forced to associate with others. Freedom of association is also negated if other people are forced to join up with the individual. In other words, freedom of association i8mplies freedom to associate and freedom not to associate.

The Court added in paragraph 114:

> The Court therefore finds that by requiring individuals to belong to and to be sponsored by a political party in seeking election in the Presidential, Parliamentary and Local Government posts, the Respondent has violated the right to freedom of association. This is because individuals are compelled to join or form an association before seeking these elective positions.

Even more, in paragraph 115, the Court added:

> The Court is not satisfied that the social needs argument raised by the Respondent ... meets the exceptions in Articles 29 (4) and 27 (2) of the Charter to such an extent that it justifies the limitation of the right to freedom of association.

19 Judgment, para. 108.

The Court directed the Respondent to take constitutional, legislative and all other necessary measures within a reasonable time to remedy the violations found by the Court and to inform the Court of the measures taken.[20]

From the perspective of the universality of human rights, one may note the following:

- The African Court interpreted the concept of freedom of association in the African Charter in the light of international standards and of regional and international jurisprudence.
- The African Court also defined criteria for limitations on the right to freedom of association in the light of international standards and of regional and international jurisprudence.
- The African Court explicitly drew approvingly on the legal views of the UN Human Rights Committee.
- The African Court explicitly drew on universal norms of the law of treaties and of State Responsibility.

In essence, the African Court was subscribing to universal precepts of the right to freedom of association in applying the corresponding provisions of the African Charter.

4.4 The African Protection Concept

The protection concept of the African Commission and the African Court on Human and Peoples' Rights will shape the future of the continent and its peoples.[21] The functions of the African Commission, as set out in Article 45 of the Charter, are to promote human and peoples' rights, to 'ensure the protection of human and peoples' rights under conditions laid down by the present Charter', to interpret the Charter, and to perform any other tasks assigned to it. The Commission considers Government reports on their efforts to fulfil the Charter, considers petitions from States, individuals and groups, and, on occasions, make visits to States Parties.

20 Judgment, para. 126.

21 See, generally C. Anyangwe, Obligations of States Parties to the African Charter on Human and Peoples' Rights, 10. Afr, J. Int'l. and Comp. Law 1998,625. E. Bello, The Mandate of the African Commission on Human and Peoples' Rights, 1 Afr, J. Int'l L, 1988, 31. N.J. Udombana, Between Promise and Performance: Revisiting States' Obligations Under the African Human Rights Charter, Stanford Journal of International Law, Vol. 40, No. 1, 2004, 105–142. Z. Stavrindes, Human Rights Obligations Under the United Nations Charter. 3 International Journal of Human Rights, 1999, 38. American Journal of International Law, Vol. 101, No. 1,2007.

When considering communications from States, the Commission, after deliberating on a communication, prepares a report to the States concerned and communicates it also to the successor of the Assembly of Heads of State and Government of the former OAU, now the Council of the African Union. In transmitting the report, the Commission may make such recommendations as it deems useful.

When considering communications from individuals or groups, the Commission, if it considers that a communication reveals the existence of a series or serious or massive violations of human and peoples' rights, shall draw the attention of the (Council) to the situation concerned. The Council may then request the Commission to undertake an in-depth study of these cases and make a factual report, accompanied by its findings and recommendations. A case of emergency duly noticed by the Commission shall be submitted by it to the (Council) which may request it to make an in-depth study.

Under Article 54 of the Charter, the Commission shall submit to each ordinary session of the (Council) a report on its activities.

Article 60 of the Charter provides that the Commission shall draw inspiration from international law on human and peoples' rights, particularly from the provisions of various African instruments on human and peoples' rights, the Charter of the United Nations, the Charter of the then Organization of African Unity, the Universal Declaration of Human Rights, other instruments adopted by the United Nations and African countries in the field of human and peoples' rights, as well as from the provisions of various instruments adopted within the Specialized Agencies of the United Nations of which the parties to the African Charter are members.

Under Article 61 the Commission shall also take into consideration, as subsidiary measures to determine the principles of law, other general or special international conventions laying down rules expressly recognized by member states of the OAU, African practices consistent international norms on human and peoples' rights, customs generally accepted as law, general principles of law recognized by African states as well as legal precedents and doctrine.

The African Commission has held that not only do the States Parties to the African Charter recognise the rights, obligations and freedoms proclaimed in the Charter. They also commit themselves to respect them and take measures to give effect to them.[22] The Commission has had a long-standing practice of holding that in cases of human rights violations, the burden of proof rests on

22 See Case Digest, Decisions of the African Commission on Human and Peoples' Rights 2010 – 2014, published by the Open Society Justice Initiative, September, 2015, p. 59.

the government. If the government provides no evidence to contradict an allegation of human rights violation made against it, the Commission will take it as proven, or at the least probable or plausible. [346:52] Where allegations of human rights abuse go uncontested by the Government concerned, the Commission must decide on the facts provided by the complainant and treat those facts as given. This principle conforms with the practice of other international human rights adjudicatory bodies and the Commission's duty to protect human rights.[23]

4.4.1 *General Obligation of the State to Respect, Protect, Promote and Fulfil Rights*[24]

In Social and Economic Rights Action Centre (SERAC) v. Nigeria, the African Commission stated that "Internationally accepted ideas of the various obligations engendered by human rights indicate duties that all rights – both civil and political rights and social and economic – generate at least four levels of duties for a state that undertakes to adhere to a rights regime: namely the duty to respect, protect, promote, and fulfil these rights. These obligations universally apply to all rights and entail a combination of negative and positive"[25]

In its General Comment No. 2, the African Commission elaborated on this as follows:

> 41. Article 14.1 (a), (b), (c) and (f) and Article 14.2 (a) and (c) impose four general obligations on State parties, like several provisions on human rights: respect, protect, promote and fulfil rights thereof.
> 42. *The obligation to respect rights* requires State parties to refrain from hindering, directly or indirectly, women's rights and to ensure that women are duly informed on family planning/contraception and safe abortion services, which should be available, accessible, acceptable and of good quality.
> 42. *The obligation to protect* requires States parties to take the necessary measures to prevent third parties from interfering with the enjoyment of women's sexual and reproductive rights. Particular attention must be given to prevention, as regards the interference of third parties concerning the rights of vulnerable groups such as

23 Ibid, p. 75.

24 ACHPR, General Comment No. 2 on Article 14.1 (a), (b), (c) and (f) and Article 14.2 (a) and (c) of Protocol to the African Charter on Human and Peoples' Rights on the Rights of Women in Africa.

25 Social and Economic Rights Action Ctr. V. Nigeria, Comm. No. 155/96, para. 44.

adolescent girls, women living with disabilities, women living with HIV and women in situations of conflict. The obligation entails the formulation of standards and guidelines containing the precision that the consent and involvement of third parties, including but limited to parents, guardians, spouses and partners, is not required when adult women and adolescent girls want to access family planning/contraception and safe abortion services in the cases provided for in the Protocol.

44. *The obligation to promote* obliges State parties to create the legal, economic and social conditions that enable women to exercise their sexual and reproductive rights with regard to family planning/contraception and safe abortion, as well as to enjoy them. An essential step towards eliminating stigmatization and discrimination related to reproductive health incudes, but is not limited to, supporting women's empowerment, sensitizing and educating communities, religious leaders, traditional chiefs and political leaders on women's sexual and reproductive rights as well as training health-care workers.

45. *The obligation to fulfil rights* requires that State Parties adopt relevant laws, policies and programmes that ensure the fulfilment *de jure* and *de facto* of women's sexual and reproductive rights, including the allocation of sufficient and available resources for the full realization of those rights.

4.4.2 *Supremacy of International Law and of the African Charter over National Law*

In its jurisprudence, the African Commission on Human and Peoples' Rights has repeatedly drawn upon international human rights law broadly in grounding its decisions. Among the statements made by the Commission are the following:

- In the task of interpretation and application of the African Charter, the Commission is enjoined by Articles 60 and 61 to "draw inspiration from international law on human and peoples' rights" as reflected in the instruments of the OAU/AU and the UN as well as other international standard setting principles.[26]

26 See Case Digest, Decisions of the African Commission on Human and Peoples' Rights 2010 – 2014, published by the Open Society Justice Initiative, September, 2015, p. 58.

- International human rights standards must always prevail over contradictory national law.[27]
- The duties of a government, whatever system of governance may be in place, are to abide by the international norms as well as the duties established in international human rights law. The Commission has held that a basic premise of international human rights law is that certain standards must be constant across national borders and governments must be held accountable to these standards. For example, the criteria for what constitutes free and fair elections are internationally agreed upon.[28]
- Principles of international law stipulate that a new government inherits the previous government's international obligations.[29]
- The prohibition of torture, cruel, inhuman or degrading treatment or punishment is absolute.[30]
- Freedom of expression is a basic human right, vital to an individual's personal development and political consciousness, and to his participation in the conduct of public affairs in his/her country.[31]
- International human rights law and the community of States accord a certain importance to the eradication of discrimination in all its guises.
- The obligations of national courts and tribunals in international standards of ensuring fair trial.[32]
- International law prohibits states from relying on their national law as justification for their non-compliance with international human rights obligations.[33]
- The competent authorities should not override constitutional provisions or undermine fundamental rights guaranteed by the constitution or international human rights standards.[34]
- The Commission has called in aid Views and General Comments of the UN Human Rights Committee. It has also called in aid decisions of the former European Commission on Human Rights and the European Court of Human Rights and the Inter-American Commission and Court of Human Rights.
- The Commission has expressly invoked UN instruments such as the UN Basic Principles on the Independence of the Judiciary and the Body of Principles

27 Ibid, p. 66.
28 Ibid, p. 231.
29 Ibid, p. 157.
30 Ibid, p. 306.
31 Ibid, p. 253.
32 Ibid., p. 60.
33 Ibid, p. 391.
34 Ibid, p. 117.

for the Protection of All Persons Under Any Form of Imprisonment; the UN Safeguards Guaranteeing Protection of the Rights of Those Facing the Death Penalty; the UN Declaration on the Rights of Persons Belonging to National, Ethnic, Religious or Linguistic Minorities. The Commission has also cited the Vienna Declaration and programme of Action adopted by the Vienna World Conference on Human Rights (1993)

The African Commission has consistently held that the international law of the African Charter takes precedence over national law. In CRP v. Nigeria, the Commission held that to permit national law to take precedence over international law would defeat the purpose of codifying certain rights in international law and indeed, the whole essence of treaty making.[35]

In Media Rights Agenda and Constitutional Rights Project v. Nigeria, the Commission declared that Governments should avoid restricting rights and have special care with regard to those rights protected by constitutional or international human rights law. No situation justifies the wholesale violation of human rights law. In fact, general restrictions on rights diminish public confidence in the rule of law and are often counter-productive.

The Commission recalled that in contrast to other international human rights instruments, the African Charter does not contain a derogation clause. Therefore, limitations on the rights and freedoms enshrined in the Charter cannot be justified by emergencies or special circumstances. The only legitimate reasons for limitations to the rights and freedoms of the African Charter are found in Article 27(2), namely that the rights in the Charter 'shall be exercised with due regard to the rights of others, collective security, morality and common interest.' The reasons for possible limitations must be grounded in a legitimate State interest and the evils of limitations of rights must be strictly proportionate with and absolutely necessary for the advantages which are to be obtained. Even more important, a limitation may never have as a consequence that the right itself becomes illusory.[36]

The African Commission has held that when a state ratifies the Charter it is responsible for upholding the rights in it even if it has not yet enacted domestic legislation to give effect to the Charter. It has held that international treaties which are not part of domestic law and which may not be directly enforceable in the national courts nonetheless impose obligations on States Parties.[37]

35 Constitutional Rights Project v. Nigeria, Comm. No. 140/94, para. 40.

36 Malcolm Evans and Rachel Murray, The African Charter on Human and Peoples' Rights: The System in Practice. Cambridge, Cambridge University Press, 2008, p. 7.

37 Legal Res. Found. V. Zambia. Comm No. 211/98, paras. 59–60. 2000–2001 Afr. Ann. Act. Rep., Annex v. See also, N.J. Udombana," Between Promise and Performance: Revisiting

4.4.3 *The Principle of Subsidiarity and the Margin of Appreciation*

In Prince v. South Africa, the African Commission recognized that the principle of subsidiarity indeed informs the African Charter and that the Commission could not substitute itself for internal or domestic procedures in the respondent state that strive to give effect to the promotion and protection of rights enshrined in the Charter. Similarly, the margin of appreciation doctrine also informs the Charter in that it recognizes a State Party as being better disposed in adopting national rules, policies and guidelines in promoting and protecting human and peoples' rights as it has direct and continuous knowledge of its society, its needs, resources, economic and political situation, legal practices and balance that needs to be struck between the competing and sometimes conflicting forces that shape its society. Both doctrines, the Commission recognized, establish the primary competence and duty of the State Party to promote and protect human and peoples' rights within its domestic order.

Nevertheless, the African Commission held:

> … Whatever discretion these two doctrines may allow Member States in promoting and protecting human and peoples' rights domestically, they do not deny the African Commission's mandate to guide, assist, supervise and insist upon Member States on better promotion and protection standards should it find domestic practices wanting. They do allow Member States to primarily take charge of the implementation of the African Charter in their respective countries. In doing so, they are informed by the trust the African Charter has on Member States to fully recognize and give effect to the rights enshrined therein. What the African Commission would not allow, however, is a restrictive reading of these doctrines, like that of the Respondent State, which advocates for the hands-off approach by the African Commission on the mere assertion that its domestic procedures meet more than the minimum requirement of the Charter.[38]

4.4.4 *The Responsibility to Protect*

In Commission National des droits de l'homme v. Chad, the African Commission recalled that the Charter specified in Article 1 that the States Parties shall not only recognize the rights and duties and freedoms enshrined in the Charter,

States' Obligations Under the African Human Rights Charter", Stanford Journal of International Law, Vol. 40, No. 1, 2004, 105–142, at p. 127.

38 Case No. 255/2002, 36th Ordinary Session, 2004.

but they should also undertake measures to give effect to them. In other words, if a State neglects to ensure the rights in the Charter, this can constitute a violation, even if the State or its agents are not the immediate cause of the violation. The Commission noted that the African Charter, unlike other human rights instruments, does not allow for States Parties to derogate from their treaty obligations during emergency situations. Thus, even a civil war in Chad could not be used as an excuse by the State violating or permitting violations of rights in the Charter.[39]

On the national responsibility to protect, the African Commission stated in Commission National des ddh et des libertes v. Chad. :

> 20. The Charter specifies in Article 1 that the States Parties shall not only recognize the rights and duties and freedoms adopted by the Charter, but they should also "undertake ... measures to give effect to them". In other words, if a State neglects to ensure the rights in the African Charter, this can constitute a violation, even if the State or its agents are not the immediate cause of the violation.
>
> 21. The African Charter, unlike other human rights instruments, does not allow for States Parties to derogate from their treaty obligations during emergency situations. Thus, even a civil war in Chad cannot be used as an excuse by the State violating or permitting violations of rights in the African Charter.[40]

4.4.5 *The Responsibility to Prevent*

In Commission National des droits de l'homme v. Chad, the African Commission held that Chad had failed to provide security and stability in the country, thereby allowing serious and massive violations of human rights. The national armed forces were participants in the civil war and there had been several instances in which the Government had failed to intervene to prevent the assassination and killing of specific individuals. Even where it could not be proved that violations were committed by Government agents, the Government had a responsibility to secure the safety and the liberty of its citizens, and to conduct investigations into murders. Chad therefore was responsible for the violations of the African Charter.[41]

---

39 Henry J. Steiner and Philip Alston, International Human Rights in Context. Law, Politics, Morals. Second Edition. Oxford, Oxford University Press, (2000), pp. 934–935.

40 Steiner and Alston, *op. cit.*, pp 934–935.

41 Steiner and Alston, op. cit., pp. 934–935.

4.4.6 *The Right to a Clean Environment*

In the Ogoni case, which involved the desecration of Ogoni lands in the extraction of oil, the African Commission found several violations and appealed to the government of Nigeria to protect fully the environment, health and livelihood of the people in Ogoniland. The Government, it held, should take measures to ensure that appropriate environmental and social impact assessment are undertaken in case of future oil development activities.

4.4.7 *The Right to Development*

The African Commission handed down a path-breaking decision on the right to development of the Endorois community in Kenya, which contains valuable guidance on principles and policies required to guarantee the development of indigenous communities. The Commission had earlier, in 2001, delivered a decision of great importance on the situation of the people of Ogoniland in Nigeria, which addressed the right of that people to livelihood and protection.

The Commission found that that community had suffered a violation of its right to development at the hands of the Kenyan government. They had been moved off their land without proper consultations, denied compensation, and not given matching land to pursue their livelihood. The Commission took the view that the right to development is both constitutive and instrumental, both a means and an end. A violation of either the procedural or substantive element violates the right to development. The Commission endorsed the submissions of the complainants in the case that giving effect to the right to development requires fulfilling five main criteria: policies must be equitable, non-discriminatory, participatory, accountable and transparent, with equity and choice as important over-arching themes. A government, the African Commission continued, bears the burden for creating conditions favourable to a people's development. It is obliged to ensure that the indigenous community is not left out of the development process or its benefits.

The Commission underlined the importance of free choice of development for indigenous peoples. It endorsed the view that indigenous peoples must not be coerced, pressurised or intimidated in their choice of development. It stressed the importance of participation and empowerment. It drew attention to the fact that the UN Declaration includes in the right to development active, free and meaningful participation in development. The results of development should be empowerment of the indigenous community. It is not sufficient for the authorities merely to give food aid. The capabilities and choices of the indigenous people must improve in order for the right to development to be realised.

The African Commission pointed out that closely allied with the right to development is the issue of participation. It cited with approval a decision of the Inter-American Court of Human Rights in the Saramaka case, which concerned Surinam, that in ensuring the effective participation of the Saramaka people in development or investment plans within their territory, the State has a duty to actively consult the said community according to their customs and traditions. This duty requires the State to both accept and disseminate information, and entails constant communication between the parties.

Consultations, the Commission determined, must be in good faith, through culturally appropriate procedures and with the objective of reaching an agreement. The Commission noted that according to the UN declaration, the right to development includes active participation in development. The result of development should be the empowerment of the indigenous community involved. It was not sufficient for the Kenyan authorities merely to give food aid. The capabilities and choices of the Endorois must improve for the right to development to be realised.

The Commission found that Kenya did not obtain the prior, informed consent of all the Endorois before designating their land a Game Reserve and commencing their eviction. A government must consult with respect to indigenous peoples, especially when dealing with sensitive issues such as land. The community representatives must not be in an unequal bargaining position. It is incumbent on the government to conduct the consultation process in such a manner that allows their representatives to be fully informed of the issues at stake and participate in developing parts crucial to the life of the community. The Kenyan Government did not impress upon the Endorois any understanding that they would be denied all rights of return to their land, including unfettered access to their grazing lnd and the medicinal salt licks for their cattle. The African Commission took the view that any as regards any development or investment projects that would have a major impact within the Endorois territory the State had a duty not only to consult with the community, but also to obtain their free, prior and informed consent, according to their customs and traditions. To the contrary, the Endorois representatives who represented the community in discussions with the Government had been illiterates, impairing their ability to understand the documents produced by the Government. The Commission held that the Government did not ensure that the Endorois were accurately informed of the nature and consequences of the process, a minimum requirement that had been set out by the Inter-American Commission of Human Rights in the Dann case (2002). Free, prior and informed consent is essential for the protection of indigenous peoples in relation to major development projects.

The Commission, endorsing earlier decisions of the Inter-American Court of Human Rights, held that benefit sharing is vital both in relation to the right to development and the right to property. The right to development will be violated when the development in question decreases the well-being of the community. The African Commission cited with approval a recommendation of the Committee on the Elimination of Racial Discrimination that not only the prior informed consent of communities must be sought when major exploitation activities are planned in indigenous territories but also that the equitable sharing of benefits to be derived from such exploitation be ensured.

4.5 Conclusion

As stated earlier in this chapter, the universality of human rights leaps out from the jurisprudence of the African Commission when considering petitions brought before it under the African Charter. The decisions of the African Commission invoke standards of justice quite well-known in United Nations human rights treaty bodies, the European Court of Human Rights, the Inter-American Commission, and Court, of Human Rights. They also invoke universal norms such as the UN Basic Principles and Guidelines on the Right to a Remedy and Reparation for Victims of Gross Violations of International Human Rights Law and Serious Violations of International Humanitarian Law. The jurisprudence of the African Court similarly contains ringing affirmations of the universality of human rights.

And then, there are the realities on the ground. In a statement to the 48th Ordinary Session of the ACHPR, 10 November, 2010, the Network of African National Human Rights Institutions declared:

> Human rights violations are not only occurring in one country but are rampant in varying forms and degrees across the continent. *"Human rights violations are exacerbated by the lack of implementation of the international and regional human rights obligations".*

CHAPTER 5

The African Union

Abstract

Foundational documents and policies of the African Union support democracy, the rule of law, and respect for human rights and fundamental freedoms. The African Union is striving on an ongoing basis to entrench peace and the prevention of conflicts in respect for democracy, the rule of law and respect for human rights.

5.1 Introduction

The African Union's commitment to universal human rights is evident in its Charter on Democracy, Elections and Governance; its African Charter on Human and Peoples' Rights and its Protocols and related conventions, the mandate of its Peace and Security Council, its conflict prevention arrangements, and its efforts for climate justice, economic and social justice, arms control and disarmament. In this chapter we look at these different facets.

5.2 African Charter on Democracy, Elections and Governance

The African Charter on Democracy, Elections and Governance was adopted by the Eighth Ordinary Session of the Assembly of the African Union, held in Addis Ababa, on 30 January, 2007. *In adopting the 'democracy charter', Member States of the African Union affirmed their commitment "to promote the universal values and principles of democracy, good governance, human rights and the right to development."* The 'democracy charter' has inspiring provisions on democracy, rule of law and human rights; a culture of democracy and peace; democratic institutions; democratic elections; and political, economic and social governance. The following is a summary of each of these themes drawn up by the Secretariat of the African Union:

5.2.1 *Democracy, Rule of Law and Human Rights*

The 'democracy charter' requires States Parties to commit to democracy, rule of law and human rights; recognize and ensure universal suffrage; take measures to ensure constitutional rule and constitutional transfer of power; take

 | DOI:10.1163/9789004520646_006

steps to strengthen the Organs of the African Union that protect and promote human rights; eliminate all forms of discrimination, especially based on political opinion, gender, ethnic, religious and racial grounds; protect vulnerable groups such as minorities, migrants, and people with disabilities; respect ethnic, cultural, and religious diversity; respect the supremacy of the constitution; any amendment or revision of the constitution should be done through national consensus or, if need be, through referendum; protect equality before the law.

5.2.2 *A Culture of Democracy and Peace*

The 'democracy charter' requires that in order to create and strengthen a culture of peace and democracy, States Parties shall promote good governance through transparency and accountability; strengthen political institutions; provide support for the existence and operation of civil society within the law; ensure there is civic education in the education system; put in place relevant legislation and policies; and ensure and main political and social dialogue.

5.2.3 *Democratic Institutions*

The 'democracy charter ' requires States Parties to ensure constitutional civilian control over the army and security forces; to put in place legal measures to deal with the unconstitutional removal of an elected government; establish public institutions that support democracy and constitutionalism, ensure that such institutions are independent and accountable to competent national organs and that they have sufficient resources; to cooperate regionally and continentally to build and consolidate democracy.

5.2.4 *Democratic Elections*

The 'democracy charter' requires States Parties to hold regular, transparent, free and fair elections in terms of the AU's Declaration on the Principles Governing Democratic Elections in Africa. To achieve this States Parties shall establish and strengthen independent and impartial national election bodies; ensure that there are mechanisms that resolve election disputes in a timely manner; ensure that political parties can equitably access state controlled media during election periods; and ensure that there is a legally enforceable code of conduct for all those involved in elections.

5.2.5 *Political, Economic and Social Governance*

The 'democracy charter' states that in order to advance political, economic and social governance, States Parties shall: strengthen parliaments and legally recognized political parties; promote citizen participation and partnerships with civil society; undertake regular reforms of the legal and justice systems; improve the performance of the public sector and combat corruption; promote the private sector through an enabling legal framework; develop information communication technologies; promote freedom of expression and freedom of the press; promote democratic values in traditional institutions; prevent the spread of diseases and combat their impact; recognise and support the full participation of women in decision making structures and processes; consolidate sustainable multiparty political systems; prevent and combat crime; implement economic development strategies that include public-private partnerships; work towards generating productive employment, alleviate poverty and illiteracy and lessen the impact of diseases; implement environmental protection policies and encourage accession to treaties and international legal instruments; and work towards providing free and compulsory education to all and especially vulnerable groups.[1]

5.2.6 *Enforcement*

States Parties to the Charter agree that the use illegal means of accessing or maintaining power, such as those listed below, constitute an unconstitutional change of government and shall draw appropriate sanctions by the African Union:

1. Any putsch or coup d'etat against a democratically elected government.
2. Any intervention by mercenaries to replace a democratically elected government.
3. Any replacement of a democratically elected government by armed dissidents or rebels.
4. Any refusal by an incumbent government to relinquish power to the winning party or candidate after free, fair and regular elections; or
5. Any amendment or revision of the constitution or legal instruments, which is an infringement on the principles of democratic change of government.[2]

When a situation arises in a State Party that may affect its democratic political institutional arrangements or the legitimate exercise of power, Peace and Security Council of the African Union is authorized to exercise its responsibilities in order to maintain the constitutional order.[3]

---

1 This summary is taken from an information packet obtained from the African Union Commission, Addis Ababa, in the summer of 2019. See, generally, www.africa-union.org.

2 Article 23.

3 Article 24.

5.2.7 *Protocol Relating to the Establishment of the Peace and Security Council of the African Union*

The Peace and Security Council of the African Union was established with great hopes that it would contribute to the prevention of conflicts, the upholding of democracy and human rights, and the spread of a universal culture of human rights in the African continent. Its objectives, as stated in Article 3(f) are to promote and encourage democratic practices, good governance and the rule of law, protect human rights and fundamental freedoms, respect for the sanctity of human life and international humanitarian law, as part of efforts for preventing conflicts.

The Principles guiding it, as stated in Article 4 (c) include respect for the rule of law, fundamental human rights and freedoms, the sanctity of human life and international humanitarian law. Article 4(j) of the Protocol establishes the right of the Union to intervene in a Member State pursuant to a decision of the Assembly in respect of grave circumstances, namely, war crimes, genocide and crimes against humanity, in accordance with Article 4(h) of the Constitutive Act.

The powers of the Council, as stated in Article 7(e) are to recommend to the African Union Assembly, pursuant to Article 4(h) of the Constitutive Act, intervention on behalf of the Union, in a Member State in respect of grave circumstances, namely war crimes, genocide and crimes against humanity, *as defined in relevant international conventions and instruments*. Article 7(f) gives it the competence to approve the modalities for intervention by the Union in Member State, following a decision by the Assembly, pursuant to article 4(j) of the Constitutive Act.

5.2.8 *Preventive Diplomacy*

Contemporary preventive diplomacy in Africa includes a broad range of visionary, structural, policy, promotional, advocacy, alert, institutional, and cooperative approaches aiming at halting current conflicts and laying the ground for long-term peace and prosperity on the continent. We summarise each of these aspects below.

The African Union vision for security and development in Africa is contained in its Agenda 2063, which contains seven African aspirations for a prosperous Africa, based on inclusive growth and sustainable development; an integrated continent, politically united, based on the ideals of Pan Africanism and the vision of Africa's Renaissance; an Africa of good governance, democracy, respect for human rights, justice and the rule of law; a peaceful and secure Africa; an Africa with a strong cultural identity, common heritage, values and ethics; An Africa whose development is is people driven, relying on the potential offered by people, especially its women and youth and caring for children; and an Africa as a strong, resilient and influential global player and partner.

The structural dimension is to implement the UN Sustainable Development Goals in the continent and to deal with the root causes of conflicts. The illicit flow of foreign-produced arms into the continent is considered a key driver of conflict.

The African Union (AU), faced with repeated, persistent and complex conflicts on the continent, engages in crisis management while developing an elaborate, multi-pronged strategy for the long-term prevention of conflicts. It has elaborated a Master Roadmap of Practical Steps to Silence the Guns in Africa. It strives to control the proliferation of weapons of mass destruction (WMD). It works on controlling Small Arms and Light Weapons (SALW) as well as dealing with land mines. It promotes Security Sector Reform and has a programme on Disarmament, Demobilization and Reintegration. It has a Post-Conflict, Reconstruction Development Policy as well as a Common Defence Policy.[4]

Pursuant to the AU Master Road Map of Practical Action to Silence the Guns in Africa and its Silencing the Guns Continental Plan of Action, the AU has so far organized a workshop to develop and validate the West Africa chapter of the plan and the East Africa chapter of the plan.

The AU initiative on controlling Small Arms and Light Weapons (SALW) rests on recognition that small arms and light weapons (SALW) constitute a serious threat to safety, security and stability in Africa. In recent years, arms diversion and trafficking have aggravated violent conflicts in Africa, fueled terrorism and enabled a range of human rights and humanitarian violations. The flow of weapons into conflict zones can intensify violence, remove incentive for reconciliation, and undermine the AU's conflict management and resolution efforts. Outside the immediate context of armed conflict, illicit small arms have aggravated inter-communal conflict, competition over natural resources, and facilitated a spectrum of criminal activities in urban setting. The AU, in response, adopted in 2013 an Action Plan on the Control of Illicit Proliferation, Circulation and Trafficking of SALW. The AU also adopted in 2017 the AU Ammunition Safety Management Initiative to assist member states in preventing diversion of ammunition and accidental explosions that can have

4 This account of the efforts of the AU is based on interviews conducted, and documents obtained, at the AU Headquarters in Addis Ababa in June 2019. The author is grateful to all those who helped him in his research. The Annual Newsletter 2018 of the AU Defense and Security Division was informative and some of the information used was taken from it ...

serious human and financial costs. Support to Member States is provided upon request and in close collaboration with implementing partners, including the UN and the Geneva Center for Humanitarian Demining (GICHD). AU Peace Support Operations (PSOs), by virtue of their mandates, have the responsibility for handling significant amounts of recovered weapons and ammunition.

The AU has conducted the first-ever continental mapping study on illicit arms flows. The study was presented to the Peace and Security Council in 2019.

Mines and explosive remnants of war (ERW) continue to pose the threat of death and injury long after conflict is over. Their presence obstructs emergency assistance, impedes the free movement of people and trade, and limits the amount of land that can be used for agriculture and development projects. The AU has organized meetings to discuss options for improving IED mitigation approaches, including standardization, interoperability, coordination platforms, political and material support needs.

The aim of the AU Security Sector Reform programme is to assist Member States to formulate and reorient the policies, structures and capacities of institutions and groups engaged in the security sector, in order to make them more effective, efficient and responsive to democratic control. It is guided by the AU Policy Framework on Security Sector Reform, adopted in January, 2013. Within this framework, the Defence and Security Division provides direct technical assistance to Member States and works with RECs to promote coherent and effective SSR approaches at the sub-regional level. Furthermore, DSD provides capacity building support through tailored training activities and the production of operational guidelines.

The AU programme on Disarmament, Demobilization and Reintegration was established in 2012 to provide political, technical and operational support to Member States in implementing DDR; generate and manage knowledge on DDR, and provide a continental platform for African dialogue on DDR. The programme derives its strength from the key partnerships developed with a range of actors, including the World Bank, the United Nations, and sub-regional organizations. It promotes the concept of African ownership over DDR processes and considers national governments as holding primary responsibility for implementation of DDR programmes. The AU also has a Post-Conflict, Reconstruction and Development Policy.

The AU Common Defence Policy has identified WMD as a common threat facing all Member States and should be addressed in a collective manner. The African Nuclear-Weapons-Free Zone Treaty (Pelindaba Treaty) entered into force in 2009. An African Commission on Nuclear Energy (AFONE) works for the implementation of the treaty.

The AU contributes to WMD disarmament and non-proliferation by supporting the ratification and implementation of the regional and global instruments, including through developing the required human and technical capacities of Member States while ensuring that they benefit fully from the peaceful application of related sciences and technologies for socio-economic development.

The AU Secretariat has initiated work on a model law on chemical, biological, radiological and nuclear security. It is intended to assist Member States with both common law and civil law systems in setting up legislation in full compliance with the regional and international instruments to strengthen national controls and prevent access and acquisition by criminals and terrorists. It will be tailored to the African context and will serve as a working tool to understand the full scope of obligations, and assess and address the gaps in domestic legislation.

The Charter of the African Union established a Peace and Security Council consisting of representatives of ten Member States. The African Union Commissioner for Peace and Security supervises a Conflict Prevention and Early Warning Division; a Crisis Management and Post-Conflict Reconstruction Division; a Peace Support Operations Division; a Defense and Security Division; an African Centre for the Study and Research on Terrorism; the AU Mechanism for Police Cooperation; and the African Commission on Nuclear Energy. The AU Commissioner for Peace and Security and the Secretariat of the Peace and Security Council also cooperates closely with Regional Economic Communities (RECs) and Regional Mechanisms for Conflict Prevention, Management and Resolution.

The authors of a book on the African Union discussed the intricate web of African institutions aimed at exercising preventive diplomacy and, in respect of the Continental Early Warning System (CEWS), came to the conclusion that "There is no evidence showing that the CEWS has effectively prevented any conflict, or contributed to a mediation and preventive diplomacy effort."[5] We think that this is an inaccurate assessment. One should look for the results achieved not in formal activities or pronouncements but in the discreet, behind-the-scenes activities such as those which led to the conclusion of a peace agreement in Sudan in July, 2019 after violence that threatened to spiral out of control.

The broad policy dimensions were stated in Agenda 2063 but there are some policies of more immediate application such as the African Peace Fund.

5 Samuel M. Makinda, F. Wafula Okumu and David Mickler, The African Union. Addressing the challenges of peace, security and governance. Second Edition. London, Routledge, 2016, p. 110.

On the promotional side, the African Union, together with the United Nations, has been seeking to mobilise Africa's population, Governments and organizations about the importance of working for peace and the prevention of conflicts.

Advocacy efforts are targeted, among others, at fostering the role of women in peace and development.

The alert role is carried out by African Union leaders particularly the AU Secretary-General, special representatives and envoys.

Institutionally, the African Union Peace and Security Council, supported by regional and sub-regional organizations, endeavour to provide alerts about potential conflicts, to help to head them off and to mediate and conciliate them in cases of need. On the peacekeeping front, the African Union has been working on an African Stand-by Force. On the cooperation front, the African Union and the United Nations have an active plan of cooperation to help prevent conflicts on the continent.

The story of efforts for early warning and preventive diplomacy on the African continent is thus one of striving. There have been worthwhile initiatives and quite a few blueprints on paper that still have to get off the ground. Within the African Union, a Panel of the Wise (PoW) has gone on 'confidence-building missions' to some countries and has issued statements on crises in Guinea, Guinea-Bissau, Zimbabwe, Madagascar, Somalia and Sudan (Darfur). The PoW has also convened meetings on thematic issues such as 'Election Related Conflicts'.

The Economic Community of West African States (ECOWAS) has a Council of the Wise which has interceded in conflicts in Liberia, Sierra Leone, Niger, Guinea, Guinea-Bissau and Togo.[6] CENSAD has a Permanent High Level Mediator for Peace and Security that has been deployed to mediate peace in Chad, Mali, Niger and the Central African Republic. COMESA plans to establish a Committee of Elders as part of its preventive diplomacy strategy. IGAD has been interested in establishing a Mediation Support Unit while the Economic Community of Central African States has its eyes on a Council of Eminent Persons as part of its Conflict Prevention, Management and Resolution Protocol.[7]

6 Samuel M. Makinda, F. Wafula Okumu and David Mickler, The African Union. Addressing the challenges of peace, security and governance. Second Edition. London, Routledge, 2016, pp. 108–112.

7 Ibid.

5.4 Conclusion

This chapter has brought out emphatically:

- The African Union's affirmations of adherence to democratic governance and to universal human rights
- The African Union's anchoring of its efforts for development, conflict prevention, peace-making, peacekeeping and peacebuilding in respect for fundamental human rights.
- ECOWAS' mirroring of the AU's democracy, human rights and peace strategies
- Africa's profound faith in the entrenchment of an ethos of democracy and human rights in the continent.

CHAPTER 6

Sub-regional Institutions and Courts

Abstract

Sub-regional African institutions and courts strongly support the universality of human rights and the application of international human rights law in Africa alongside the norms of the African Charter on Human and Peoples' Rights. Policies and norms in support of democracy have been enshrined in democracy charters. Regional courts of ECOWAS and the East African Community have consistently invoked international human rights norms.

6.1 Introduction

In the preceding chapter we visited the African Union's Charter on Democracy, Elections and Governance, of 2007. In fact, the African Union's Charter had been preceded in 2001 by the ECOWAS Protocol on Democracy and Good Governance which strongly reaffirmed universal principles of democracy and good governance. In this chapter we shall look at the practice of sub-regional African institutions, notably ECOWAS, the East African Community, and SADC.

6.2 ECOWAS Protocol on Democracy and Good Governance (2001)

On 21 December, 2001, ECOWAS Heads of State and Government signed a Supplementary Protocol on Democracy and Good Governance to the ECOWAS founding Treaty of 24 July, 1993, 1993 as well as to the ECOWAS Protocol of 10 December, 1993 relating to the Mechanism for Conflict Prevention, Management, Resolution, Peacekeeping and Security. The ECOWAS Protocol on Democracy and Good Governance situates itself squarely within the stream of universal human rights principles and values as we shall see presently.

In the Preamble to the Protocol on Democracy and Good Governance the heads of State and Government were mindful of the principles set out in the then OAU Solemn Declaration on Security, Stability, Development and Cooperation of 2000 and the framework for OAU's reaction to unconstitutional change of government, adopted in July 1999. The Heads of State and Government also recalled the Harare Declaration adopted by the

 | DOI:10.1163/9789004520646_007

Commonwealth on 20 December, 1991 and the Bamako Declaration adopted by the member countries of the Francophonie on 3 November 2000. The Heads of State and Government further had in view: the Cotonou Declaration adopted on 6 December, 2000 at the end of the fourth international conference on new and restored democracies; the Universal Declaration of Human Rights and the African Charter on Human and Peoples' Rights.

Section 1 of the Protocol on Democracy and Good Governance declared the following as constitutional principles shared by all Member States of ECOWAS:

a) ...
   - Separation of powers – the Executive, Legislative and Judiciary.
   - Empowerment and strengthening of parliaments and guarantee of parliamentary immunity.
   - Independence of the Judiciary: Judges shall be independent in the discharge of their duties.
   - The freedom of the members of the Bar shall be guaranteed; without prejudice to their penal or disciplinary responsibility in the event of contempt of court or breaches of the common law.

b) Every accession to power must be made through free, fair and transparent elections.

c) Zero tolerance for power obtained or maintained by unconstitutional means.

d) Popular participation in decision-making, strict adherence to democratic principles and decentralization of power at all levels of governance.

e) The armed forces must be apolitical and must be under the command of a legally constituted political authority, no serving member of the armed forces may seek to run for elective political [office].

f) Secularism and neutrality of the State in all matters relating to religion, freedom for each individual to practise, within the limits of existing laws, the religion of his/her choice everywhere on the national territory. The secularism shall extend to all parts of the State, but shall not deprive the State of the right to regulate, with due respect to human rights, the different religions practiced on the national territory or to inte4rvene when law and order break down as a result of any religious activity.

g) The State and all its institutions belong to all the citizens, therefore none of their decisions and actions shall involve any form of discrimination, be it on an ethnic, racial, religious or regional basis.

h) *The rights set out in the African Charter on Human and Peoples' Rights and other international instruments shall be guaranteed in each of the ECOWAS Member States; each individual or organization shall be free to have recourse to the common or civil law courts, a court of special jurisdiction, or any other national institution established within the framework of an international instrument on Human Rights, to ensure the protection of his/her rights. In the absence of a court of special jurisdiction, the present Supplementary Protocol shall be regarded as giving the necessary powers to common or civil law judicial bodies.*

i) Political parties shall be formed and shall have the right to carry out their activities freely, within the limits of the law. Their formation and activities shall not be based on ethnic, religious, regional or racial considerations. They shall participate freely and without hindrance or discrimination in any electoral process. The freedom of the opposition shall be guaranteed. Each Member State may adopt a system for financing political parties, in accordance with criteria set under the law.

j) The freedom of association and the right to meet and organize peaceful demonstrations shall also be guaranteed.

k) The freedom of the press shall be guaranteed.

l) All former Heads of State shall enjoy a special status including freedom of movement. They shall enjoy special benefits compatible to their status as former Heads of State.

The other Sections of the Protocol have extensive provisions on the conduct of elections, election monitoring, the role of the armed forces, the police and the security forces in a democracy, and on the rule of law, human rights and good governance. In Section VII on the rule of law, human rights and good governance, Member States agreed that good governance and press freedom are essential for preserving social justice, preventing conflict, guaranteeing political stability and peace and for strengthening democracy (Article 33).

Member States recognized that the rule of law involves not only the promulgation of good laws that are in conformity with the provisions on human rights, but also a good judicial system, a good system of administration, and good management of the State apparatus. They expressed the conviction that a system that guarantees smooth running of the State and its administrative and judicial services contributes to the consolidation of the rule of law. (Article 33)

Member States and the Executive Secretariat of ECOWAS undertook to endeavour to adopt at national and regional levels, practical modalities for the enforcement of the rule of law, human rights for the enforcement of the rule of law, human rights, justice and good governance. Member States undertook an obligation to ensure accountability, professionalism, transparency and expertise in the public and private sectors. (Article 34).

Member States undertook to establish independent national institutions to promote and protect human rights. The Executive Secretariat of ECOWAS undertook to take measures to strengthen their capacities. The institutions shall be organized into a regional network. Within the framework of this network, each national institution shall systematically submit to the Executive Secretariat any report on human rights violations observe on its territory. Such reports and reactions of governments shall be widely disseminated through the most appropriate means (Article 35). Article added that "member States shall institutionalize a national mediation system."

Each Member State undertook to work towards ensuring pluralism of the information sector and the development of the media. Each Member State may give financial assistance to privately-owned media. The distribution and allocation of such assistance shall be done by an Independent national body or by a body freely instituted by the journalists themselves. (Article 37).

Member States undertook to fight corruption and manage their national resources in a transparent manner, ensuring that they are equitably distributed. In this regard, Member States and the ECOWAS Executive Secretariat undertook to establish appropriate mechanisms to address issues of corruption within the Member States and at the Community level. (Article 38)

Article 39 authorized the ECOWAS Community Court of Justice to hear cases relating to violations of human rights, after all attempts to resolve the matter at the national level have failed.

6.3 ECOWAS and East African Community Courts of Justice

6.3.1 *ECOWAS Community Court of Justice*

> The ECOWAS Community Court of Justice was established pursuant to the provisions of Articles 6 and 15 of the Revised Treaty of ECOWAS. The Court is composed of five independent Judges who are persons of high moral character appointed for a four-year term of office upon recommendation of the Community Judicial Council. Its mandate is to ensure the observance of law and of the principles of equity and in the interpretation and application of the provisions of the ECOWAS Revised Treaty and all other subsidiary legal instruments adopted by the Community.[1]

6.3.2 *East African Community and the East African Court of Justice*

While the East African Court of Justice does not yet have an explicit jurisdiction to hear human rights cases, it has nevertheless addressed cases involving

1 https://www.ecowas.int/institutions/community-court-of-justice/.

individual rights.[2] In the case of Katabazi v. Secretary-General of the East African Community, the Court, while noting its lack of jurisdiction to hear human rights cases, went on to state that "it will not abdicate from exercising its jurisdiction of interpretation under Article 27(1) merely because the reference includes allegation of human rights violations." While the EACJ did not evaluate the claims within a human rights framework, the Court found that that the respondent had violated *the principle of the rule of law* and consequently contravened the founding Treaty.

In 2010, the EACJ further decided in Sitenda Sebalu v. Secretary-General of the East African Community et al, that the failure to extend the jurisdiction to cover human rights cases *contravened the principles of good governance* stipulated in Article 6 of the founding treaty. The extension of the Court's jurisdiction to cover human rights cases has been the subject of consideration subsequently within the East African Community.[3]

It will be noted that the Court's affirmation of the principle of the rule of law and the principles of good governance fall squarely within the stream of universal human rights principles.

6.4 IGAD: Democracy, Governance, Elections, Early Warning

The Intergovernmental Authority on Development (IGAD) covering the Horn of Africa,[4] was established in 1996, succeeding the former Intergovernmental Authority on Drought and Development. Its objectives include to promote joint development strategies, harmonize policies with regard to trade, create an enabling environment for foreign, cross-border and domestic trade and investments, achieve regional food security, promote sustainable development of natural resources and environment protection, engage in early warning and conflict prevention efforts, and promote democracy and free and fair elections. We shall here focus on two areas of its activities: early warning and promotion of democracy and fair elections.

The Conflict Early Warning and Response Mechanism (CEWARN), established by IGAD in 2002, carries out some of the most hands-on preventive diplomacy of all the international, regional and sub-regional organizations around. CEWARN's mandate is to receive and share information concerning

2 See International Justice Resource Center, East African Court of Justice.

3 Ibid.

4 Its members are Djibouti, Ethiopia, Eritrea, Kenya, Somalia, the Sudan, South Sudan, and Uganda.

potentially violent conflicts as well as their outbreak and escalation in the IGAD region, undertake and share analyses of that information, develop case scenarios and formulate options for response, share and communicate information analyses and response options, carry out studies on specific types and areas of conflict in the IGAD region.

At the heart of the functioning of the CEWARN mechanism is data collection, analysis and the timely dissemination of information and knowledge to the right people and institutions. The network of actors steered by a secretariat based in Addis Ababa was from the beginning designed to join government and civil society. It also joins regional, national and local dimensions in data collection, analysis and decision making.[5]

Since its establishment, CEWARN has gained valuable experience and credibility with officials and peace workers in its areas of operation for supporting local institutions and expanding their capabilities for conflict prevention.[6] CEWARN's operations have been credited with significant reduction of violent conflict particularly along Kenya-Uganda as well as Ethiopia-Kenya-Somalia borders. CEWARN has built a valuable body of data and knowledge on violent conflicts along IGAD Member State borders and it has built the ability to implement on the ground development projects that entrench peace by reducing the incentive for violent conflict.

Conflicts over the scarce resources of land, water and pasture are prevalent in the IGAD region, where pastoralism is predominant, and they often lead to deadly violence. CEWARN opted from the beginning for regional, cross, cross-border cooperation to tackle the root of the problem.

The following real-life example was recounted by Ms Tigist Hailu in an article in Rural 21: At 7.00 pm on a Sunday evening in 2012, the CEWARN Director received an SMS message from the co-ordinator of CEWARN's national early warning and response structure in Kenya. The co-ordinator relayed a report received from field reporters on the killing of 22 Kenyan pastoralists and the theft of their cattle that had allegedly been driven across the border into Ethiopia by armed attackers. The attackers were believed to be from a neighbouring community in Ethiopia.

As the evening wore on, details of the attack were updated through SMS, telephone calls and email amongst field reporters, national co-ordinators of

5 See on this, Tigist Hailu, "Data-based conflict early warning- a vital instrument in peacebuilding", New Routes 4/2012, 24–26.

6 This account of the activities of CEWARN is based on interviews conducted and information obtained at IGAD's headquarters in Addis-Ababa in June, 2019. I am particularly grateful to Ms Tigist Hailu for her insights and assistance.

Ethiopia and Kenya as well as the CEWARN Director. In less than two hours, CEWARN had briefed senior officials in both capitals. "The conversations of updates, clarifications, questions and developments continues for the next four days until the perpetrators have been arrested, their weapons seized and the stolen livestock recovered."[7]

Thereafter, there was a handover ceremony, carried out with the help of local officials that blended the legal state approach with the local practices of reconciliation. At the end, the relationship between the countries was strengthened by their ability to agree on a version of what had happened in an area where communication was poor, while the violence was prevented from escalating to claim even more lives and property. As Tigist Hailu wrote, the anecdote was based on an actual event and gave a glimpse of CEWARN in action.

CEWARN expanded its focus in 2012 following the launch of the CEWARN Strategic Framework 2012–2019. The new strategy brought in a significant expansion of CEWARN's thematic focus, that is to say, on the types, causes and drivers of violent conflicts beyond pastoral conflicts. Before working out the new strategy CEWARN engaged in extensive local consultations with up to 5000 citizens and local level officials. This was followed by extensive consultations with national officials and NGOs in each Member State. The new strategy identified 60 high priority typologies themes, with detailed specification of potential problems in each of the IGAD Member States.

The new CEWARN strategy framework recognizes that the risks and structures of violent conflict in the IGAD region are increasingly complex and interwoven. It is mindful of rapid urbanization and the conflict implications of the networks and proximities of cities, Climate extremes and the growing nexus between resource competition and violent conflict need to be addressed. Governance structures on the national, regional and international level affect the pace of socio-political change and evolution, A large youth population is difficult to absorb in the formal sectors of governance and economic life and growing populations and economic development have increased the demands for natural resources and contributed to environmental degradation. The socio-cultural values that inform cooperation, competition and conflict are increasingly divorced from long-standing traditions and are driven by ideals, appetites and worldviews from distant lands. Historical inequality among regions or center-periphery conflicts in political and socio-economic terms. The rapid evolution of communications and weapons technology and its democratization.

7 See Tigist Hailu, "Anticipate and prevent violent conflicts", Rural 21, 01/2012, 18–21 at 18.

On democracy and free elections, IGAD undertook a Study on Democracy, Governance and Election and has under consideration a Draft Protocol on Democracy, Governance and Elections. It also has a Draft Code of Conduct on Election Observation, as well as Draft Guidelines for elections observers. A meeting of IGAD's Committee of Ambassadors, held from 3–6 June, 2014 thoroughly examined these drafts, endorsed them, and recommended their presentation to the next regular session of the IGAD Council of Ministers for approval. The Committee of Ministers "underscored the importance of Democracy, Governance and Elections and commended the Secretariat for the initiative taken" on these topics.

6.5 SADC: Southern African Development Community and ECCAS: Economic Community of Central African States

The Southern African Development Community provides a mirror image of the universalist human rights aspirations of African countries and peoples and the practical problems realized on the ground in realising those aspirations. At the end of the day, it is a story of continuous struggle for the vindication of human rights.

In August, 1992, in Windhoek, Namibia, ten founding members signed the SADC treaty, which committed them to act in accordance with the principles of 'human rights, democracy and the rule of law'. In 2008, SADC leaders made efforts to protect women's rights by adopting the SADC Protocol on Gender and Development, which obliged members states to include women's equality in their constitutions as a safeguard to prevent the use of other lower laws, including religious and customary laws, to undermine women's equality.

However, as the body marked its twenty-fifth anniversary in 2017, Human Rights Watch called upon SADC to reaffirm its commitment to improve respect for human rights among its Member States.[8] The sub-region, Human Rights Watch complained, continued to have high rates of forced and child marriages. Human Rights Watch noted that in recent years SADC governments had taken regressive steps to weaken and undermine key rights protection mechanisms such as the SADC Tribunal, which we discuss in the next section.

Human Rights Watch recounted extensive gross violations of human rights in Angola, Malawi, South Africa, Swaziland and Zimbabwe. In Zimbabwe, at the time, the government of then President Robert Mugabe had ignored the

8 Human Rights Watch, "SADC: Recommit to Human Rights Protection", 7 August, 2017.

rights provisions in the country's new constitution, neither enacting laws to put the new constitution into effect nor amending existing laws to bring them in line with the constitution and Zimbabwe's obligations under regional and international human rights conventions. In addition, NGOs had reported that the police used outdated and abusive laws to violate basic rights.

On 29 September, 2020, the Third Annual Regional Summit of Civil Society Organizations on Democracy expressed concern about the continued shrinking of democratic space in the SADC region, in particular the entrenchment of authoritarian rule in Zimbabwe, Zambia, Tanzania and eSwatini, and the worrying presence of vigilante groups in Cabo Delgado, Mozambique. The Summit "recommended to the SADC Heads of State … the re-establishment of the SADC Tribunal and the setting up of a SADC Human Rights Commission which will address issues relating to human rights abuses in the region …".[9]

6.5.1 *SADC Tribunal*

The SADC Tribunal was created in 1992 and people in the region hoped that the Tribunal's mission would extend beyond questions of economic cooperation to include human rights protection, similar to the ECOWAS Community Court of Justice. According to Mia Swart, "Africa-wide civil society and academia agree upon the need for citizens to be able to resort toa regional tribunal when their domestic legal systems fail to provide relief. Indeed, the first president of the tribunal called the institution a 'House of Justice for Africa.' "[10]

Unfortunately, the SADC Tribunal heard only one case in 2007–2008 in which it held that there had been breaches of fundamental rights in Zimbabwe. The sharp opposition of the government of President Robert Mugabe of Zimbabwe resulted in the disbanding of the Tribunal in 2012. At the time of writing there are hopes that SADC might be able to re-instate the Tribunal.

In the one case that it decided, the SADC Tribunal courageously upheld universal human rights. The case involved 79 white Zimbabwean commercial farmers who took the Mugabe government to the Tribunal to stop the compulsory acquisition of their farms. The Tribunal found for the farmers on the basis

---

9 "Whither democracy and human rights in SADC?: COVID-19, lockdowns and basic rights: Communique of the Third Annual Regional Summit of Civil Society Organizations on Democracy", 29 September, 2020. https://www.thezimbabwean.co/2020/10/whithe-democracy-and-human-rights-in sadc-covid-19-lockdowns-and basic-rights/.

10 Mia Swart, A house of justice for Africa: Resurrecting the SADC Tribunal", the Brookings Institution, 2 April, 2018: https://www.brookings.edu/blog/africa-in-focus/2018/04/02/a-house-of-justice-for-africa-resurrecting-the-sadc-tribunal/.

that they had been deprived of their land without the right of access to the courts and the right to a fair hearing, both which it held were essential human rights. In this way, the tribunal held that the Zimbabwean government had breached the provisions of the SADC Treaty.

The Zimbabwean government of President Roberg Mugabe refused to enforce the judgment, and the Supreme Court of Zimbabwe decided that its government had an inherent right to compulsorily acquire property. In the words of Mia Swart, "As a direct result of the Zimbabwean opposition to the Campbell decision, the heads of state and government of SADC decided to suspend the Tribunal until August 2012. Then, in August 2012, the doors of the tribunal closed to individuals. Since the court was primarily set up to hear individual cases, this meant that it effectively came to a standstill."[11]

6.5.2 *ECCAS: Economic Community of Central African States*

Created in 1983, The Economic Community of Central African States (ECCAS) strives to make Central Africa a region of peace, prosperity and solidarity for its citizens. ECCAS seeks to promote economic growth, social well-being and preservation of nature among its eleven member countries.

Preserving peace and collective security is a strong focus of the organization in a "hostile environment combining terrorism, organized crime and religious radicalism against which ECCAS and its partners have structured an early warning mechanism, multinational force and protocol of action."[12]

6.5.3 *ECCAS: Economic Community of Central African States*

Created in 1983, The Economic Community of Central African States (ECCAS) strives to make Central Africa a region of peace, prosperity and solidarity for its citizens. ECCAS seeks to promote economic growth, social well-being and preservation of nature among its eleven member countries.

Preserving peace and collective security is a strong focus of the organization in a "hostile environment combining terrorism, organized crime and religious radicalism against which ECCAS and its partners have structured an early warning mechanism, multinational force and protocol of action."[13]

---

11 Ibid.

12 https://ceeac-eccas.org/en/#presentation.

13 https://ceeac-eccas.org/en/#presentation.

6.6 Conclusion

As in the preceding chapter on the African Union, this chapter has also brought out emphatically:

- The regional organizations' affirmations of adherence to democratic governance and to universal human rights
- The regional organizations' anchoring of their efforts for development, conflict prevention, peace-making, peacekeeping and peacebuilding in respect for fundamental human rights.
- The regional organizations' mirroring of the AU's democracy, human rights and peace strategies
- Africa's profound faith in the entrenchment of an ethos of democracy and human rights in the continent – even if many problems still continue to be felt on the ground.

CHAPTER 7

National Human Rights Institutions and Courts

Abstract

There is abundant evidence that African national human rights institutions and Courts strongly support the universality of human rights and the application of international human rights norms in Africa, alongside the norms of the African Charter on Human and Peoples' Rights. Leading African courts, such as the South African Constitutional Court have consistently upheld the validity of international human rights norms, as this chapter will show.

7.1 Introduction

This chapter will present evidence that African national human rights institutions are very much committed to the universality of human rights, as are leading national courts, such as the South African Constitutional Court, the Kenyan Supreme Court, and the Malawi Constitutional Court, all of which have delivered decisions and taken stances very much in support of universal precepts of democracy, the rule of law, and respect for fundamental human rights and freedoms. We begin with African National Human Rights Institutions.

7.2 African National Human Rights Institutions (ANHRIs)

African National Human Rights Institutions, like African Human Rights Defenders, have been doing their utmost to promote implementation of international and African norms of human rights. Stated summarily, there are numerous challenges still to achieving optimal respect for, and protection of human rights in Africa – as indeed in the rest of the world, and African National Human Rights Institutions are using both United Nations fora and African fora in their quest for human rights protection. In fact, it is the United Nations framework that has led to the establishment and promotion of ANHRIs, as we shall see presently.

The Network of African National Human Rights Institutions (NANHRI) is a regional umbrella body that brings together 46 African National Human Rights Institutions. NHRIs generally refer to bodies established by governments to aid

 | DOI:10.1163/9789004520646_008

in promotion and protection of human rights within their respective jurisdictions through handling complaints and conducting investigations, conducting research, advocacy and educational programmes in line with the Paris Principles. The Network seeks to support and strengthen national Human Rights Institutions in Africa as well as to facilitate coordination and cooperation among themselves and between them and other key human rights actors at the regional and international levels.[1]

NANHRI's vision is of a continent with effective NHRIS, contributing to an enhanced human rights culture and justice for every African. Its Mission is to support, through national, sub-regional, regional and international cooperation, the establishment, strengthening and development of national human rights institutions in order to enable them to more effectively undertake their mandate of human rights monitoring, promotion, protection and advocacy. NANHRI's values and guiding principles are: transparency, accountability, openness, cooperation, professionalism, and gender equity.[2]

NANHRI has been working to support the establishment if NHRIS in accordance with the Paris Principles, which are principles endorsed by the UN General Assembly for the establishment and functioning of independent national human rights institutions.[3] NANHRI works with NHRIS to build their capacity and address gaps that hinder effective implementation of their mandates. It promotes strong links amongst and between NHRIS and regional and international key human rights stakeholders. It provides platforms for peer-to-peer learning and sharing of best practices at national, regional and international levels. It coordinates research on various human rights thematic areas and fosters the gathering of human rights documentation and knowledge management.[4]

NANHRI strives to advance the principles of equality and non-discrimination, which are universal human rights principles:

> Equality and non-discrimination are central concepts in the promotion and protection of human rights; they are woven into the application of

1 See Network of African National Human Rights Institutions, https://www.nanhri.org/about-nanhri/, accessed 26 July, 2020.

2 Ibid.

3 The Paris Principles set out the minimum standards required by national human rights institutions to be considered credible and to operate effectively. The Paris Principles relating to the status of national institutions was adopted by the UN General Assembly in its resolution 48/134 of 20 December, 1993. It states competences and responsibilities which should attach to national institutions. See https://www.nanhri.org/our-work/paris-principles/.

4 See https://www.nanhri.org/our-history/, accessed 26 July, 2020.

> al human rights standards as key guiding principles. Since 2013, NANHRI, with the support f rom Raoul Wallenberg Institute of Human Rights and Humanitarian Law (RWI) has been working on equality and non-discrimination with the aim of enhancing the capacity of National Human Rights Institutions (NHRIs) to deal with issues of equality and non-discrimination within their respective countries[5]

NANHRI has also been working on the issue of business and human rights:

> Business is one of the economic activities promoting good life through strong economies, jobs, production of quality goods and services, infrastructure, among others. But over the past few decades, business activities have emerged as contributors to deterioration of human rights; hence the need for accountability for sustainable development. NANHRI identified that National Human Rights Institutions are key in monitoring and reporting, advocating legal reforms, facilitating dialogue and handling complaints in business and human rights (BHR)[6]

The support of African National Human Rights Institutions for universal human rights norms may be seen in the positions they have consistently taken at the UN Human Rights Council and in other international and African fora. In a statement to the UN Human Rights Council at its 16th session, in 2011, NANHRI spoke out unmistakeably against torture. NANHRI, they declared, "is firmly committed to increasingly fight against torture and other cruel, inhuman or degrading treatment in Africa, to promote the role of African NHRIs in the prevention of torture, to strengthen their commitments on issues of torture and to strengthen the capacities of their staff for this purpose."

They added: "In Africa, NHRI play an important role at national level in promoting the ratification of the Optional Protocol to the Convention Against Torture (OPCAT) and contribute to reflection and consultation on various options for NPM [national preventive mechanisms]. This is the case, for example, in South Africa, Ghana and Togo. Similarly, national human rights commissions in Mali and Mauritius have been designated as NPM. Both institutions are also part of the Network."[7]

5 Ibid.

6 Ibid.

7 Statement by the Network of African National Human Rights Institutions ... Human Rights Council, 16th Session, 28th February to 25th March, 2011. NANHRI, accessed on the internet 26 July, 2020.

NANHRI has sought to advance implementation of the UN's Sustainable Development Goals (SDGs) on the foundation of human rights. A regional exchange workshop on African National Human Rights Institutions' Engagement in Sustainable Development processes was held on 22–23 February, 2020 in Zimbabwe. The workshop, among other topics, "involved an exchange of experiences on: adoption of a Human Rights-Based Approach (HRBA) to Sustainable Development processes at national level;.."

Among the Key messages and recommendations from the Network to the sixth session of the African Regional Forum on Sustainable Development (ARFSD) were the following:

> 1. People
>
> All issues addressed in the 'People' cluster can be linked to human rights standards, which can therefore guide the implementation of the concerned Goals. A human rights based approach can support the achievement of all goals in this cluster through ensuring accountability, transparency, participation and non-discrimination in the process of achieving sustainable development. Therefore duty-bearers should seek to safeguard active and meaningful pubic participatory process with rights-holders, and in particular with vulnerable groups in these processes , to ensure that no one is left behind.
>
> Encourage Parliaments to exercise effective oversight over government departments and involve National Human Rights Institutions (NHRIs) during such processes to ensure that there is an added level of accountability.
>
> Education for sustainable development is a critical component of ensuring sustainability and longevity of impact. Build national capacity to conduct human rights education in relation to the SDGs across all government departments and state actors to ensure that their policies, actions and activities are couched in human rights and encourage a human rights-based approach in their work.[8]

The foregoing is convincing evidence of the support of African National Human Rights Institutions for universal as well as African regional norms of

8 Key messages and recommendations from the Network of African National Human Rights Institutions (NANHRI) to the sixth session of the African Regional Forum on Sustainable Development (ARFSD), on the People, Prosperity, Planet, Peace and partnerships. NANHRI, accessed on the internet on 26 July, 2020.

human rights. We shall see next a similar stance by the premier Constitutional Court in Africa, that of South Africa.

7.3 South African Constitutional Court

Universal human rights norms are at the heart of the South African Bill of Rights. As *apartheid* was being dismantled, South Africans consulted the Universal Declaration of Human Rights, the various other United Nations treaties and normative instruments, as well as international and regional human rights norms and jurisprudence and drew upon them liberally in drafting the South African Bill of Rights.[9]

Section 8 of the South African Constitution provides that "the Bill of Rights applies to all law, and binds the legislative, the executive, the judiciary and all organs of state." Section 39 (1) specifies that when interpreting the Bill of Rights, a court, tribunal or forum must promote the values that underlie an *open and democratic society based on human dignity, equality freedom*; must consider international law; and may consider foreign law.

Hennie Styrdom and Kevin Hopkins have written:

> In recognition of the important influence that international human rights law has had on the drafting of our Bill of Rights, FC's s 39(1)(b) makes it mandatory for our courts to consider international law when interpreting the Bill of Rights .... [T]here has been significant reference to international human rights jurisprudence in a number of the judgments of the Constitutional Court. In S v Makwanyane, Chaskalson P set out the approach that ought to be employed by a court when considering how to use international law in interpreting the meaning of a provision in the Bill of Rights:
>
> In the course of the arguments addressed to us, we were referred to books and articles on the death sentence, and to judgments dealing with challenges made to capital punishment in the courts of other countries and in international tribunals. The international and foreign authorities are of value because they analyse arguments for and against the death sentence and show how courts of other jurisdictions have dealt with the vexed issue. For that reason alone they require our attention. They may

9 See, generally, M. Olivier, "South Africa and International Human Rights Agreements. Policy, Policy and Practice", (2003) 2 Journal of SA Law, 293.

> also have to be considered because of their relevance to section 35(1) of the Constitution …
>
> In the context of section 35(1) public international law would include non-binding as well as binding law. They may both be used under section as tools of interpretation. International agreements and customary international law accordingly provide a framework within which [the Bill of Rights] can be evaluated and understood and for that purpose decisions of tribunals dealing with comparable instruments, such as the United Nations Committee on Human Rights, the Inter-American Commission on Human Rights, the European Commission of Human Rights, and the European Court of Human Rights and in appropriate cases, reports of specialized agencies such as the International Labour Organization may provide guidance as to the correct interpretation of particular provisions of [the Bill of Rights]. …
>
> In dealing with comparative law, we must bear in mind that we are required to construe the South African Constitution, and not an international instrument or the constitution of some foreign country, and that this has to be done with due regard to our legal system, our legal history and circumstances, and the structure and language of our own Constitution. We can derive assistance from public international law and foreign case law, but we are in no way bound to follow it.[10]

The South African common law has long regarded international law as part of South African domestic law.[11] Customary international law is thus law in the Republic of South Africa unless it is inconsistent with the Constitution or an Act of Parliament.[12] When interpreting any legislation, every court must prefer any reasonable interpretation of the legislation that is consistent with international law over any alternative interpretation that is inconsistent with international law.[13] An international agreement binds the Republic of South

10 S v Makwanyane 1995 (3) SA 391 (CC). 1995 (6) BCLR 665 (CC) (Makwanyane) at paras. 34, 35, and 39. LoSA, Constitutinal Law of South Africa, Chapter 30 on International Law by Hennie Styrdom and Kevin Hopkins accessed on the internet on 26 July, 2020, #30 (3). See, generally, M. Olivier, "South Africa and International Human Rights Agreements. Policy, Policy and Practice", (2003) 2 Journal of SA Law, 293. See also, Government of the Republic of South Africa and Others v. Grootboom 2001 (1) SA 46 (CC), 2000 (11) BCLR 1160 (CC) Grootboom.

11 LoSA, Constitutinal Law of South Africa, Chapter 30 on International Law by Hennie Styrdom and Kevin Hopkins accessed on the internet on 26 July, 2020, #30 (2).

12 Ibid #232.

13 Ibid, #233.

Africa after it has been approved by resolution in both the National Assembly and the National Council of provinces.[14]

Section 39(2) of the Constitution provides that: "When interpreting any legislation, and when developing the common law or customary law, every court, tribunal or forum must promote the spirit, purport and objects of the Bill of Rights. In other words, in the view of Cornell and Friedman, whenever a court is dealing with the common law it must test the common law against the demands of the Bill of Rights. Only thus can the Constitution's promise be delivered of a legal system founded on dignity, freedom and substantive equality.[15]

In *Thebus,* Moseneke DCJ said that the common law is developed either when it is inconsistent with a specific constitutional provision or when it falls short of the Constitution's 'objective normative value system' (that is to say the spirit, purport and objects of the Bill of Rights).[16]

In Makwanyane, the Constitutional Court noted that "What the Constitution expressly aspires to is to provide a transition from ... grossly unacceptable features of the past to a conspicuously contrasting future founded on the recognition of human rights, democracy, and peaceful co-existence and development opportunities for all South Africans, irrespective of color, race, class, belief or sex."[17]

In Mhlungu, Justice Albie Sachs considered the existence of the South African Constitutional Court "as part of a global development of constitutionalism and human rights."[18]

Lawfare is the title of a 2019 book on judging politics in South Africa, written by two eminent South African constitutional lawyers, that would be well worth consulting by those interested in constitutional governance and the rule of law in countries such as ours.

By 'lawfare', the authors signify that as society increasingly uses law as a means of control, those targeted invoke the claim of human rights to persuade the courts that law has an intrinsic quality of accountability, certainty and recognition of the basic freedom of the individual citizen. In this way, citizens

14 Ibid, #231.

15 Drucilla Cornell and Nick Friedman, "In Defence of the Constitutional Court: Human Rights and the South African Common Law", 5 Malawi Law Journal (2011), Issue 1, pp. 1–31, at p. 18.

16 S v Thebus & Another, 2003 (10) BCLR 1100 (CC), para. 27.

17 Makwanyane,para 261, per Judge Mahomed.

18 Para. 127.

fight attempts to control them through abusive use of the law by using the law in turn.

Lawfare, they explain, can be a good thing when it advances the constitutional project and is undertaken by litigants and judges as an instrument to ensure that the constitutional vision is realized. It can be a bad thing when courts become the site of pure political contestation and when politicians seek to usurp judicial powers to achieve their objectives.

The South African Constitution of 1994, the authors point out, is the plan for a new society. It enshrines the foundational values of dignity, equality and freedom. Basic to the implementation of the Constitution is the principle of legality, namely the notion that all public power is sourced in the Constitution, expressed in national legislation and exercised in a way that needs to be rational, fair and reasonable.

The Constitution is a bridge away from a culture of arbitrary authority and to a culture of justification – a culture in which every exercise of power is expected to be justified; in which the leadership given by government rests on the cogency of the case offered in defence of its decisions, not the fear inspired by the force at its command. In this spirit, the Constitutional Court held in 2017 that President Zuma had to disclose the reasons for his 2017 Cabinet reshuffle – a spectacular application of the principles of justification and accountability.

In the Glenister case, the Constitutional Court of South Africa sourced an obligation to establish a viable, and thus independent, anti-corruption unit in a reading of South Africa's international obligations coupled with the Constitution. This case exemplified the principle that constitutional provisions should be given good faith interpretation in the light of relevant international law.

In the *Makwanyane* case, the Constitutional Court held that the death penalty was unconstitutional, again on grounds of incompatibility with constitutional law coupled with international law.

In the remarkable case of Daniels v. Scribante, the Constitutional Court upheld a claim Ms. Daniels, a farm worker who occupied a cottage on the farm she worked, that the right to reside accorded to her included the right to make improvements in her dwelling -even if the owners did not agree to the improvements.. Justice Fronemen declared in his judgment:

> Before we can make substantial and lasting progress in making the ideals of the Constitution a reality, at least three things must happen: (a) an honest and deep recognition of past injustice; (b) a re-appraisal of our conception of the nature of ownership and property; and (c) an

> acceptance, rather than avoidance or obfuscation of the consequences of constitutional change.

In a case where the South African government let former Sudanese President Bashir leave South Africa notwithstanding a legitimate request from the Prosecutor of the International Criminal Court to arrest him, the Government was roundly criticized by the Courts. When, in an act of pique, the Government sought to withdraw its ratification of the Statute of the International Criminal Court without the prior consent of Parliament, the Courts held that this was unlawful. The South African Government eventually complied with this ruling and revoked its notification of withdrawal. As the authors of the book put it:

> The court was saying that South Africa's Constitution promotes human rights and a human rights perspective on the world. The Courts, as the custodians of the Constitution, will not support an executive that seeks to aid and abet a war criminal evading accountability and justice for his victims.

The jurisprudence of the South African Constitutional Court has deep relevance for other countries in Africa, and indeed world-wide. It brings out well the bold experiment to uphold the traditional rule of law inherited from the Common Law while giving it contemporary meaning in light of Constitutional provisions and the economic and social realities of the country.

One can only hope that the standard set by the South African Constitutional Court will be emulated by similar courts elsewhere in Africa, and indeed in the world at large. In recent years there have been encouraging reeds in places such as Kenya and Malawi that we shall look at next, in turn.

7.3.1 *Supreme Court of Kenya*

On [1] September, 2017, Kenya's Supreme Court annulled the result of the previous month's presidential election, citing irregularities and ordered a new election within 60 days.[19] The BBC commented at the time, "Other elections in Africa have been annulled or cancelled but this appears to be the first time on the continent that an opposition court challenge against a presidential poll result has been successful."[20]

19 See https://www.bbc,com/news/world-africa-41123329, 1 September, 2017: Kenya presidential election cancelled by Supreme Court.

20 Idem.

In delivering the decision, Chief Justice David Maraga said that the 8 August 2017 election had not been "conducted in accordance with the constitution" and declared it "invalid, null and void." He added that the Elections Commission had failed "to conduct the presidential election in a manner consistent with the dictates of the constitution." The Commission had committed irregularities "in the transmission of results".[21]

According to the bbc, the Chairman of the Electoral Commission Wafula Chebukati noted the ruling and said that there would be "changes to personnel" ahead of the new election. He invited the Director of Public Prosecutions "to prosecute any of our staff that may have been involved in violations."[22]

In the re-run of the elections, President Uhuru Kenyatta was returned to power.

7.3.2 *Constitutional Court of Malawi*

On 3 February, 2020, the Constitutional Court of Malawi ordered the Electoral Commission to organise fresh Presidential elections before July the same year. A panel of five judges led by Justice Healy Potani cited widespread irregularities in the conduct of the elections as the reason for declaring the outcome of the polls as null and void. Justice Potani declared in delivering the judgment: "In every election there will be irregularities but in the present matter, it has been our finding that the irregularities were so widespread, systematic and grave that the results of the elections have been compromised and cannot be trusted as a reflection of the votes"

Some of the irregularities included failure by the Malawi Electoral Commission to adhere to statutory requirements on handling tally sheets and log books, delegation of statutory powers belonging to the Electoral Commission to the chief elections officer and accepting tally sheets that had been altered using correction fluid.[23]

In the re-run of the elections, Opposition candidate Lazarus Chakwera, won instead of the previous incumbent Peter Mutharika.

---

21 Idem.

22 Idem.

23 See Tanaka Chitsa, "Court orders rerun of Malawi presidential elections", https://www.sardc.net/en/southern-african-news-features/court-orders-rerun-of-malawi-presidential-elections/.

7.4 Conclusion

This chapter has presented convincing evidence that African National Human Rights Institutions stand firmly behind universal norms of human rights as reflected in United Nations treaties and other normative documents. The South African Constitutional Court has placed its authority firmly behind the universal groundings of the human rights provisions of the South African Bill of Rights. The Supreme Court of Kenya and the Constitutional Court of Malawi have handed down landmark decisions in support of the principles of democratic legitimacy and the rule of law. Africa's normative human rights heritage thus anchors itself firmly in universal human rights principles, even as it expands on those principles in order to take account of African specificities

In the chapter following we shall present evidence of the strong support of civil society organizations in Africa for universal human rights norms.

CHAPTER 8

Civil Society

Abstract

African civil society has resoundingly supported international human rights norms and the universality of human rights, while calling for gross violations of human rights to cease. African publicists have also marshalled evidence that the universality of human rights is grounded in African philosophical systems such as Ubuntu and those of the Akan people.

8.1 Introduction

This chapter will adduce evidence of support for the universality of human rights by important sectors of African society, including pronouncements of Human Rights Defenders (HRDs), senior African judges, The Elders, a grouping established by the late Nelson Mandela to promote peace, democracy and justice, African NGOs, and African publicists. We begin with as powerful an African statement of universality as could be imagined, the Harare Declaration of Human Rights, adopted on 22 April, 1989.

8.2 Kampala Declaration of Human Rights Defenders (2009); Kampala Plan of Action for Human Rights Defenders (2019)

As we shall see presently, African Human Rights Defenders continue to plead for protection and support from universal as well as regional African human rights mechanisms. A lynch-pin of their work is the UN Declaration on Human Rights Defenders which they see as the basis for their efforts regionally and internationally. In sum, what is crucial for African Human Rights Defenders is effective protection, from wherever it comes.

From 20–23 April, 2009, 85 human rights defenders (HRD) from 45 African States and 33 partners from across the world met at an All-Africa Human Rights Defenders Conference held in Kampala. On 23 April, 2009, the conference adopted the Kampala Declaration on Human Rights Defenders in which they condemned the significant number of HRDs who had been killed *in*

 | DOI:10.1163/9789004520646_009

their efforts to promote and protect universal human rights since the All-Africa Human Rights Defenders Conference of November 1998 held in Johannesburg.

The Conference affirmed the rights of HRDs to effectively continue their work in accordance with the UN Declaration on HRDs. They acknowledged the contribution of the UN and ACHPR human rights protection mechanisms in their efforts to protect HRDs, including the practices of urgent communications and country visits, and their collaboration with NGOs and UN peacekeeping operations.

Conference participants remained deeply concerned by the challenges HRDs continued to face in the various sub-regions of Africa whose rights as defenders continued to be violated and to be subjected to summary execution, torture, arbitrary detention, legislative restrictions, unfair trials, harassment and stigmatization. They remained particularly concerned by the threats against vulnerable HRDs, including women HRDs, HRDs working in armed conflict areas or under oppressive regimes, journalists, lesbian, gay, bisexual, transgender and intersex (LGBT) and minority rights activists.

The participants noted "the challenges of international and regional mechanisms in the field of HRDs protection, and those mechanisms' shortcomings which include: few country visits, insufficient follow-up on HRD cases, insufficient capacity and inadequate or non-responsiveness by States on these cases." The participants therefore decided to: build on existing sub-regional networks and create new ones where needed; undertake an updated assessment of HRDs' needs in all Africa; and design accordingly a national, regional and international strategy for their protection, and strengthen national HRD coalitions and sub-regional networks to render them more dynamic and effective.

Ten years later, at an African Human Rights Defenders Convention held in Zanzibar, Tanzania, from 12–14 June, 2019, participants adopted the Kampala Plan of Action for Human Rights Defenders in which they: urged continued collaboration to reinforce the work of sub-regional networks, national coalitions and key interest groups; *enhanced collaboration of HRDs with regional and international mechanisms*; enhanced sub-regional networks and national coalitions' *active use of an engagement with the regional and international human rights systems*; wide dissemination of the UN Declaration on the Right and Responsibility of Individuals, Groups and Organs of Society to Promote and Protect Universally Recognized Human Rights and Fundamental Freedoms and the manual on the use of these mechanisms; supporting efforts by sub-regional networks to enhance the capacity of national coalitions in their advocacy activities aimed at pushing for county visits, helping to create space for an active collaboration of civil society with the African human rights mechanisms and the UN Human Rights Council; supporting systematic reporting to the African human rights mechanisms and the United nations Human Rights Council special procedures, including advocacy on state reporting.

8.3 Harare Declaration of Human Rights 1989

Between 19 and 22 April, 1989 there was convened in Harare Zimbabwe a high level judicial colloquium on the Domestic Application of International Human Rights Norms. This meeting was in continuation of a similar one convened the previous year in Bangalore, India, by the former Indian Chief Justice, P.N. Bhagwati.

The Convenor of the Harare meeting was the Hon. Chief Justice E. Dumbutshena, Chief Justice of Zimbabwe, acting with the approval of the Government of Zimbabwe. The Colloquium was honoured by the attendance at the first session of His Excellency the Hon. R.G. Mugabe, President of Zimbabwe, who opened the colloquium with a speech in which he reaffirmed the commitment of his Government to respect for human rights, the independence of the judiciary, the rule of law and a bill of rights which is justiciable in the courts. This was President Mugabe or earlier vintage.

The participants in the Colloquium included a stellar cross-section of African Chief Justices and other Justices:

Chief Justice E. Dumbutshena, Zimbabwe (Convenor)
Justice A. Ademola, Nigeria.
Chief Justice E.O. Ayoola, the Gambia
Justice P.R. Bhagwati, India
Chief Justice B.P. Cullinan, Lesotho
Justice A.R. Gubbay, Zimbabwe
Justice M.D. Kirby, CMG, Australia
Justice Rajsoomer Lallah, Mauritius
Mr Recorder Anthony Lester, Q.C., United Kingdom
Chief Justice E. Livesey Luke, Botswana
Chief Justice F.L. Makuta, Malawi
Chief Justice Cecil H.E. Miller, Kenya
Chief Justice F.L. Nyalali, Tanzania
Justice E.W. Sansole, Zimbabwe
Chief Justice E.A. Seaton, Seychelles
Chief Justice A.M. Silungwe, Zambia
Justice J.N.K. Taylor, Ghana
Justice L.E. Unyolo, Malawi

The Participants agreed as follows:

1. Fundamental human rights and freedoms are inherent in humankind. In some cases, they are expressed in the constitutions, legislation and principles of common law and customary law of each country. They are also expressed in customary international law, international instruments on human rights and in the developing international jurisprudence on human rights.
2. The coming into force of the African Charter on Human and Peoples' Rights is a step in the ever widening effort of humanity to promote and protect fundamental human rights declared both in universal and regional instruments. The gross violations of human rights and fundamental freedoms which have occurred around the world in living memory (and which still occur) provide the impetus in a world of diminishing distances and growing interdependence, for such effort to provide effectively for their promotion and protection.
3. But fine statements in domestic laws or international and regional instruments are not enough. Rather it is essential to develop a culture of respect for internationally stated human rights norms which sees these norms applied in domestic laws of all nations and given full effect. They must not be seen as alien to domestic law in national courts. It is in this context that the principles on the Domestic Application of International Human Rights Norms stated in Bangalore in February 1988 are warmly endorsed by participants. In particular, they reaffirmed that, subject always to any clearly applicable domestic law to the contrary, it is within the proper nature of the judicial process for national courts to have regard to international human rights norms – whether or not incorporated into domestic law and whether or not a country is a party to a particular convention where it is declaratory of customary international law – for the purpose of resolving ambiguity or uncertainty in national constitutions and legislation or filling gaps in the common law. The participants noted many recent examples in countries of the Commonwealth where this had been done by courts of the highest authority – including in Australia, India, Mauritius, the United Kingdom and Zimbabwe.
4. There is a particular need to ensure that judges, lawyers, litigants and others are made aware of applicable human rights norms – stated in international instruments and otherwise. In this respect, the participants endorsed the spirit of Article 25 of the African Charter. Under that Article, States Parties to the Charter have the duty to promote and ensure through teaching, education and publication, respect for the rights and freedoms (and corresponding duties) expressed in the Charter. The participants

looked forward to the Commission established by the African Charter developing its work of promoting an awareness of human rights. The work being done in this regard by the publication of the Commonwealth Law Bulletin, the Law Reports of the Commonwealth and the Bulletin of Interrights (The International Centre for the Legal Protection of Human Rights) was especially welcomed. But to facilitate the domestic application of international human rights norms more needed to be done. So much was recognized in the Principles stated after the Bangalore Colloquium which called for new initiatives in legal education, provision of material in libraries and better dissemination of information abut developments in this field to judges, lawyers and law enforcement officers in particular. There is also a role of non-government organisations in these as in other regards, including the development of public interest litigation.

5. As a practical measure to carrying forward the objectives of the Principles stated in Bangalore, the participants requested that the Legal Division of the Commonwealth Secretariat arrange for a handbook for judges and lawyers in all parts of the Commonwealth to be produced, containing at least the following:
   - The basic texts of the most relevant international and regional human rights instruments;
   - A table for ease of reference to and comparison of applicable provisions in each instrument; and
   - Up to date references to the jurisprudence of international and national courts relevant to the meaning of the provisions in such instrument

6. If the judges and lawyers in Africa – and indeed of the Commonwealth and of the wider world – have ready access to reference material of this kind, opportunities will be enhanced for the principles of international human rights norms to be utilised in proper ways by judges and lawyers performing their daily work. In this way, the long journey to universal respect of basic rights will be advanced. Judges and lawyers have a duty to familiarise themselves with the growing international jurisprudence of human rights. So far as they may lawfully do so, they have a duty to reflect the basic norms of human rights in the performance of their duties.

In this way the noble words of international instruments will be translated into legal reality for the benefit of the people we serve but also ultimately for that of people in every land.

Harare,
Zimbabwe
22 April, 1989."

The Harare Declaration of Human Rights was a moving affirmation of African support for the universality of human rights. Another example would be seen a quarter of a century later in the report of the Global Commission on Elections, Democracy and Security established by The Elders, led after the passing of Nelson Mandela by Kofi Annan, former Secretary-General of the United Nations.

8.4 Civil Society

8.4.1 *The Elders' Global Commission on Elections, Democracy and Security*

In September 2012, former UN Secretary-General Kofi Annan, Chairman of the Elders, launched the Global Commission on Elections, Democracy and Security. Speaking at the launch of the report of the Commission the following year, Annan noted that elections with integrity are the foundation of democracy. In a true democracy, elected leaders are simply the temporary custodians of political power, the power ultimately resting with the people. The Global Commission defined an election with integrity as one that is "based on the democratic principles of universal suffrage and political equality as reflected in international standards and agreements, and is professional, impartial and transparent in its preparation and administration through the electoral cycle." At its core the ideal of electoral integrity means that all voters should have an equal opportunity to participate in public debate and cast their ballots, all votes are counted equally, and all candidates seeking election do so on a level playing field.

In its report the Global Commission stressed that democracy is a universal value. The ideal and appeal of democracy is found across the world and does not belong to any country, region or culture. It is enshrined in the Universal Declaration of Human Rights, which states that 'everyone has the right to take part in the government of his country' and that the will of the people 'shall be expressed in periodic and genuine elections.' At the World Summit in 2005,the Member States of the United Nations reaffirmed that democracy is a universal value.[1]

The Global Commission identified five challenges that must be overcome if elections are to be held with integrity:

---

1 See, The Elders, Opinion: "Deepening Democracy: why elections with integrity matter", Monday 4 March, 2013. https://wwww.theelders.org/news/deepening-democracy-why-elections-integrity-matter.

- Strengthening the rule of law so that the rights of voters and candidates are protected;
- Building competent, professional and independent electoral management bodies that can organise free, fair and credible elections;
- …
- …
- …

8.4.2 *Electoral Institute for Sustainable Democracy in Africa*

The Electora l Institute for Sustainable Democracy in Africa (EISA) is a not-for-profit organization established in 1996, based in Johannesburg, South Africa, with field offices across the continent. Its vision is for an African continent where democratic governance, human rights and citizen participation are upheld in a peaceful environment. According to its Mission Statement, EISA strives for excellence in the promotion of credible elections, citizen participation, and strong political institutions for sustainable democracy in Africa …

8.5 Publicists

8.5.1 *An Akan Perspective on Human Rights*

Kwasi Wiredu[2] has written authoritatively on the human rights perspectives of the Akan people in West Africa. A right, he notes, is a claim that people are entitled to make on others or on society at large by virtue of their status. Human rights are claims that people are entitled to make simply by virtue of their status as human beings. The question naturally arises, what is it about a human being that makes him or her entitled to make the latter kind of claim.

Wiredu explored the answer to this question by looking principally at the Akan conception of a person. The word 'Akan' refers both to a group of intimately related languages found in West Africa and to the people who speak them. This ethnic group lives predominantly in Ghana and in parts of adjoining Cote d'Ivoire.

8.5.2 *The Akan Conception of a Person*

The Akan conception of a person, Wiredu writes, has both descriptive and normative aspects that are directly relevant not only to the idea that there are

2 This presentation is based on Kwasi Wiredu, "An African perspective on human rights", in his Cultural universals and particulars: An African perspective. Bloomington: Indiana University Press, 1996, pp. 157–171.

human rights but also to the question of what those rights are. In this conception a person is the result of the union of three elements. There is the life principle (*okra*), the blood principle (*mogya*),and the personality principle (*sunsum*). By virtue of possessing an *okra*, divine element, all persons have an intrinsic value, the same in each, which they do not owe to any earthly circumstance. Associated with this value is a concept of human dignity, which implies that every human being is entitled in an equal measure to a certain basic respect.

8.5.3 *The Akan Political System*

Every Akan is obligated by birth to contribute to defence in one way or another. There is also the complementary fact that he had a right to the protection of his person, property, dignity, not only in his own state but also outside it. And states were known to go to war to secure the freedom of their citizens abroad or avenge their mistreatment. The ruling body of an Akan town is a council consisting of the lineage heads with the chief of the town in the capacity of chairman. The functions of the council are to preserve law, order, and peace in the town, to ensure its safety, and to promote its welfare.

8.5.4 *Rights of Political Participation*

In principle citizens have a say, first in the question of who would exercise political power over them, and second in the issue of what specific policies are to be implemented in the town and, derivatively, in the state and nation. The people's freedom of thought and expression goes beyond the device of any chief or council. A cherished principle of Akan politics is that those who served the chief could also destool him.

8.5.5 *The Right to a Fair Trial*

It is an absolute principle of Akan justice that no human being could be punished without trial.

8.5.6 *The Right to Land*

[A]ny human being is held, by virtue of his/her blood principle (*mogya*), to be entitled to some land. For the duration of his/her life any Akan had the right to the use of a piece of the lineage land. However, land is supposed to belong to the whole lineage, conceived as including the ancestors, the living members, and those as yet to be born. For this reason, in traditional times the sale of land was prohibited.

8.5.7 *Religious Freedom*

Religion consisted simply of belief and trust in, and reverence for, a Supreme being regarded as the architect of the cosmos. The Akan take it to be obvious even to children that such a being exists.

From their tolerant attitude toward other people's religious beliefs, it is sufficiently clear that the Akans make no exceptions of subject matter in the question of the freedom of thought.

Wiredu summed up:

> In summary, one finds a veritable harvest of human rights. Akan thought recognized the right of a new-born to be nursed and educated, the right of an adult to a plot of land from the ancestral holdings, the right of any well-defined unit of political organization to self-government, the right of all to have a say in the enstoolment or destoolment of their chiefs or their elders and to participate in the shaping of governmental policies, the right of al to freedom of thought and expression in all matters, political, religious and metaphysical, the right of everybody to trial before punishment, the right of a person to remain at any locality or to leave, and so on ...[3]

8.5.8 *African Ubuntu on Human Rights*

Dr Tim Murithi has written cogently on the human rights content of the African philosophy of Ubuntu.[4] Are human rights, he asked, truly universal or do they merely represent the historically dominant Western civilization's world view? Faced with issues of safeguarding and protecting human dignity, both at home and abroad, he commented that this question is more compelling than ever. Since the adoption of the Universal Declaration of Human Rights (UDHR) by the United Nations General Assembly on 10 December 1948, there has been an ongoing debate about whether human rights – in the way that they have been formulated and codified – are truly representative of a culturally global consensus on the fundamental provisions for securing human dignity.

Summarising different positions, he notes that there are those who maintain that the articles of the UDHR are representative of what the international community should universally aspire to; but there are also those who argue that the Universal Declaration is incomplete. A key argument advanced in this regard is that the UDHR should include additional values and insights from different

3 Ibid.

4 Formerly Programme Officer, United Nations Institute for Training and research, Geneva. Published in Human Rights Tribune, Vol. 10, No. 1, March 2004.

cultures. In contrast, for those who re-affirm its universality, the UDHR does an adequate job in categorizing and classifying rights in a way that is acceptable to everyone. Those who adhere to this point of view challenge the idea that the Universal Declaration is 'Western' by indicating that the 18 members of the original Human Rights Commission that drafted the document included influential international scholars such as P.C. Chang from China, Charles Malik from Lebanon, and Hernan Santa Crus from Chile. In this sense the UDHR did in fact have substantial input from developing and non-Western countries. They do, however, concede that there are parts of the world that were not represented, particularly from sub-Saharan Africa and other countries that were still colonies at the time the Universal Declaration was drafted.

Groups and individuals who criticize the Universal Declaration for its exclusion, Murithi notes, also argue that the very absence of marginalized voices during the drafting phase of the UDHR makes it an incomplete formulation. In particular, with reference to the contribution of Africa to the human rights debate, academics have suggested there has been an inadequate recognition of the way in which African thought systems contribute towards advancing the cause of human dignity for all. He cites Makau Mutua, a Professor of Law and Director of the Human Rights Centre at the State University of New York at Buffalo Law School, who argued in his book, *Human Rights: A Political and Cultural Critique*[5] that what was needed was a more extended understanding of human rights, one that takes into account alternative ways of thinking about and articulating human dignity.

Mutua argued for what he calleds the "multiculturalization" of human rights in an effort to make them truly universal. By this he alluded to the need to open the space of dialogue on what human rights entail within the various cultural communities around the world. By virtue of the fact that colonizing forces had marginalized these communities, oppressed people were not in a position to input and contribute towards the formulation of a global code of human rights. Mutua emphasized that the indigenous, non-European traditions of Asia, Africa, the Pacific and the Americas must be deployed and referred to in order to deconstruct what we understand by human rights. Only once this has been achieved could we reconstruct a genuinely universal bundle of rights that all human societies could unequivocally claim as their own.

In the context of this debate, Murithi counsels, lessons can be learnt from the African worldview known as *ubuntu*. Ubuntu is an ancient African code of ethics that emphasizes the importance of hospitality, generosity, respect for

5 University of Pennsylvania Press, 2002.

all members of the community, and embraces the view that we all belong to one human family. This notion of ubuntu is found in diverse forms in many societies throughout Africa. More specifically, among the Bantu languages of the regions of Eastern, Central and Southern Africa, the notion of ubuntu is a cultural worldview that tries to capture the essence of what it means to be human. In southern Africa its earliest formulation is found amongst the Nguni group of languages. In terms of its definition, Desmond Tutu in his book *No Future Without Forgiveness* (Pinter, 1999) observes:

> Ubuntu is very difficult to render into a Western language. It speaks to the very essence of being human. When you want to give high praise to someone we say, '*Yu, u nobuntu*', he or she has ubuntu. This means that they are generous, hospitable, friendly, caring and compassionate. They share what they have. It also means that my humanity is caught up, is inextricably bund up, in theirs. We belong in a bundle of life.We say, 'person is a person through other people.' (In Xhosa, *Ubuntu ungamntu ngabanye abantu* and in Zulu *Umuntu ngumuntu ngabanuye*). I am human because I belong, I participate, and I share. A person with ubuntu is open and available to others, affirming of others, does not feel threatened that others are able and good; for he or she has a proper self-assurance that comes with knowing tht he or she belongs in a greater whole and is diminished when others are humiliated or diminished, when others are tortured or oppressed, or treated as if they were less than who they are.

This notion of ubuntu, Murithi continues, sheds light on the importance of the promotion of human rights through the principles of reciprocity and a sense of shared destiny between peoples. It provides a value system for giving and receiving forgiveness, which in turn advances human rights in war-affected societies and countries in transition from authoritarian regimes. It provides a rationale for sacrificing or letting go of the desire for revenge for past wrongs. It provides an inspiration and suggests guidelines for societies, and their governments, on how to legislate and establish laws that promote human rights. In short, it can culturally re-inform and reconstruct practical efforts to establish a more effective and relevant human rights regime in Africa and other parts of the world. Murithi comments that the principles found in ubuntu are not unique; they are found in diverse forms in other cultures and traditions. Nevertheless, an ongoing reflection and re-appraisal of this notion of ubuntu could serve to re-emphasize the essential unity of humanity. It could achieve this gradually by promoting attitudes and values predicated on the promotion and protection of human rights, including emphasizing the sharing of resources and reinforcing a collective commitment to cooperation as the means for resolving humanity's common problems.

Ubuntu societies, Murithi notes, maintain institutions that have at their very core concern for the human dignity of the individual; but they also combine that principle with an individual's obligation towards the community. Such institutions also serve as mechanisms for maintaining law and order within society. The wisdom of ubuntu lies in the recognition that it is not possible to build a healthy community at peace with itself unless the human dignity of all members of the community is safeguarded. The principle of ubuntu (*I am because we are*) can help to guide us as we advocate, monitor and promote the human rights of others, both at home and abroad.

Ubuntu can provide us with a basis for the promotion of human rights: Its principles are primarily geared towards promoting the recognition of our collective humanity and advocating for an attitude of solidarity towards our fellow human beings. The ethics of Ubuntu suggest to us that all cultures have principles that can serve as a basis for re-emphasizing our collective human rights and reinforcing the idea that these rights are inclusive and truly universal. In keeping with the tradition of how ubuntu societies function. Recognition of our collective humanity is also a call to action. There is no point, Murithi comments, in recognizing the principles of ubuntu merely for the sake of recognition only; we also have to internalize these principles and then act upon them. Recognition of our 'ubuntuness' is a call to put our principles in action, to practice politics with principle; it is also a call to rebuild our societies upon the foundations of tolerance and equal access to resources for the improvement of our collective well- being.

The recognition and practice of the norms of ubuntu, Murithi pointed out, pre-dated the drafting of the UDHR. It goes without saying that similar values-systems exist or have existed in most cultures in the world and can, in their own way, serve to promote and maintain standards of human rights. It is therefore necessary to research the wisdom of these cultures and create opportunities for sharing and exchanging ideas on how we can work towards the genuine multi-cultural perspective of the human rights movement. Advancing an ubuntu perspective on human rights can facilitate the inclusion of the African voice in a dialogue on rights and responsibilities. It can also enhance the ongoing efforts to re-emphasize the universality of human rights through the recognition of local or cultural interpretations. Finally, it will enable us to establish us to establish human rights standards that cannot be discredited because of the nature of their organs.

Murithi pleaded:

> The moment has come for new life to be given to the global campaign for human rights by reformulating the Universal Declaration of Human Rights. We should note that the provisions relating to social and economic justice have been virtually neglected over the last five decades as focus has stayed on the civic and political dimensions of human rights. As we make in-roads into the twenty-first century we need to re-articulate our aspirations toward human rights in the language of obligations and as a call to action. In essence, a re-articulation of human rights from an ubuntu perspective adds value to the human rights movement by placing more of an emphasis on the obligations that we have towards the 'other'.[6]

8.6 Conclusion

This chapter has shown solid evidence of the commitment of African civil society and academics to fundamental human rights and their universality. As senior African jurists emphasized in the Harare Declaration many years ago:

> Fundamental human rights and freedoms are inherent in humankind. In some cases, they are expressed in the constitutions, legislation and principles of common law and customary law of each country. They are also expressed in customary international law, international instruments on human rights and in the developing international jurisprudence on human rights.

On the ground, young Africans who will shape the continent's future have embraced universal human rights as evidenced by their enthusiastic participation in human rights studies programs, such as the Master in Human Rights and Democratisation in Africa of the Centre for Human Rights of the University of Pretoria, South Africa. Students from all parts of Africa have flocked to programmes such as this one and others in search of ways of further entrenching the protection of human rights on their continent. In this and other programs across the continent African international law scholars, such as Professor Michelo Hansungule of Zambia, Evance Kalula of Zambia and South Africa, and Tiyanjana Maluwa of Malawi and South Africa, have opined

6 Loc. Cit. supra.

that many of the norms and practices that accompany contemporary international human rights, and international law more generally, may also be found in African history, though this has been obscured by colonial domination and the marginalization of the oral traditions of Africa. Young African students embrace the universality of human rights and seek to localise them in their own time and ways.

CHAPTER 9

Conclusion

Abstract

This chapter seals the argument that Africa supports the universality of human rights by highlighting the adoption of democracy charters, continental and regional human rights instruments, the jurisprudence of the African Commission and African Court, and the insistence of the African Union that it would not accept, or recognize military coups against democratically elected Governments. It also recalls ringing affirmations of universality at the highest levels of the African Union.

9.1 Introduction

It is a sad reality that gross violations of human rights are rampant in numerous parts of the world and that democracy is under pressure world-wide. Africa has not escaped these trends. Conflicts, displacements, and gross violations of human rights continue to take their toll in some parts of Africa – as indeed elsewhere in the world.

But this book has brought forth convincing evidence of the commitment of African peoples, governments and institutions to the pursuit of democracy and to the promotion and protection of human rights. In a wider world where the universality of human rights is under explicit challenge from some powerful quarters, Africa has adopted a firm position of principle in support of universal human rights, while mindful of the historical characteristics of the continent.

In South Africa, already in the 1920s, the African National Congress framed the struggle against racial oppression as a fight for freedom and adopted its Freedom Charter. After the adoption of the Universal Declaration of Human Rights in 1948, Nelson Mandela, Kwame N'krumah, Julius Nyerere, Kenneth Kaunda, and other leaders fighting for freedom embraced the Universal Declaration and pleaded the cause of freedom invoking the Declaration.

The founding Charter of the OAU, the predecessor of today's African Union, specifically drew on the Universal Declaration. Subsequently, the African Charter of Human and People's Rights built on the foundations of the Universal Declaration.

 | DOI:10.1163/9789004520646_010

It has not been plain sailing to uphold human rights in practice. One party states, dictatorships, oppression, injustices, gross violations of human rights have all taken their toll on Africa's peoples. Yet, we have seen in this book:

- The adoption of, and commitment to, democracy charters.
- The adoption of continental and regional human rights instruments.
- The establishment of continental and regional human rights bodies.
- Consistent jurisprudence of continental and regional human rights bodies upholding the norms of international human rights law and explicitly affirming that universal human rights are binding on African Governments.
- The insistence of the African Union that its Members would not accept, or recognize, military coups against democratically elected African Governments.
- Consistent efforts to build peace in troubled areas on the foundations of human rights and also to prevent conflicts through respecting human rights.

There are fifty-four African States in the United Nations, well over one quarter of the membership of the world body. It is without doubt that the views of African States, peoples, and institutions upholding the universality of human rights count when it comes to upholding the tenets of the Universal Declaration of Human Rights world-wide.

9.2 Grand Bay Declaration

It would be fitting to conclude this book by recalling the Declaration and plan of action adopted by the first African Ministerial conference on human rights in Africa, held at Grand Bay, Mauritius from 12–16 April, 1999. "Determined to consolidate the gains made in Africa in the promotion and protection of human rights":

1. The Ministerial Conference affirms the principle that human rights are universal, indivisible, interdependent and inter-related and urges governments, in their policies, to give parity to economic, social and cultural rights as well as civil and political rights.
2. The Conference also affirms that the right to development, the right to a generally satisfactory healthy environment and the right to national and international peace and security are universal and inalienable rights which form an integral part of fundamental rights.
3. The Conference further affirms the interdependence of the principles of good governance, the rule of law, democracy and development.

4. The Conference recognizes that the development of the rule of law, democracy and human rights calls for an independent, open, accessible and impartial judiciary, which can deliver justice promptly and at an affordable cost. To this end, such a system requires a body of professional and competent judges enjoying conducive conditions.
5. The Conference recognizes that the core values on which human rights are founded, particularly (a) respect for the sanctity of life and human dignity; (b) tolerance of differences; and (c) desire for liberty, order, fairness, prosperity and stability, are shared across all cultures. In this connection, integrating positive traditional and cultural values of Africa into the human rights debate will be useful in ensuring their transmission to future generations.

All of Africa, at the Ministerial level, thus spoke eloquently in support of the universality of human rights: "human rights are universal", they said; furthermore, "the core values on which human rights are founded … are shared across all cultures."

9.3 Algiers Declaration

Later in the year, the Assembly of Heads of State and Government of the OAU [the predecessor of the African Union], meeting for their thirty-fifth ordinary session in Algiers, Algeria, from 12–14 July, 1999, declared:

> We believe that human rights have undergone major positive changes since the independence of African countries. The liberation movements of our peoples, the efforts of our countries and of the OAU to codify and implement these rights, as well as the current dynamic process of establishing new democratic spaces in Africa have contributed to a very large extent to these changes. The African Charter on Human and Peoples' Rights and the Protocol on African Court on Human and Peoples' Rights as well as the Declaration and Plan of Action, recently adopted in Mauritius, eloquently testify to Africa's contribution to the promotion and protection of the noble cause of human rights. We, however, recognize that much remains to be done to bring these developments to the level of our own expectations and the legitimate aspirations of our peoples. We are aware of these limitations and are determined not to relent in our efforts to transcend them.

> In this spirit, we reiterate our commitment to the protection and promotion of human rights and fundamental freedoms. We emphasize the indivisibility, universality and interdependence of all human rights, by they political and civil or economic, social and cultural, or even individual and collective. We call upon the international community to ensure that they are not used for political purposes.
>
> We are convinced that the increase in, and expansion of the spaces of freedom and the establishment of democratic institutions that are representative of our peoples and receiving their active participation, would further contribute to the consolidation of modern African States underpinned by the rule of law, respect for the fundamental rights and freedoms of the citizens and the democratic management of public affairs.[1]

Echoing Nietzsche in Zarathustra, "Thus spoke Africa", eloquently, in affirmation of universal human rights. As senior African jurists had emphasized in the Harare Declaration many years earlier:

> Fundamental human rights and freedoms are inherent in humankind. In some cases, they are expressed in the constitutions, legislation and principles of common law and customary law of each country. They are also expressed in customary international law, international instruments on human rights and in the developing international jurisprudence on human rights.

The African Commission and the African Court on human rights have both eloquently and firmly upheld the universality of human rights, and all African Governments participating in the UN Human Rights Council's Universal Periodic Review provide ringing affirmations of their adherence to universal human rights norms anchored in the Universal Declaration of Human Rights.

9.4 Conclusion

The final word may be given to the International Criminal Tribunal for Rwanda (ICTY). At a commemorative event on the twentieth anniversary of the tribunal, its President told a commemorative even on 8 November, 2014:

---

1 AHG/Decl.1 (XXXV), pp. 4–5.

> [T]he international community has witnessed an evolution of international law since 1994, an evolution that saw the ICTR at the forefront of many 'firsts'. The ICTR became the first international tribunal to enter a judgement for genocide and the first to interpret the definition of genocide set forth in the Genocide Convention.
>
> The ICTR defined for the first time the crime of rape in international criminal law, and it recognized rape as a means of perpetuating genocide and significantly expanded the law with respect to sexual violence crimes ...
>
> In 1998, the ICTR became the first international tribunal since Nuremberg and Tokyo to issue a judgement against a former head of government and demonstrated that in the fight against impunity no person is immune from accountability. The Tribunal also rendered the first judgement examining the role of the media with respect to direct and public incitement to commit genocide. It is now recognized that civilians can also be prosecuted for international crimes when they participate in hostilities.
>
> Many of these firsts represent the foundation of international legal concepts that continue to be used by other courts and demonstrate the ICTR's impact on codifying numerous facets of international criminal law and humanitarian that were undeveloped 20 years ago.[2]

Africa thus contributed magisterially to shaping the content of the international law of human rights and the universality of human rights.

2 See A Compendium on the Legacy of the ICTR and the Development of International Law. https://unictr.irmct.org/en/compendium-legacy-ictr-and-development-international-law. Address by the President of the ICTR, pp.2–3.

ANNEX I

African Charter on Human and Peoples' Rights (Banjul Charter, 1981)

Preamble[1]

The African States members of the Organisation of African Unity, parties to the present Convention entitled "African Charter on Human and Peoples' Rights

Recalling Decision 115 (XVI) of the Assembly of Heads of State and Government at its Sixteenth Ordinary Session held in Monrovia, Liberia, from 17 to 20 July 1979 on the preparation of "a preliminary draft on an African Charter on Human and Peoples' Rights, providing inter alia for the establishment of bodies to promote and protect human and peoples' rights";

Considering the Charter of the Organisation of African Unity, which stipulates that "freedom, equality, justice and dignity are essential objectives for the achievement of the legitimate aspirations of the African peoples";

Reaffirming the pledge they solemnly made in Article 2 of the said Charter to eradicate all forms of colonialism from Africa, to coordinate and intensify their cooperation and efforts to achieve a better life for the peoples of Africa and to promote international cooperation having due regard to the Charter of the United Nations and the Universal Declaration of Human Rights;

Taking into consideration the virtues of their historical tradition and the values of African civilization which should inspire and characterize their reflection on the concept of human and peoples' rights;

Recognizing on the one hand, that fundamental human rights stem from the attitudes of human beings, which justifies their international protection and on the other hand that the reality and respect of peoples' rights should necessarily guarantee human rights;

Considering that the enjoyment of rights and freedoms also implies the performance of duties on the part of everyone;

Convinced that it is henceforth essential to pay particular attention to the right to development and that civil and political rights cannot be dissociated from economic,

1 African Commission on Human and People's Rights, Accessed on 28 July 2021. https://www.achpr.org/legalinstruments/detail?id=49.

 | DOI:10.1163/9789004520646_011

social and cultural rights in their conception as well as universality and that the satisfaction of economic, social and cultural rights is a guarantee for the enjoyment of civil and political rights;

Conscious of their duty to achieve the total liberation of Africa, the peoples of which are still struggling for their dignity and genuine independence, and undertaking to eliminate colonialism, neo-colonialism, apartheid, zionism and to dismantle aggressive foreign military bases and all forms of discrimination, language, religion or political opinions;

Reaffirming their adherence to the principles of human and peoples' rights and freedoms contained in the declarations, conventions and other instruments adopted by the Organisation of African Unity, the Movement of Non-Aligned Countries and the United Nations;

Firmly convinced of their *duty* to promote and protect human and peoples' rights and freedoms and taking into account the importance traditionally attached to these rights and freedoms in Africa;

HAVE AGREED AS FOLLOWS:

Part I Rights and Duties

Chapter I Human and Peoples' Rights

ARTICLE 1

The Member States of the Organisation of African Unity, parties to the present Charter shall recognise the rights, duties and freedoms enshrined in the Charter and shall undertake to adopt legislative or other measures to give effect to them.

ARTICLE 2

Every individual shall be entitled to the enjoyment of the rights and freedoms recognised and guaranteed in the present Charter without distinction of any kind such as race, ethnic group, colour, sex, language, religion, political or any other opinion, national and social origin, fortune, birth or any status.

ARTICLE 3

1. Every individual shall be equal before the law
2. Every individual shall be entitled to equal protection of the law

ARTICLE 4

Human beings are inviolable. Every human being shall be entitled to respect for his life and the integrity of his person. No one may be arbitrarily deprived of this right.

ARTICLE 5

Every individual shall have the right to the respect of the dignity inherent in a human being and to the recognition of his legal status. All forms of exploitation and degradation of man, particularly slavery, slave trade, torture, cruel, inhuman or degrading punishment and treatment shall be prohibited.

ARTICLE 6

Every individual shall have the right to liberty and to the security of his person. No one may be deprived of his freedom except for reasons and conditions previously laid down by law. In particular, no one may be arbitrarily arrested or detained.

ARTICLE 7

1. Every individual shall have the right to have his cause heard. This comprises:
    1. The right to an appeal to competent national organs against acts of violating his fundamental rights as recognized and guaranteed by conventions, laws, regulations and customs in force;
2. The right to be presumed innocent until proved guilty by a competent court or tribunal;
    1. The right to defence, including the right to be defended by counsel of his choice;
    2. The right to be tried within a reasonable time by an impartial court or tribunal.
    3. No one may be condemned for an act or omission which did not constitute a legally punishable offence at the time it was committed. No penalty may be inflicted for an offence for which no provision was made at the time it was committed. Punishment is personal and can be imposed only on the offender.

ARTICLE 8

Freedom of conscience, the profession and free practice of religion shall be guaranteed. No one may, subject to law and order, be submitted to measures restricting the exercise of these freedoms.

ARTICLE 9

1. Every individual shall have the right to receive information.
2. Every individual shall have the right to express and disseminate his opinions within the law.

ARTICLE 10

1. Every individual shall have the right to free association provided that he abides by the law.
2. Subject to the obligation of solidarity provided for in Article 29, no one may be compelled to join an association.

ARTICLE 11

Every individual shall have the right to assemble freely with others. The exercise of this right shall be subject only to necessary restrictions provided for by law, in particular those enacted in the interest of national security, the safety, health, ethics and rights and freedoms of others.

ARTICLE 12

1. Every individual shall have the right to freedom of movement and residence within the borders of a State provided he abides by the law.

2. Every individual shall have the right to leave any country including his own, and to return to his country.
3. This right may only be subject to restrictions, provided for by law for the protection of national security, law and order, public health or morality.
4. Every individual shall have the right, when persecuted, to seek and obtain asylum in other countries in accordance with the law of those countries and international conventions.
5. A non-national legally admitted in a territory of a State Party to the present Charter, may only be expelled from it by virtue of a decision taken in accordance with the law.
6. The mass expulsion of non-nationals shall be prohibited. Mass expulsion shall be that which is aimed at national, racial, ethnic or religious groups.

ARTICLE 13

1. Every citizen shall have the right to participate freely in the government of his country, either directly or through freely chosen representatives in accordance with the provisions of the law.
2. Every citizen shall have the right of equal access to the public service of the country.
3. Every individual shall have the right of access to public property and services in strict equality of all persons before the law.

ARTICLE 14

The right to property shall be guaranteed. It may only be encroached upon in the interest of public need or in the general interest of the community and in accordance with the provisions of appropriate laws.

ARTICLE 15

Every individual shall have the right to work under equitable and satisfactory conditions, and shall receive equal pay for equal work.

ARTICLE 16

1. Every individual shall have the right to enjoy the best attainable state of physical and mental health.
2. State Parties to the present Charter shall take the necessary measures to protect the health of their people and to ensure that they receive medical attention when they are sick.

ARTICLE 17

1. Every individual shall have the right to education
2. Every individual may freely take part in the cultural life of his community.
3. The promotion and protection of morals and traditional values recognized by the community shall be the duty of the State.

ARTICLE 18

1. The family shall be the natural unit and basis of society. It shall be protected by the State which shall take care of its physical health and moral.

2. The State shall have the duty to assist the family which is the custodian of morals and traditional values recognized by the community.
3. The State shall ensure the elimination of every discrimination against women and also ensure the protection of the rights of women and the child as stipulated in international declarations and conventions.
4. The aged and the disabled shall also have the right to special measures of protection in keeping with their physical or moral needs.

ARTICLE 19

All peoples shall be equal; they shall enjoy the same respect and shall have the same rights. Nothing shall justify the domination of a people by another.

ARTICLE 20

1. All peoples shall have the right to existence. They shall have the unquestionable and inalienable right to self-determination. They shall freely determine their political status and shall pursue their economic and social development according to the policy they have freely chosen.
2. Colonized or oppressed peoples shall have the right to free themselves from the bonds of domination by resorting to any means recognized by the international community.
3. All peoples shall have the right to the assistance of the State Parties to the present Charter in their liberation struggle against foreign domination, be it political, economic or cultural.

ARTICLE 21

1. All peoples shall freely dispose of their wealth and natural resources. This right shall be exercised in the exclusive interest of the people. In no case shall a people be deprived of it
2. In case of spoilation, the dispossessed people shall have the right to the lawful recovery of its property as well as to an adequate compensation.
3. The free disposal of wealth and natural resources shall be exercised without prejudice to the obligation of promoting international economic cooperation based on mutual respect, equitable exchange and the principles of international law.
4. State Parties to the present Charter shall individually and collectively exercise the right to free disposal of their wealth and natural resources with a view to strengthening African Unity and solidarity.
5. State Parties to the present Charter shall undertake to eliminate all forms of foreign exploitation particularly that practised by international monopolies so as to enable their peoples to fully benefit from the advantages derived from their national resources.

ARTICLE 22

1. All peoples shall have the right to their economic, social and cultural development with due regard to their freedom and identity and in the equal enjoyment of the common heritage of mankind.
2. States shall have the duty, individually or collectively, to ensure the exercise of the right to development.

ARTICLE 23

1. All peoples shall have the right to national and international peace and security. The principles of solidarity and friendly relations implicitly affirmed by the Charter of the United Nations and reaffirmed by that of the Organisation of African Unity shall govern relations between States.
2. For the purpose of strengthening peace, solidarity and friendly relations, State Parties to the present Charter shall ensure that:
   1. any individual enjoying the right of asylum under Article 12 of the present Charter shall not engage in subversive activities against his country of origin or any other State Party to the present Charter;
   2. their territories shall not be used as bases for subversive or terrorist activities against the people of any other State Party to the present Charter.

ARTICLE 24

All peoples shall have the right to a general satisfactory environment favourable to their development.

ARTICLE 25

State Parties to the present Charter shall have the duty to promote and ensure through teaching, education and publication, the respect of the rights and freedoms contained in the present Charter and to see to it that these freedoms and rights as well as corresponding obligations and duties are understood.

ARTICLE 26

State Parties to the present Charter shall have the duty to guarantee the independence of the Courts and shall allow the establishment and improvement of appropriate national institutions entrusted with the promotion and protection of the rights and freedoms guaranteed by the present Charter.

Chapter II Duties

ARTICLE 27

1. Every individual shall have duties towards his family and society, the State and other legally recognised communities and the international community.
2. The rights and freedoms of each individual shall be exercised with due regard to the rights of others, collective security, morality and common interest.

ARTICLE 28

Every individual shall have the duty to respect and consider his fellow beings without discrimination, and to maintain relations aimed at promoting, safeguarding and reinforcing mutual respect and tolerance.

ARTICLE 29

The individual shall also have the duty:

1. To preserve the harmonious development of the family and to work for the cohesion and respect of the family; to respect his parents at all times, to maintain them in case of need.
2. To serve his national community by placing his physical and intellectual abilities at its service;
3. Not to compromise the security of the State whose national or resident he is;
4. To preserve and strengthen social and national solidarity, particularly when the latter is strengthened;
5. To preserve and strengthen the national independence and the territorial integrity of his country and to contribute to his defence in accordance with the law;
6. To work to the best of his abilities and competence, and to pay taxes imposed by law in the interest of the society;
7. To preserve and strengthen positive African cultural values in his relations with other members of the society, in the spirit of tolerance, dialogue and consultation and, in general, to contribute to the promotion of the moral well being of society;
8. To contribute to the best of his abilities, at all times and at all levels, to the promotion and achievement of African unity.

Part II Measures of Safeguard

Chapter I Establishment and Organisation of the African Commission on Human and Peoples' Rights

ARTICLE 30

An African Commission on Human and Peoples' Rights, hereinafter called "the Commission", shall be established within the Organisation of African Unity to promote human and peoples' rights and ensure their protection in Africa.

ARTICLE 31

1. The Commission shall consist of eleven members chosen from amongst African personalities of the highest reputation, known for their high morality, integrity, impartiality and competence in matters of human and peoples' rights; particular consideration being given to personshaving legal experience.
2. The members of the Commission shall serve in their personal capacity.

ARTICLE 32

The Commission shall not include more than one national of the same State.

ARTICLE 33

The members of the Commission shall be elected by secret ballot by the Assembly of Heads of State and Government, from a list of persons nominated by the State Parties to the present Charter.

ARTICLE 34

Each State Party to the present Charter may not nominate more than two candidates. The candidates must have the nationality of one of the State Parties to the present Charter. When two candidates are nominated by a State, one of them may not be a national of that State.

ARTICLE 35

1. The Secretary General of he Organisation of African Unity shall invite State Parties to the present Charter at least four months before the elections to nominate candidates;
2. The Secretary General of the Organisation of African Unity shall make an alphabetical list of the persons thus nominated and communicate it to the Heads of State and Government at least one month before the elections;

ARTICLE 36

The members of the Commission shall be elected for a six year period and shall be eligible for re-election. However, the term of office of four of the members elected at the first election shall terminate after two years and the term of office of three others, at the end of four years.

ARTICLE 37

Immediately after the first election, the Chairman of the Assembly of Heads of State and Government of the Organisation of African Unity shall draw lots to decide the names of those members referred to in Article 36.

ARTICLE 38

After their election, the members of the Commission shall make a solemn declaration to discharge their duties impartially and faithfully.

ARTICLE 39

1. In case of death or resignation of a member of the Commission, the Chairman of the Commission shall immediately inform the Secretary General of the Organisation of African Unity, who shall declare the seat vacant from the date of death or from the date on which the resignation takes effect.
2. If, in the unanimous opinion of other members of the Commission, a member has stopped discharging his dutiesfor any reason other than a temporary absence, the Chairman of the Commission shall inform the Secretary General of the Organisation of African Unity, who shall then declare the seat vacant.

3. In each of the cases anticipated above, the Assembly of Heads of State and Government shall replace the member whose seat became vacant for the remaining period of his term, unless the period is less than six months.

ARTICLE 40

Every member of the Commission shall be in office until the date his successor assumes office.

ARTICLE 41

The Secretary General of the Organisation of African Unity shall appoint the Secretary of the Commission. He shall provide the staff and services necessary for the effective discharge of the duties of the Commission. The Organisation of African Unity shall bear cost of the staff and services.

ARTICLE 42

1. The Commission shall elect its Chairman and Vice Chairman for a two-year period. They shall be eligible for re-election.
2. The Commission shall lay down its rules of procedure.
3. Seven members shall form the quorum.
4. In case of an equality of votes, the Chairman shall have a casting vote.
5. The Secretary General may attend the meetings of the Commission. He shall neither participate in deliberations nor shall he be entitled to vote. The Chairman of the Commission may, however, invite him to speak.

ARTICLE 43

In discharging their duties, members of the Commission shall enjoy diplomatic privileges and immunities provided for in the General Convention on the Privileges and Immunities of the Organisation of African Unity.

ARTICLE 44

Provision shall be made for the emoluments and allowances of the members of the Commission in the Regular Budget of the Organisation of African Unity.

Chapter II Mandate of the Commission

ARTICLE 45

The functions of the Commission shall be:

1. To promote human and peoples' rights and in particular:
    1. to collect documents, undertake studies and researches on African problems in the field of human and peoples' rights, organise seminars, symposia and conferences, disseminate information, encourage national and local institutions concerned with human and peoples' rights and, should the case arise, give its views or make recommendations to Governments.
    2. to formulae and lay down, principles and rules aimed at solving legal problems relating to human and peoples' rights and fundamental freedoms upon which African Governments may base their legislation.

3. cooperate with other African and international institutions concerned with the promotion and protection of human and peoples' rights.
2. Ensure the protection of human and peoples' rights under conditions laid down by the present Charter.
3. Interpret all the provisions of the present Charter at the request of a State Party, an institution of the OAU or an African Organisation recognised by the OAU.
4. Perform any other tasks which may be entrusted to it by the Assembly of Heads of State and Government.

Chapter III Procedure of the Commission

ARTICLE 46

The Commission may resort to any appropriate method of investigation; it may hear from the Secretary General of the Organisation of African Unity or any other person capable of enlightening it.

COMMUNICATION FROM STATES

ARTICLE 47

If a State Party to the present Charter has good reasons to believe that another State Party to this Charter has violated the provisions of the Charter, it may draw, by written communication, the attention of that State to the matter. This Communication shall also be addressed to the Secretary General of the OAU and to the Chairman of the Commission. Within three months of the receipt of the Communication, the State to which the Communication is addressed shall give the enquiring State, written explanation or statement elucidating the matter. This should include as much as possible, relevant information relating to the laws and rules of procedure applied and applicable and the redress already given or course of action available.

ARTICLE 48

If within three months from the date on which the original communication is received by the State to which it is addressed, the issue is not settled to the satisfaction of the two States involved through bilateral negotiation or by any other peaceful procedure, either State shall have the right to submit the matter to the Commission through the Chairman and shall notify the other States involved.

ARTICLE 49

Notwithstanding the provisions of Article 47, if a State Party to the present Charter considers that another State Party has violated the provisions of the Charter, it may refer the matter directly to the Commission by addressing a communication to the Chairman, to the Secretary General of the Organisation of African unity and the State concerned.

ARTICLE 50

The Commission can only deal with a matter submitted to it after making sure that all local remedies, if they exist, have been exhausted, unless it is obvious to the Commission that the procedure of achieving these remedies would be unduly prolonged.

ARTICLE 51

1. The Commission may ask the State concerned to provide it with all relevant information.
2. When the Commission is considering the matter, States concerned may be represented before it and submit written or oral representation.

ARTICLE 52

After having obtained from the States concerned and from other sources all the information it deems necessary and after having tried all appropriate means to reach an amicable solution based on the respect of human and peoples' rights, the Commission shall prepare, within a reasonable period of time from the notification referred to in Article 48, a report to the States concerned and communicated to the Assembly of Heads of State and Government.

ARTICLE 53

While transmitting its report, the Commission may make to the Assembly of Heads of State and Government such recommendations as it deems useful.

ARTICLE 54

The Commission shall submit to each Ordinary Session of the Assembly of Heads of State and Government a report on its activities.

ARTICLE 55

1. Before each Session, the Secretary of the Commission shall make a list of the Communications other than those of State Parties to the present Charter and transmit them to Members of the Commission, who shall indicate which Communications should be considered by the Commission.
2. A Communication shall be considered by the Commission if a simple majority of its members so decide.

ARTICLE 56

Communications relating to Human and Peoples' rights referred to in Article 55 received by the Commission, shall be considered if they:

1. Indicate their authors even if the latter requests anonymity,
2. Are compatible with the Charter of the Organisation of Afri- can Unity or with the present Charter,
3. Are not written in disparaging or insulting language directed against the State concerned and its institutions or to the Organisation of African Unity,
4. Are not based exclusively on news disseminated through the mass media,

5. Are sent after exhausting local remedies, if any, unless it is obvious that this procedure is unduly prolonged,
6. Are submitted within a reasonable period from the time local remedies are exhausted or from the date the Commission is seized with the matter, and
7. Do not deal with cases which have been settled by those States involved in accordance with the principles of the Charter of the United Nations, or the Charter of the Or- ganisation of African Unity or the provisions of the present Charter.

ARTICLE 57

Prior to any substantive consideration, all communications shall be brought to the knowledge of the State concerned by the Chairman of the Commission.

ARTICLE 58

1. When it appears after deliberations of the Commission that one or more Communications apparently relate to special cases which reveal the existence of a series of serious or massive violations of human and peoples' rights, the Commission shall draw the attention of the Assembly of Heads of State and Government to these special cases.
2. The Assembly of Heads of State and Government may then request the Commission to undertake an in-depth study of these cases and make a factual report, accompanied by its finding and recommendations.
3. A case of emergency duly noticed by the Commission shall be submitted by the latter to the Chairman of the Assembly of Heads of State and Government who may request an in-depth study.

ARTICLE 59

1. All measures taken within the provisions of the present Chapter shall remain confidential until the Assembly of Heads of State and Government shall otherwise decide.
2. However the report shall be published by the Chairman of the Commission upon the decision of he Assembly of Heads of State and Government.
3. The report on the activities of the Commission shall be published by its Chairman after it has been considered by the Assembly of Heads of State and Government.

Chapter IV: Applicable Principles

ARTICLE 60

The Commission shall draw inspiration from international law on human and peoples' rights, particularly from the provisions of various African instruments on Human and Peoples' Rights, the Charter of the United Nations, the Charter of the Organisation of African Unity, the Universal Declaration of Human Rights, other instruments adopted by the United Nations and by African countries in the field of Human and Peoples' Rights, as well as from the provisions of various instruments adopted within the

Specialised Agencies of the United Nations of which the Parties to the present Charter are members.

ARTICLE 61

The Commission shall also take into consideration, as subsidiary measures to determine the principles of law, other general or special international conventions, laying down rules expressly recognised by Member States of the Organisation of African Unity, African practices consistent with international norms on Human and Peoples' Rights, customs generally accepted as law, general principles of law recognised by African States as well as legal precedents and doctrine.

ARTICLE 62

Each State Party shall undertake to submit every two years, from the date the present Charter comes into force, a report on the legislative or other measures taken, with a view to giving effect to the rights and freedoms recognised and guaranteed by the present Charter.

ARTICLE 63

1. The present Charter shall be open to signature, ratification or adherence of the Member States of the Organisation of African Unity.
2. The instruments of ratification or adherence to the present Charter shall be deposited with the Secretary General of the Organisation of African Unity.
3. The present Charter shall come into force three months after the reception by the Secretary General of the instruments of ratification or adherence of a simple majority of the Member States of the Organisation of African Unity.

Part III General Provisions

ARTICLE 64

1. After the coming into force of the present Charter, members of the Commission shall be elected in accordance with the relevant Articles of the present Charter.
2. The Secretary General of the Organisation of African Unity shall convene the first meeting of the Commission at the Headquarters of the Organisation within three months of the constitution of the Commission. Thereafter, the Commission shall be convened by its Chairman whenever necessary but at least once a year.

ARTICLE 65

For each of the States that will ratify or adhere to the present Charter after its coming into force, the Charter shall take effect three months after the date of the deposit by that State of the instrument of ratification or adherence.

ARTICLE 66

Special protocols or agreements may, if necessary, supplement the provisions of the present Charter.

ARTICLE 67

The Secretary General of the Organisation of African Unity shall inform members of the Organisation of the deposit of each instrument of ratification or adherence.

ARTICLE 68

The present Charter may be amended if a State Party makes a written request to that effect to the Secretary General of the Organisation of African Unity. The Assembly of Heads of State and Government may only consider the draft amendment after all the State Parties have been duly informed of it and the Commission has given its opinion on it at the request of the sponsoring State. The amendment shall be approved by a simple majority of the State Parties. It shall come into force for each State which has accepted it in accordance with its constitutional procedure three months after the Secretary General has received notice of the acceptance.

Adopted by the eighteenth Assembly of Heads of State and Government, June 1981 – Nairobi, Kenya

Reservations and Declarations to the African Charter

Egypt

Having considered the African Charter on Human and Peoples' Rights, the Arab Republic of Egypt signed the said Charter on 16 November 1981 and attached hereto is the following instrument of ratification:

Having accepted all the provisions of the African Charter on Human and Peoples' Rights with the approval of the People's Assembly and with the reservation that article 8 and paragraph 3 of article 8 and paragraph 3 of article 18 be implemented in accordance with the Islamic Law and that, as far as the Arab Republic of Egypt is concerned, the provision of the first paragraph of article 9 should be [confined] to such information as could be obtained within the limits of the Egyptian laws and regulations;

We hereby declare acceptance and ratification of the said Charter.

South Africa

While acceding to the African Charter on Human and Peoples' Rights it is the view of the Republic of South Africa that there should be consultation between States parties to the Charter, inter alia, to:

1. consider possible measures to strengthen the enforcement mechanisms of the Charter;
2. clarify the criteria for the restrictions of rights and freedoms recognised and guaranteed in the Charter; and
3. bring the Charter into line with the United Nations' resolutions regarding the characterisation of Zionism.

Zambia

WHEREAS the African Charter on Human and Peoples' Rights was adopted by the Assembly of Heads of State and Government of the Member States of the Organisation of African Unity held at Nairobi in June 1981:

AND WHEREAS the Government of the Republic of Zambia signed the Charter on 17th January 1983;

AND WHEREAS the Charter provides that the Charter is subject to ratification by the States Parties which are signatories to the Charter;

AND WHEREAS the Republic of Zambia is a State Party to the Charter on whose behalf the Charter has been signed;

NOW THEREFORE the Government of the Republic of Zambia having considered the aforesaid Charter hereby

CONFIRMS AND RATIFIES the same on behalf of the Republic of Zambia and undertakes faithfully to observe the provisions and carry out all the stipulations therein contained subject to the following amendments or reservations:

1. Article 13 paragraph 3 should read:- "Every individual shall have the right of access to any place, services or public property intended for use by the general public."
2. (Explanation: The purpose of this reservation is to exclude any claim for the right to use by all citizens of all public property other than as fairly established.)
3. Article 37 should read:- "Immediately after the first election the Chairman of the Assembly of Heads of State of the Organisation of African Unity shall announce the names of those members referred to in Article 36."
4. (Explanation: This is to avoid calling on the Chairman, who is after all a Head of State, carrying out the rather menial exercise of drawing lots. It being understood that the Secretary-General of the Organisation of African Unity would draw such lots.)
5. There should be an extra article which should read:- "After the establishment of the Commission all members of the OAU not ratifying or adhering to the Charter shall submit reports to the Commission, at appropriate intervals, on the position of their laws and practices in regard to the matters dealt with in the Charter, showing the extent to which effort has been given, or is proposed to be given, to any of the provisions of the Charter by legislation or administrative action and stating the difficulties which prevent or delay ratification or adherence to the Charter."

(Explanation:- In the interest of early universal ratification of the Charter by the Organisation of African Unity Countries and also since all Heads of State of the OAU will together tackle the problems of administering or enforcing the Charter including, where necessary, criticising fellow Heads of State who are proved to have violated the Charter, all members of the OAU should carry some responsibility, under the Charter, for the state of human and peoples' rights in their respective countries.)

The African Charter on Human and Peoples' Rights (also known as the Banjul Charter) is an international human rights instrument that is intended to promote and protect human rights and basic freedoms in the African continent.

Oversight and interpretation of the Charter is the task of the African Commission on Human and Peoples' Rights, which was set up in 1987 and is now headquartered in Banjul, Gambia. A protocol to the Charter was subsequently adopted in 1998 whereby an African Court on Human and Peoples' Rights was to be created. The protocol came into effect on 25 January 2005.

ANNEX II

Protocol to the African Charter on Human and Peoples' Rights on the Rights of Women in Africa

The States Parties to this Protocol,[1]

CONSIDERING that Article 66 of the African Charter on Human and Peoples' Rights provides for special protocols or agreements, if necessary, to supplement the provisions of the African Charter, and that the Assembly of Heads of State and Government of the Organization of African Unity meeting in its Thirty-first Ordinary Session in Addis Ababa, Ethiopia, in June 1995, endorsed by resolution AHG/Res.240 (XXXI) the recommendation of the African Commission on Human and Peoples' Rights to elaborate a Protocol on the Rights of Women in Africa;

CONSIDERING that Article 2 of the African Charter on Human and Peoples' Rights enshrines the principle of non-discrimination on the grounds of race, ethnic group, colour, sex, language, religion, political or any other opinion, national and social origin, fortune, birth or other status;

FURTHER CONSIDERING that Article 18 of the African Charter on Human and Peoples' Rights calls on all States Parties to eliminate every discrimination against women and to ensure the protection of the rights of women as stipulated in international declarations and conventions;

NOTING that Articles 60 and 61 of the African Charter on Human and Peoples' Rights recognise regional and international human rights instruments and African practices consistent with international norms on human and peoples' rights as being important reference points for the application and interpretation of the African Charter;

RECALLING that women's rights have been recognised and guaranteed in all international human rights instruments, notably the Universal Declaration of Human Rights, the International Covenant on Civil and Political Rights, the International Covenant on Economic, Social and Cultural Rights, the Convention on the Elimination of All Forms of Discrimination Against Women and its Optional Protocol, the African Charter on the Rights and Welfare of the Child, and all other international and regional conventions and covenants relating to the rights of women as being inalienable, interdependent and indivisible human rights;

1 African Commission on Human and People's Rights, Accessed on 28 July 2021. https://www.achpr.org/legalinstruments/detail?id=37.

 | DOI:10.1163/9789004520646_012

NOTING that women's rights and women's essential role in development, have been reaffirmed in the United Nations Plans of Action on the Environment and Development in 1992, on Human Rights in 1993, on Population and Development in 1994 and on Social Development in 1995;

RECALLING ALSO United Nations Security Council's Resolution1325 (2000) on the role of Women in promoting peace and security;

REAFFIRMING the principle of promoting gender equality as enshrined in the Constitutive Act of the African Union as well as the New Partnership for Africa's Development, relevant Declarations, Resolutions and Decisions, which underline the commitment of the African States to ensure the full participation of African women as equal partners in Africa's development;

FURTHER NOTING that the African Platform for Action and the Dakar Declaration of 1994 and the Beijing Platform for Action of 1995 call on all Member States of the United Nations, which have made a solemn commitment to implement them, to take concrete steps to give greater attention to the human rights of women in order to eliminate all forms of discrimination and of gender-based violence against women;

RECOGNISING the crucial role of women in the preservation of African values based on the principles of equality, peace, freedom, dignity, justice, solidarity and democracy;

BEARING IN MIND related Resolutions, Declarations, Recommendations, Decisions, Conventions and other Regional and Sub-Regional Instruments aimed at eliminating all forms of discrimination and at promoting equality between women and men;

CONCERNED that despite the ratification of the African Charter on Human and Peoples' Rights and other international human rights instruments by the majority of States Parties, and their solemn commitment to eliminate all forms of discrimination and harmful practices against women, women in Africa still continue to be victims of discrimination and harmful practices;

FIRMLY CONVINCED that any practice that hinders or endangers the normal growth and affects the physical and psychological development of women and girls should be condemned and eliminated;

DETERMINED to ensure that the rights of women are promoted, realised and protected in order to enable them to enjoy fully all their human rights;

HAVE AGREED AS FOLLOWS:

Article 1 Definitions

For the purpose of the present Protocol:

a) "African Charter" means the African Charter on Human and Peoples' Rights;

b) "African Commission" means the African Commission on Human and Peoples' Rights;
   - "Assembly" means the Assembly of Heads of State and Government of the African Union;
   - "AU" means the African Union;
   - "Constitutive Act" means the Constitutive Act of the African Union;
   - "Discrimination against women" means any distinction, exclusion or restriction or any differential treatment based on sex and whose objectives or effects compromise or destroy the recognition, enjoyment or the exercise by women, regardless of their marital status, of human rights and fundamental freedoms in all spheres of life;
   - "Harmful Practices" means all behaviour, attitudes and/or practices which negatively affect the fundamental rights of women and girls, such as their right to life, health, dignity, education and physical integrity;
   - "NEPAD" means the New Partnership for Africa's Development established by the Assembly;
   - "States Parties" means the States Parties to this Protocol;
   - "Violence against women" means all acts perpetrated against women which cause or could cause them physical, sexual, psychological, and economic harm, including the threat to take such acts; or to undertake the imposition of arbitrary restrictions on or deprivation of fundamental freedoms in private or public life in peace time and during situations of armed conflicts or of war;
   - "Women" means persons of female gender, including girls;

Article 2 Elimination of Discrimination against Women

1. States Parties shall combat all forms of discrimination against women through appropriate legislative, institutional and other measures. In this regard they shall:
   a) include in their national constitutions and other legislative instruments, if not already done, the principle of equality between women and men and ensure its effective application;
   b) enact and effectively implement appropriate legislative or regulatory measures, including those prohibiting and curbing all forms of discrimination particularly those harmful practices which endanger the health and general well-being of women;
   c) integrate a gender perspective in their policy decisions, legislation, development plans, programmes and activities and in all other spheres of life;
   d) take corrective and positive action in those areas where discrimination against women in law and in fact continues to exist;

   e) support the local, national, regional and continental initiatives directed at eradicating all forms of discrimination against women.
2. States Parties shall commit themselves to modify the social and cultural patterns of conduct of women and men through public education, information, education and communication strategies, with a view to achieving the elimination of harmful cultural and traditional practices and all other practices which are based on the idea of the inferiority or the superiority of either of the sexes, or on stereotyped roles for women and men.

Article 3 Right to Dignity

- Every woman shall have the right to dignity inherent in a human being and to the recognition and protection of her human and legal rights;
- Every woman shall have the right to respect as a person and to the free development of her personality;
- States Parties shall adopt and implement appropriate measures to prohibit any exploitation or degradation of women;
- States Parties shall adopt and implement appropriatemeasures to ensure the protection of every woman's right to respect for her dignity and protection of women from all forms of violence, particularly sexual and verbal violence.

Article 4 The Rights to Life, Integrity and Security of the Person

1. Every woman shall be entitled to respect for her life and the integrity and security of her person. All forms of exploitation, cruel, inhuman or degrading punishment and treatment shall be prohibited.
2. States Parties shall take appropriate and effective measures to:
   a) enact and enforce laws to prohibit all forms of violence against women including unwanted or forced sex whether the violence takes place in private or public;
   b) adopt such other legislative, administrative, social and economic measures as may be necessary to ensure the prevention, punishment and eradication of all forms of violence against women;
   c) identify the causes and consequences of violence against women and take appropriate measures to prevent and eliminate such violence;
   d) actively promote peace education through curricula and social communication in order to eradicate elements in traditional and cultural beliefs, practices and

stereotypes which legitimise and exacerbate the persistence and tolerance of violence against women;

e) punish the perpetrators of violence against women and implement programmes for the rehabilitation of women victims;

f) establish mechanisms and accessible services for effective information, rehabilitation and reparation for victims of violence against women;

g) prevent and condemn trafficking in women, prosecute the perpetrators of such trafficking and protect those women most at risk;
   - prohibit all medical or scientific experiments on women without their informed consent;
   - provide adequate budgetary and other resources for the implementation and monitoring of actions aimed at preventing and eradicating violence against women;
   - ensure that, in those countries where the death penalty still exists, not to carry out death sentences on pregnant or nursing women.
   - e nsure that women and men enjoy equal rights in terms of access to refugee status, determination procedures and that women refugees are accorded the full protection and benefits guaranteed under international refugee law, including their own identity and other documents;

Article 5 Elimination of Harmful Practices

States Parties shall prohibit and condemn all forms of harmful practices which negatively affect the human rights of women and which are contrary to recognised international standards. States Parties shall take all necessary legislative and other measures to eliminate such practices, including:

- creation of public awareness in all sectors of society regarding harmful practices through information, formal and informal education and outreach programmes;
- prohibition, through legislative measures backed by sanctions, of all forms of female genital mutilation, scarification, medicalisation and para-medicalisation of female genital mutilation and all other practices in order to eradicate them;
- provision of necessary support to victims of harmful practices through basic services such as health services, legal and judicialsupport, emotional and psychological counselling as well as vocational training to make them self-supporting;
- protection of women who are at risk of being subjected to harmful practices or all other forms of violence, abuse and intolerance.

Article 6 Marriage

States Parties shall ensure that women and men enjoy equal rights and are regarded as equal partners in marriage. They shall enact appropriate national legislative measures to guarantee that:

- no marriage shall take place without the free and full consent of both parties;
- the minimum age of marriage for women shall be 18 years;
- monogamy is encouraged as the preferred form of marriage and that the rights of women in marriage and family, including in polygamous marital relationships are promoted and protected;
- every marriage shall be recorded in writing and registered in accordance with national laws, in order to be legally recognised;
- the husband and wife shall, by mutual agreement, choose their matrimonial regime and place of residence;
- a married woman shall have the right to retain her maiden name, to use it as she pleases, jointly or separately with her husband's surname;
- a woman shall have the right to retain her nationality or to acquire the nationality of her husband;
- a woman and a man shall have equal rights, with respect to the nationality of their children except where this is contrary to a provision in national legislation or is contrary to national security interests;
- a woman and a man shall jointly contribute to safeguarding the interests of the family, protecting and educating their children;
- during her marriage, a woman shall have the right to acquire her own property and to administer and manage it freely.

Article 7 Separation, Divorce and Annulment of Marriage

States Parties shall enact appropriate legislation to ensure that women and men enjoy the same rights in case of separation, divorce or annulment of marriage. In this regard, they shall ensure that:

- separation, divorce or annulment of a marriage shall be effected by judicial order;
- women and men shall have the same rights to seek separation, divorce or annulment of a marriage;
- in case of separation, divorce or annulment of marriage, women and men shall have reciprocalrights and responsibilities towards their children. In any case, the interests of the children shall be given paramount importance;
- in case of separation, divorce or annulment of marriage, women and menshall have the right to an equitable sharing of the joint property deriving from the marriage.

Article 8 Access to Justice and Equal Protection before the Law

Women and menare equal before the law and shall have the right to equal protection andbenefit of the law. States Parties shall take all appropriate measures to ensure:
- effective access by women to judicial and legal services, including legal aid;
- support to local, national, regional and continental initiatives directed at providing women access to legal services, including legal aid;
- the establishment of adequate educational and other appropriate structures with particular attention to women and to sensitise everyone to the rights of women;
- that law enforcement organs at all levels are equipped to effectively interpret and enforce gender equality rights;
- that women are represented equally in the judiciary and law enforcement organs;
- reform of existing discriminatory laws and practices in order to promote and protect the rights of women.

Article 9 Right to Participation in the Political and Decision-Making Process

1. States Parties shall take specific positive action to promote participative governance and the equal participation of women in the political life of their countries through affirmative action, enabling national legislation and other measures to ensure that:
   a) women participate without any discrimination in all elections;
   b) women are represented equally at all levels with men in all electoral processes;
   c) women are equal partners with men at all levels of development and implementation of State policies and development programmes .
2. States Parties shall ensure increased and effective representation and participation of women at all levels of decision-making.

Article 10 Right to Peace

1. Women have the right to a peaceful existence and the right to participate in the promotion and maintenance of peace.
2. States Parties shall take all appropriate measures to ensure the increased participation of women:
   a) in programmes of education for peace and a culture of peace;
   b) in the structures and processes for conflict prevention, management and resolution at local, national, regional, continental and international levels;

- in the local, national, regional, continental and international decision making structures to ensure physical, psychological, social and legal protection of asylum seekers, refugees, returnees and displaced persons, in particular women;
- in all levels of the structures established for the management of camps and settlements for asylum seekers, refugees, returnees and displaced persons, in particular, women;
- in all aspects of planning, formulation and implementation of post conflict reconstruction and rehabilitation.

3. States Parties shall take the necessary measures to reduce military expenditure significantly in favour of spending on social development in general, and the promotion of women in particular.

Article 11 Protection of Women in Armed Conflicts

- States Parties undertake to respect and ensure respect for the rules of international humanitarian law applicable in armed conflict situations which affect the population, particularly women.
- States Parties shall, in accordance with the obligations incumbent upon them under the international humanitarian law, protect civilians including women, irrespective of the population to which theybelong, in the event of armedconflict.
- States Parties undertake to protect asylum seeking women, refugees, returnees and internally displaced persons, against all forms of violence, rape and other forms of sexual exploitation, and to ensure that such acts are considered war crimes, genocide and/or crimes against humanity and that their perpetrators are brought to justice before a competent criminal jurisdiction.
- States Parties shall take all necessary measures to ensure that no child, especially girls under 18 years of age, take a direct part in hostilities and thatno child is recruited as a soldier.

Article 12 Right to Education and Training

1. States Parties shall take all appropriate measures to:
   a) eliminate all forms of discrimination against women and guarantee equal opportunity and access in the sphere of education and training;
   b) eliminate all stereotypes in textbooks, syllabuses and the media, that perpetuate such discrimination;

- protect women, especially the girl-child from all forms of abuse, including sexual harassment in schools and other educational institutions and provide for sanctions against the perpetrators of such practices;
- provide access to counselling and rehabilitation services to women who suffer abuses and sexual harassment;
- integrate gender sensitisation and human rights education at all levels of education curricula including teacher training.

2. States Parties shall take specific positive action to:
   a) promote literacy among women;
   b) promote education and training for women at all levels and in all disciplines, particularly in the fields of science and technology;
   c) promote the enrolment and retention of girls in schools and other training institutions and the organisation of programmes for women who leave school prematurely.

Article 13 Economic and Social Welfare Rights

States Parties shall adopt and enforce legislative and other measures to guarantee womenequal opportunities in work and career advancement and other economic opportunities. In this respect, they shall:

a) promote equality of access to employment;
b) promote the right to equal remuneration for jobs of equal value for women and men;
c) ensure transparency in recruitment, promotion and dismissal of women and combat and punish sexual harassment in the workplace;
d) guarantee women the freedom to choose their occupation, and protect them from exploitation by their employers violating and exploiting their fundamental rights as recognised and guaranteed by conventions, laws and regulations in force;
e) create conditions to promote and support the occupations and economic activities of women, in particular, within the informal sector;
f) establish a system of protection and social insurance for women working in the informal sector and sensitise them to adhere to it;
g) introduce a minimum age for work and prohibit the employment of children below that age, andprohibit, combat and punish all forms of exploitation of children, especially the girl-child;
h) take the necessary measures to recognise the economic value of the work of women in the home;

i) guarantee adequate and paid pre and post-natal maternity leave in both the private and public sectors;
j) ensure the equal application of taxation laws to women and men;
k) recognise and enforce the right of salaried women to the same allowances and entitlements as those granted to salaried men for their spouses and children;
l) recognise that both parents bear the primary responsibility for the upbringing and development of children and that this is a social function for which the State and the private sector have secondary responsibility;
m) take effective legislative and administrative measures to prevent the exploitation and abuse of women in advertising and pornography.

Article 14 Health and Reproductive Rights

1. States Parties shall ensure that the right to health of women, including sexual and reproductive health is respected and promoted. This includes:
   a) the right to control their fertility;
   b) the right to decide whether to have children, the number of children and the spacing of children;
   c) the right to choose any method of contraception;
   d) the right toselfprotectionand to be protected against sexually transmitted infections, including HIV/AIDS;
   e) the right to be informed on one's health status and on the health status of one's partner, particularly if affected with sexually transmitted infections, including HIV/AIDS, in accordance with internationally recognised standards and best practices;
   f) the right to have family planning education.
2. States Parties shall take all appropriate measures to:
   a) provide adequate, affordable and accessible health services, including information, education and communication programmes to women especially those in rural areas;
   b) establish and strengthen existing pre-natal, delivery and post-natal health and nutritional services for women during pregnancy andwhile they are breast-feeding;
   c) protect the reproductive rights of women by authorising medical abortion in cases of sexual assault, rape, incest, and where the continued pregnancy endangers the mental and physical health of the mother or the life of themother or the foetus.

Article 15 Right to Food Security

a) provide women with access to clean drinking water, sources of domestic fuel, land, and the means of producing nutritious food;
b) establish adequate systems of supply and storage to ensure food security.

Article 16 Right to Adequate Housing

Women shall have the right to equal access to housing and to acceptable living conditions in a healthy environment. To ensure this right, States Parties shall grant to women, whatever their marital status, access to adequate housing.

Article 17 Right to Positive Cultural Context

1. Women shall have the right to live in a positive cultural context and to participate at all levels in the determination of cultural policies.
2. States Parties shall take all appropriate measures to enhance the participation of women in the formulation of cultural policies at all levels.

Article 18 Right to a Healthy and Sustainable Environment

1. Women shall have the right to live in a healthy and sustainable environment.
2. States Parties shall take all appropriate measures to:
   a) ensure greater participation of women in the planning, management and preservation of the environment and the sustainable use of natural resources at all levels;
   b) promote research and investment in new and renewable energy sources and appropriate technologies, including information technologies and facilitate women's access to, and participation in their control;
   c) protect and enable the development of women's indigenous knowledge systems;
   d) regulate the management, processing, storage and disposal of domestic waste;
   e) ensure that proper standards are followed for the storage, transportation and disposal of toxic waste.

Article 19 Right to Sustainable Development

Women shall have the right to fully enjoy their right to sustainable development. In this connection, the States Parties shall take all appropriate measures to:

a) introduce the gender perspective in the national development planning procedures;
b) ensure participation of women at all levels in the conceptualisation, decision-making, implementation and evaluation of development policies and programmes;
c) promote women's access to and control over productive resources such as land and guarantee their right to property;
d) promote women's access to credit, training, skills development and extension services at rural and urban levels in order to provide women with a higher quality of life and reduce the level of poverty among women;
e) take into account indicators of human development specifically relating to women in the elaboration of development policies and programmes; and
f) ensure that the negative effects of globalisation and any adverse effects of the implementation of trade and economic policies and programmes are reduced to the minimum for women.

Article 20 Widows' Rights

States Parties shall take appropriate legal measures to ensure that widows enjoy all human rights through the implementation of the following provisions:

a) that widows are not subjected to inhuman, humiliating or degrading treatment;
b) a widow shall automatically become the guardian and custodian of her children, after the death of her husband, unless this is contrary to the interests and the welfare of the children;
c) a widow shall have the right to remarry, and in that event, to marry the person of her choice.

Article 21 Right to Inheritance

1. A widow shall have the right to an equitable share in the inheritance of the property of her husband. A widow shall have the right to continue to live in the matrimonial house. In case of remarriage, she shall retain this right if the house belongs to her or she has inherited it.
2. Women and men shall have the right to inherit, in equitable shares, their parents' properties.

Article 22 Special Protection of Elderly Women

The States Parties undertake to:

a) provide protection to elderly women and take specific measures commensurate with their physical, economic and social needs as well as their access to employment and professional training;
b) ensure the right of elderly women to freedom from violence, including sexual abuse, discrimination based on age and the right to be treated with dignity.

Article 23 Special Protection of Women with Disabilities

The States Parties undertake to:

a) ensure the protection of women with disabilities and take specific measures commensurate with their physical, economic and social needs to facilitate their access to employment, professional and vocational training as well as their participation in decision-making;
b) ensure the right of women with disabilities to freedom from violence, including sexual abuse, discrimination based on disability and the right to be treated with dignity.

Article 24 Special Protection of Women in Distress

The States Parties undertake to:

a) ensure the protection of poor women and women heads of families including women from marginalized population groups and provide the an environment suitable to their condition and their special physical, economic and social needs;
b) ensure the right of pregnant or nursing women or women in detention by providing them with an environment which is suitable to their condition and the right to be treated with dignity.

Article 25 Remedies

States Parties shall undertake to:

a) provide for appropriate remedies to any woman whose rights or freedoms, as herein recognised, have been violated;
b) ensure that such remedies are determined by competent judicial, administrative or legislative authorities, or by any other competent authority provided for by law.

Article 26 Implementation and Monitoring

1. States Parties shall ensure the implementation of this Protocol at national level, and in their periodic reports submitted in accordance with Article 62 of the African Charter, indicate the legislative and other measures undertaken for the full realisation of the rights herein recognised.
2. States Parties undertake to adopt all necessary measures and in particular shall provide budgetary and other resources for the full and effective implementation of the rights herein recognised.

Article 27 Interpretation

The African Court on Human and Peoples' Rights shall be seized with matters of interpretation arising from the application or implementation of this Protocol.

Article 28 Signature, Ratification and Accession

1. This Protocol shall be open for signature, ratification and accession by the States Parties, in accordance with their respective constitutional procedures.
2. The instruments of ratification or accession shall be deposited with the Chairperson of the Commission of the AU.

Article 29 Entry into Force

1. This Protocol shall enter into force thirty (30) days after the deposit of the fifteenth (15) instrument

ANNEX III

African Charter on the Rights and Welfare of the Child

Preamble[1]

The African Member States of the Organization of African Unity, Parties to the present Charter entitled African Charter on the Rights and Welfare of the Child,

CONSIDERING that the Charter of the Organization of African Unity recognizes the paramountcy of Human Rights and the African Charter on Human and People's Rights proclaimed and agreed that everyone is entitled to all the rights and freedoms recognized and guaranteed therein, without distinction of any kind such as race, ethnic group, colour, sex, language, religion, political or any other opinion, national and social origin, fortune, birth or other status,

RECALLING the Declaration on the Rights and Welfare of the African Child (AHG/ST.4 Rev.l) adopted by the Assembly of Heads of State and Government of the Organization of African Unity, at its Sixteenth Ordinary Session in Monrovia, Liberia, from 17 to 20 July 1979, recognized the need to take appropriate measures to promote and protect the rights and welfare of the African Child,

NOTING WITH CONCERN that the situation of most African children, remains critical due to the unique factors of their socio-economic, cultural, traditional and developmental circumstances, natural disasters, armed conflicts, exploitation and hunger, and on account of the child's physical and mental immaturity he/she needs special safeguards and care,

RECOGNIZING that the child occupies a unique and privileged position in the African society and that for the full and harmonious development of his personality, the child should grow up in a family environment in an atmosphere of happiness, love and understanding,

RECOGNIZING that the child, due to the needs of his physical and mental development requires particular care with regard to health, physical, mental, moral and social development and requires legal protection in conditions of freedom, dignity and security,

1 African Commission on Human and People's Rights, Accessed on 28 July 2021. https://www.achpr.org/legalinstruments/detail?id=46.

 | DOI:10.1163/9789004520646_013

TAKING INTO CONSIDERATION the virtues of their cultural heritage, historical background and the values of the African civilization which should inspire and characterize their reflection on the concept of the rights and welfare of the child,

CONSIDERING that the promotion and protection of the rights and welfare of the child also implies the performance of duties on the part of everyone,

REAFFIRMING ADHERENCE to the principles of the rights and welfare of the child contained in the declaration, conventions and other instruments of the Organization of African Unity and in the United Nations and in particular the United Nations Convention on the Rights of the Child; and the OAU Heads of State and Government's Declaration on the Rights and Welfare of the African Child;

HAVE AGREED AS FOLLOWS:

Part 1 Rights and Duties

Chapter One Rights and Welfare Of the Child

Article 1 Obligation of State Parties

1. Member States of the Organization of African Unity, Parties to the present Charter shall recognize the rights, freedoms and duties enshrined in this Charter and shall undertake the necessary steps, in accordance with their Constitutional processes and with the provisions of the present Charter, to adopt such legislative or other measures as may be necessary to give effect to the provisions of this Charter.
2. Nothing in this Charter shall affect any provisions that are more conducive to the realization of the rights and welfare of the child contained in the law of a State Party or in any other international Convention or agreement in force in that State.
3. Any custom, tradition, cultural or religious practice that is inconsistent with the rights, duties and obligations contained in the present Charter shall, to the extent of such inconsistency, be discouraged.

Article 2 Definition of a Child

For the purposes of this Charter, a child means every human being below the age of 18 years.

Article 3 Non-discrimination

Every child shall be entitled to the enjoyment of the rights and freedoms recognized and guaranteed in this Charter irrespective of the child's or his/her parents' or legal guardians' race, ethnic group, colour, sex, language, religion, political or other opinion, national and social origin, fortune, birth or other status.

Article 4 Best Interests of the Child

1. In all actions concerning the child undertaken by any person or authority the best interests of the child shall be the primary consideration.
2. In all judicial or administrative proceedings affecting a child who is capable of communicating his/her own views, an opportunity shall be provided for the views of the child to be heard either directly or through an impartial representative as a party to the proceedings, and those views shall be taken into consideration by the relevant authority in accordance with the provisions of appropriate law.

Article 5 Survival and Development

1. Every child has an inherent right to life. This right shall be protected by law.
2. State Parties to the present Charter shall ensure, to the maximum extent possible, the survival, protection and development of the child.
3. Death sentence shall not be pronounced for crimes committed by children.

Article 6 Name and Nationality

1. Every child shall have the right from his birth to a name.
2. Every child shall be registered immediately after birth.
3. Every child has the right to acquire a nationality.

State Parties to the present Charter shall undertake to ensure that their Constitutional legislation recognize the principles according to which a child shall acquire the nationality of the State in the territory of which he has been born if, at the time of the child's birth he is not granted nationality by any other State in accordance with its laws.

Article 7 Freedom of Expression

Every child who is capable of communicating his or her own views shall be assured the rights to express his opinions freely in all matters and to disseminate his opinions subject to such restrictions as are prescribed by laws.

Article 8 Freedom of Association

Every child shall have the right to free association and freedom of peaceful assembly in conformity with the law.

Article 9 Freedom of Thought, Conscience and Religion

1. Every child shall have the right to freedom of thought conscience and religion.
2. Parents, and where applicable, legal guardians shall have the duty to provide guidance and direction in the exercise of these rights having regard to the evolving capacities, and best interests of the child.

3. State Parties shall respect the duty of parents and where applicable, legal guardians, to provide guidance and direction in the enjoyment of these rights subject to the national laws and policies.

Article 10 Protection of Privacy

No child shall be subject to arbitrary or unlawful interference with his privacy, family home or correspondence, or to the attacks upon his honour or reputation, provided that parents or legal guardians shall have the right to exercise reasonable supervision over the conduct of their children. The child has the right to the protection of the law against such interference or attacks.

Article 11 Education

1. Every child shall have the right to education.
2. The education of the child shall be directed to:
   1. the promotion and development of the child's personality, talents and mental and physical abilities to their fullest potential;
   2. fostering respect for human rights and fundamental freedoms with particular reference to those set out in the provisions of various African instruments on human and peoples' rights and international human rights declarations and conventions;
   3. the preservation and strengthening of positive African morals, traditional values and cultures;
   4. the preparation of the child for responsible life in a free society, in the spirit of understanding, tolerance, dialogue, mutual respect and friendship among all peoples, ethnic, tribal and religious groups;
   5. the preservation of national independence and territorial integrity;
   6. the promotion and achievement of African Unity and Solidarity;
   7. the development of respect for the environment and natural resources;
   8. the promotion of the child's understanding of primary health care.
3. State Parties to the present Charter shall take all appropriate measures with a view to achieving the full realization of this right and shall in particular:
   1. provide free and compulsory basic education
   2. encourage the development of secondary education in its different forms and progressively make it free and accessible to all;
   3. make higher education accessible to all on the basis of capacity and ability by every appropriate means;
   4. take measures to encourage regular attendance at schools and the reduction of drop-out rates;
   5. take special measures in respect of female, gifted and disadvantaged children, to ensure equal access to education for all sections of the community.

4. State Parties to the present Charter shall respect the rights and duties of parents, and where applicable, of legal guardians, to choose for their children schools other than those established by public authorities, which conform to such minimum standards as approved by the State, to ensure the religious and moral education of the child in a manner consistent with the evolving capacities of the child.
5. State Parties to the present Charter shall take all appropriate measures to ensure that a child who is subjected to schools or parental discipline shall be treated with humanity and with respect for the inherent dignity of the child and in conformity with the present Charter.
6. State Parties to the present Charter shall take all appropriate measures to ensure that children who become pregnant before completing their education shall have an opportunity to continue their education on the basis of their individual ability.
7. No part of this Article shall be construed as to interfere with the liberty of individuals and bodies to establish and direct educational institutions subject to the observance of the principles set out in Paragraph 1 of this Article and the requirement that the education given in such institutions shall conform to such minimum standards as may be laid down by the States .

Article 12 Leisure, Recreation and Cultural Activities

1. State Parties shall recognize the right of the child to rest and leisure, to engage in play and recreational activities appropriate to the age of the child and to participate freely in cultural life and the arts.
2. State Parties shall respect and promote the right of the child to fully participate in cultural and artistic life and shall encourage the provision of appropriate and equal opportunities for cultural, artistic, recreational and leisure activity.

Article 13 Handicapped Children

1. Every child who is mentally or physically disabled shall have the right to special measures of protection in keeping with his physical and moral needs and under conditions which ensure his dignity, promote his self-reliance and active participation in the community.
2. State Parties to the present Charter shall ensure, subject to available resources, to a disabled child and to those responsible for his care, assistance for which application is made and which is appropriate to the child's condition and in particular shall ensure that the disabled child has effective access to training, preparation for employment and recreation opportunities in a manner conducive to the child achieving the fullest possible social integration, individual development and his/her cultural and moral development.
3. The State Parties to the present Charter shall use their available resources with a view to achieving progressively the full convenience of the mentally and physically

disabled person to movement and access to public highway buildings and other places to which the disabled may legitimately want to have access to.

Article 14 Health and Health Services

1. Every child shall have the right to enjoy the best attainable state of physical, mental and spiritual health.
2. State Parties to the present Charter shall undertake to pursue the full implementation of this right and in particular shall take measures:
    1. to reduce infant and child mortality rate;
    2. to ensure the provision of necessary medical assistance and health care to all children with emphasis on the development of primary health care;
    3. to ensure the provision of adequate nutrition and safe drinking water;
    4. to combat disease and malnutrition within the framework of primary health care through the application of appropriate technology;
    5. to ensure appropriate health care for expectant and nursing mothers;
    6. to develop preventive health care and family life education and provision of service;
    7. to integrate basic health service programmes in national development plans;
    8. to ensure that all sectors of the society, in particular, parents, children, community leaders and community workers are informed and supported in the use of basic knowledge of child health and nutrition, the advantages of breastfeeding, hygiene and environmental sanitation and the prevention of domestic and other accidents;
    9. to ensure the meaningful participation of non-governmental organizations, local communities and the beneficiary population in the planning and management of basic service programmes for children;
    10. to support through technical and financial means, the mobilization of local community resources in the development of primary health care for children.

Article 15 Child Labour

1. Every child shall be protected from all forms of economic exploitation and from performing any work that is likely to be hazardous or to interfere with the child's physical, mental, spiritual, moral, or social development.
2. State Parties to the present Charter take all appropriate legislative and administrative measures to ensure the full implementation of this Article which covers both the formal and informal sectors of employment and having regard to the relevant provisions of the International Labour Organization's instruments relating to children.
3. State Parties shall in particular:
    1. provide through legislation, minimum wages for admission to every employment;

2. provide for appropriate regulation of hours and conditions of employment;
3. provide for appropriate penalties or other sanctions to ensure the effective enforcement of this Article;
4. promote the dissemination of information on the hazards of child labour to all sectors of the community.

Article 16 Protection against Child Abuse and Torture

1. State Parties to the present Charter shall take specific legislative, administrative, social and educational measures to protect the child from all forms of torture, inhuman or degrading treatment and especially physical or mental injury or abuse, neglect or maltreatment including sexual abuse, while in the care of the child.
2. Protective measures under this Article shall include effective procedures for the establishment of special monitoring units to provide necessary support for the child and for those who have the care of the child, as well as other forms of prevention and for identification, reporting referral investigation, treatment, and follow-up of instances of child abuse and neglect.

Article 17 Administration of Juvenile Justice

1. Every child accused or found guilty of having infringed penal law shall have the right to special treatment in a manner consistent with the child's sense of dignity and worth and which reinforces the child's respect for human rights and fundamental freedoms of others.
2. State Parties to the present Charter shall in particular:
    1. ensure that no child who is detained or imprisoned or otherwise deprived of his/her liberty is subjected to torture, inhuman or degrading treatment or punishment;
    2. ensure that children are separated from adults in their place of detention or imprisonment;
    3. ensure that every child accused of infringing the penal law:
        1. shall be presumed innocent until duly recognized guilty;
        2. shall be informed promptly in a language that he understands and in detail of the charge against him, and shall be entitled to the assistance of an interpreter if he or she cannot understand the language used;
        3. shall be afforded legal and other appropriate assistance in the preparation and presentation of his defence;
        4. shall have the matter determined as speedily as possible by an impartial tribunal and if found guilty, be entitled to an appeal by a higher tribunal;
    4. prohibit the press and the public from the trial.

3. The essential aim of treatment of every child during the trial and also if found guilty of infringing the penal law shall be his or her reformation, reintegration into his or her family and social rehabilitation.
4. There shall be a minimum age below which children shall be presumed not to have the capacity to infringe the penal law.

Article 18 Protection of the Family

1. The family shall be the natural unit and basis of society. It shall enjoy the protection and support of the State for its establishment and development.
2. State Parties to the present Charter shall take appropriate steps to ensure equality of rights and responsibilities of spouses with regard to children during marriage and in the event of its dissolution. In case of the dissolution, provision shall be made for the necessary protection of the child.
3. No child shall be deprived of maintenance by reference to the parents' marital status.

Article 19 Parental Care and Protection

1. Every child shall be entitled to the enjoyment of parental care and protection and shall, whenever possible, have the right to reside with his or her parents. No child shall be separated from his/her parents against his/her will, except when a judicial authority determines in accordance with the appropriate law, that such separation is in the best interest of the child.
2. Every child who is separated from one or both parents shall have the right to maintain personal relations and direct contact with both parents on a regular basis.
3. Where separation results from the action of a State Party, the State Party shall provide the child, or if appropriate, another member of the family with essential information concerning the whereabouts of the absent member or members of the family. State Parties shall also ensure that the submission of such a request shall not entail any adverse consequences for the person or persons in whose respect it is made.
4. Where a child is apprehended by a State Party, his parents or guardians shall, as soon as possible, be notified of such apprehension by that State Party.

Article 20 Parental Reponsibilities

1. Parents or other persons responsible for the child shall have the primary responsibility for the upbringing and development the child and shall have the duty:
    1. to ensure that the best interests of the child are their basic concern at all times;
    2. to secure, within their abilities and financial capacities, conditions of living necessary to the child's development; and

   3. to ensure that domestic discipline is administered with humanity and in a manner consistent with the inherent dignity of the child.
2. State Parties to the present Charter shall in accordance with their means and national conditions take all appropriate measures:
   1. to assist parents and other persons responsible for the child and in case of need, provide material assistance and support programmes particularly with regard to nutrition, health, education, clothing and housing;
   2. to assist parents and others responsible for the child in the performance of child-rearing and ensure the development of institutions responsible for providing care of children; and
   3. to ensure that the children of working parents are provided with care services and facilities.

Article 21 Protection against Harmful Social and Cultural Practices

1. State Parties to the present Charter shall take all appropriate measures to eliminate harmful social and cultural practices affecting the welfare, dignity, normal growth and development of the child and in particular:
   1. those customs and practices prejudicial to the health or life of the child; and
   2. those customs and practices discriminatory to the child on the grounds of sex or other status.
2. Child marriage and the betrothal of girls and boys shall be prohibited and effective action, including legislation, shall be taken to specify the minimum age of marriage to be 18 years and make registration of all marriages in an official registry compulsory.

Article 22 Armed Conflicts

1. State Parties to this Charter shall undertake to respect and ensure respect for rules of international humanitarian law applicable in armed conflicts which affect the child.
2. State Parties to the present Charter shall take all necessary measures to ensure that no child shall take a direct part in hostilities and refrain in particular, from recruiting any child.
3. State Parties to the present Charter shall, in accordance with their obligations under international humanitarian law, protect the civilian population in armed conflicts and shall take all feasible measures to ensure the protection and care of children who are affected by armed conflicts. Such rules shall also apply to children in situations of internal armed conflicts, tension and strife.

Article 23 Refugee Children

1. State Parties to the present Charter shall take all appropriate measures to ensure that a child who is seeking refugee status or who is considered a refugee in accordance with applicable international or domestic law shall, whether unaccompanied or accompanied by parents, legal guardians or close relatives, receive appropriate protection and humanitarian assistance in the enjoyment of the rights set out in this Charter and other international human rights and humanitarian instruments to which the States are Parties.
2. State Parties shall undertake to cooperate with existing international organizations which protect and assist refugees in their efforts to protect and assist such a child and to trace the parents or other close relatives or an unaccompanied refugee child in order to obtain information necessary for reunification with the family.
3. Where no parents, legal guardians or close relatives can be found, the child shall be accorded the same protection as any other child permanently or temporarily deprived of his family environment for any reason.
4. The provisions of this Article apply mutatis mutandis to internally displaced children whether through natural disaster, internal armed conflicts, civil strife, breakdown of economic and social order or howsoever caused.

Article 24 Adoption

State Parties which recognize the system of adoption shall ensure that the best interest of the child shall be the paramount consideration and they shall:

1. establish competent authorities to determine matters of adoption and ensure that the adoption is carried out in conformity with applicable laws and procedures and on the basis of all relevant and reliable information, that the adoption is permissible in view of the child's status concerning parents, relatives and guardians and that, if necessary, the appropriate persons concerned have given their informed consent to the adoption on the basis of appropriate counseling;
2. recognize that inter-country adoption in those States that have ratified or adhered to the International Convention on the Rights of the Child or this Charter, may, as the last resort, be considered as an alternative means of a child's care, if the child cannot be placed in a foster or an adoptive family or cannot in any suitable manner be cared for in the child's country of origin;
3. ensure that the child affected by inter-country adoption enjoys safeguards and standards equivalent to those existing in the case of national adoption;
4. take all appropriate measures to ensure that in inter-country adoption, the placement does not result in trafficking or improper financial gain for those who try to adopt a child;
5. promote, where appropriate, the objectives of this Article by concluding bilateral or multilateral arrangements or agreements, and endeavour, within this framework

to ensure that the placement of the child in another country is carried out by competent authorities or organs;
6. establish a machinery to monitor the well-being of the adopted child.

Article 25 Separation from Parents

1. Any child who is permanently or temporarily deprived of his family environment for any reason shall be entitled to special protection and assistance;
2. State Parties to the present Charter:
3. shall ensure that a child who is parentless, or who is temporarily or permanently deprived of his or her family environment, or who in his or her best interest cannot be brought up or allowed to remain in that environment shall be provided with alternative family care, which could include, among others, foster placement, or placement in suitable institutions for the care of children;
4. shall take all necessary measures to trace and re-unite children with parents or relatives where separation is caused by internal and external displacement arising from armed conflicts or natural disasters.
5. When considering alternative family care of the child and the best interests of the child, due regard shall be paid to the desirability of continuity in a child's upbringing and to the child's ethnic, religious or linguistic background.

Article 26 Protection Against Apartheid and Discrimination

1. State Parties to the present Charter shall individually and collectively undertake to accord the highest priority to the special needs of children living under Apartheid and in States subject to military destabilization by the Apartheid regime.
2. State Parties to the present Charter shall individually and collectively undertake to accord the highest priority to the special needs of children living under regimes practising racial, ethnic, religious or other forms of discrimination as well as in States subject to military destabilization.
3. State Parties shall undertake to provide whenever possible, material assistance to such children and to direct their efforts towards the elimination of all forms of discrimination and Apartheid on the African Continent.

Article 27 Sexual Exploitation

1. State Parties to the present Charter shall undertake to protect the child from all forms of sexual exploitation and sexual abuse and shall in particular take measures to prevent:
    1. the inducement, coercion or encouragement of a child to engage in any sexual activity;
    2. the use of children in prostitution or other sexual practices;
    3. the use of children in pornographic activities, performances and materials.

Article 28 Drug Abuse

State Parties to the present Charter shall take all appropriate measures to protect the child from the use of narcotics and illicit use of psychotropic substances as defined in the relevant international treaties, and to prevent the use of children in the production and trafficking of such substances.

Article 29 Sale, Trafficking and Abduction

State Parties to the present Charter shall take appropriate measures to prevent:

1. the abduction, sale of, or traffick in children for any purpose or in any form, by any person including parents or legal guardians of the child;
2. the use of children in all forms of begging.

Article 30 Children of Imprisoned Mothers

1. State Parties to the present Charter shall undertake to provide special treatment to expectant mothers and to mothers of infants and young children who have been accused or found guilty of infringing the penal law and shall in particular:
   1. ensure that a non-custodial sentence will always be first considered when sentencing such mothers;
   2. establish and promote measures alternative to institutional confinement for the treatment of such mothers;
   3. establish special alternative institutions for holding such mothers;
   4. ensure that a mother shall not be imprisoned with her child;
   5. ensure that a death sentence shall not be imposed on such mothers;
   6. the essential aim of the penitentiary system will be the reformation, integration of the mother to the family and social rehabilitation.

Article 31 Responsibility of the Child

Every child shall have responsibilities towards his family and society, the State and other legally recognized communities and the international community. The child, subject to his age and ability, and such limitations as may be contained in the present Charter, shall have the duty:

1. to work for the cohesion of the family, to respect his parents, superiors and elders at all times and to assist them in case of need;
2. to serve his national community by placing his physical and intellectual abilities at its service;
3. to preserve and strengthen social and national solidarity;
4. to preserve and strengthen African cultural values in his relations with other members of the society, in the spirit of tolerance, dialogue and consultation and to contribute to the moral well-being of society;

5. to preserve and strengthen the independence and the integrity of his country;
6. to contribute to the best of his abilities at all times, and at all levels, to the promotion and achievement of Afncan Unity.

Part II

Chapter Two Establishment and Organization of the Committee on the Rights and Welfare of the Child

Article 32 The Committee

An African Committee of Experts on the Rights and Welfare of the Child hereinafter called 'the Committee' shall be established within the Organization of African Unity to promote and protect the rights and welfare of the child.

Article 33 Composition

1. The Committee shall consist of 11 members of high moral standing, integrity, impartiality and competence in matters of the rights and welfare of the child.
2. The members of the Committee shall serve in their personal capacity.
3. The Committee shall not include more than one national of the same State.

Article 34 Election

As soon as this Charter shall enter into force the members of the Committee shall be elected by secret ballot by the Assembly of Heads of State and Government from a list of persons nominated by the State Parties to the present Charter.

Article 35 Candidates

Each State Party to the present Charter may nominate not more than two candidates. The candidates must have one of the nationalities of the State Parties to the present Charter. When two candidates are nominated by a State, one of them shall not be a national of that State.

Article 36

1. The Secretary-General of the Organization of African Unity shall invite State Parties to the present Charter to nominate candidates at least six months before the elections.
2. The Secretary-General of the Organization of African Unity shall draw up in alphabetical order, a list of persons nominated and communicate it to the Heads of State and Government at least two months before the elections.

Article 37 Term of Office

1. The members of the Committee shall be elected for a term of five years and may not be re-elected; however, the term of four of the members elected at the first election shall expire after two years and the term of six others, after four years.
2. Immediately after the first election, the Chairman of the Assembly of Heads of State and Government of the Organization of African Unity shall draw lots to determine the names of those members referred to in sub-paragraph 1 of this Article.
3. The Secretary-General of the Organization of African Unity shall convene the first meeting of the Committee at the Headquarters of the Organization within six months of the election of the members of the Committee, and thereafter the Committee shall be convened by its Chairman whenever necessary, at least once a year.

Article 38 Bureau

1. The Committee shall establish its own Rules of Procedure.
2. The Committee shall elect its officers for a period of two years.
3. Seven Committee members shall form the quorum.
4. In case of an equality of votes, the Chairman shall have a casting vote.
5. The working languages of the Committee shall be the official languages of the OAU.

Article 39 Vacancy

If a member of the Committee vacates his office for any reason other than the normal expiration of a term, the State which nominated that member shall appoint another member from among its nationals to serve for the remainder of the term – subject to the approval of the Assembly.

Article 40 Secretariat

The Secretary-General of the Organization of African Unity shall appoint a Secretary for the Committee.

Article 41 Privileges and Immunities

In discharging their duties. members of the Committee shall enjoy the privileges and immunities provided for in the General Convention on the Privileges and Immunities of the Organization of Afncan Unity.

Chapter Three Mandate and Procedure of the Committee

Article 42 Mandate

The functions of the Committee shall be:

1. To promote and protect the rights enshrined in this Charter and in particular to:

1. collect and document information, commission inter-disciplinary assessment of situations on African problems in the fields of the rights and welfare of the child, organize meetings, encourage national and local institutions concerned with the rights and welfare of the child, and where necessary give its views and make recommendations to Governments;
2. formulate and lay down principles and rules aimed at protecting the rights and welfare of children in Africa;
3. cooperate with other African, international and regional Institutions and organizations concerned with the promotion and protection of the rights and welfare of the child.

2. To monitor the implementation and ensure protection of the rights enshrined in this Charter.
3. To interpret the provisions of the present Charter at the request of a State Party, an Institution of the Organization of African Unity or any other person or Institution recognized by the Organization of African Unity, or any State Party.
4. Perform such other task as may be entrusted to it by the Assembly of Heads of State and Government, Secretary-General of the OAU and any other organs of the OAU or the United Nations.

Article 43 Reporting Procedure

1. Every State Party to the present Charter shall undertake to submit to the Committee through the Secretary-General of the Organization of African Unity, reports on the measures they have adopted which give effect to the provisions of this Charter and on the progress made in the enjoyment of these rights:
   1. within two years of the entry into force of the Charter for the State Party concerned;
   2. and thereafter, every three years.
2. Every report made under this Article shall:
   1. contain sufficient information on the implementation of the present Charter to provide the Committee with comprehensive understanding of the implementation of the Charter in the relevant country; and
   2. shall indicate factors and difficulties, if any, affecting the fullfilment of the obligations contained in the Charter.
3. A State Party which has submitted a comprehensive first report to the Committee need not, in its subsequent reports submitted in accordance with Paragraph 1 (a) of this Article, repeat the basic information previously provided.

Article 44 Communications

1. The Committee may receive communication, from any person, group or non-governmental organization recognized by the Organization of African Unity, by a Member State, or the United Nations relating to any matter covered by this Charter.
2. Every communication to the Committee shall contain the name and address of the author and shall be treated in confidence.

Article 45 Investigations by the Committee

1. The Committee may, resort to any appropriate method of investigating any matter falling within the ambit of the present Charter, request from the State Parties any information relevant to the implementation of the Charter and may also resort to any appropriate method of investigating the measures the State Party has adopted to implement the Charter.
2. The Committee shall submit to each Ordinary Session of the Assembly of Heads of State and Govenrment every two years, a report on its activities and on any communication made under Article [44] of this Charter.
3. The Committee shall publish its report after it has been considered by the Assembly of Heads of State and Government.
4. State Parties shall make the Committee's reports widely available to the public in their own countries.

Chapter Four Miscellaneous Provisions

Article 46 Sources of Inspiration

The Committee shall draw inspiration from International Law on Human Rights, particularly from the provisions of the African Charter on Human and Peoples' Rights, the Charter of the Organization of African Unity, the Universal Declaration on Human Rights, the International Convention on the Rights of the Child, and other instruments adopted by the United Nations and by African countries in the field of human rights, and from African values and traditions.

Article 47 Signature, Ratification or Adherence

1. The present Charter shall be open to signature by all the Member States of the Organization of Afncan Unity.
2. The present Charter shall be subject to ratification or adherence by Member States of the Organization of African Unity. The instruments of ratification or adherence to the present Charter shall be deposited with the Secretary-General of the Organization of African Unity.

3. The present Charter shall come into force 30 days after the reception by the Secretary-General of the Organization of African Unity of the instruments of ratification or adherence of 15 Member States of the Organization of African Unity.

Article 48 Amendment and Revision of the Charter

1. The present Charter may be amended or revised if any State Party makes a written request to that effect to the Secretary-General of the Organization of African Unity, provided that the proposed amendment is not submitted to the Assembly of Heads of State and Government for consideration until all the State Parties have been duly notified of it and the Committee has given its opinion on the amendment.
2. An amendment shall be approved by a simple majority of the State Parties.

African Charter on the Rights and Welfare of the Child, OAU Doc. CAB/LEG/24.9/49 (1990).

ANNEX IV

Protocol to the African Charter on Human and Peoples' Rights on the Establishment of the African Court on Human and Peoples' Rights, 1998

The Member States of the Organization of African Unity hereinafter referred to as the OAU,[1] States Parties to the African Charter on Human and Peoples` Rights.

Considering that the Charter of the Organization of African Unity recognizes that freedom, equality, justice, peace and dignity are essential objectives for the achievement of the legitimate aspirations of the African Peoples;

Noting that the African Charter on Human and Peoples` Rights reaffirms adherence to the principles of Human and Peoples` Rights, freedoms and duties contained in the declarations, conventions and other instruments adopted by the Organization of African Unity, and other international organizations;

Recognizing that the twofold objective of the African Commission on Human and Peoples` Rights is to ensure on the one hand promotion and on the other protection of Human and Peoples` Rights, freedom and duties;

Recognizing further, the efforts of the African Charter on Human and Peoples` Rights in the promotion and protection of Human and Peoples` Rights since its inception in 1987;

Recalling resolution AHGéRes.230 (XXX) adopted by the Assembly of Heads of State and Government in June 1994 in Tunis, Tunisia, requesting the Secretary-General to convene a Government experts` meeting to ponder, in conjunction with the African Commission, over the means to enhance the efficiency of the African commission and to consider in particular the establishment of an African Court on Human and Peoples` Rights;

Noting the first and second Government legal experts` meeting held respectively in Cape Town, South Africa (September, 1995) and Nouakchott, Mauritania (April 1997), and the third Government Legal Experts meeting held in Addis Ababa, Ethiopia (December, 1997), which was enlarged to include Diplomats;

Firmly convinced that the attainment of the objectives of the African Charter on Human and Peoples` Rights requires the establishment of an African Court on Human and Peoples` Rights to complement and reinforce the functions of the African Commission on Human and Peoples` Rights.

1 African Commission on Human and Peoples' Rights, Accessed on 28 July 2021: https://www.achpr.org/legalinstruments/detail?id=45.

 | DOI:10.1163/9789004520646_014

Have agreed as follows:

Article 1 Establishment of the Court

There shall be established within the Organization of African Unity an African Court Human and Peoples` Rights hereinafter referred to as "the Court", the organization, jurisdiction and functioning of which shall be governed by the present Protocol.

Article 2 Relationship between the Court and the Commission

The Court shall, bearing in mind the provisions of this Protocol, complement the protective mandate of the African Commission on Human and Peoples` Rights hereinafter referred to as "the Commission", conferred upon it by the African Charter on Human and Peoples` Rights, hereinafter referred to as "the Charter".

Article 3 Jurisdiction

1. The jurisdiction of the Court shall extend to all cases and disputes submitted to it concerning the interpretation and application of the Charter, this Protocol and any other relevant Human Rights instrument ratified by the States concerned.
2. In the event of a dispute as to whether the Court has jurisdiction, the Court shall decide.

Article 4 Advisory Opinions

1. At the request of a Member State of the OAU, the OAU, any of its organs, or any African organization recognized by the OAU, the Court may provide an opinion on any legal matter relating to the Charter or any other relevant human rights instruments, provided that the subject matter of the opinion is not related to a matter being examined by the Commission.
2. The Court shall give reasons for its advisory opinions provided that every judge shall be entitled to deliver a separate of dissenting decision.

Article 5 Access to the Court

1. The following are entitled to submit cases to the Court:
   a) The Commission
   b) The State Party which had lodged a complaint to the Commission
   c) The State Party against which the complaint has been lodged at the Commission
   d) The State Party whose citizen is a victim of human rights violation
   e) African Intergovernmental Organizations
2. When a State Party has an interest in a case, it may submit a request to the Court to be permitted to join.
3. The Court may entitle relevant Non Governmental organizations (NGOs) with observer status before the Commission, and individuals to institute cases directly before it, in accordance with article 34 (6) of this Protocol.

Article 6 Admissibility of Cases

1. The Court, when deciding on the admissibility of a case instituted under article 5 (3) of this Protocol, may request the opinion of the Commission which shall give it as soon as possible.
2. The Court shall rule on the admissibility of cases taking into account the provisions of article 56 of the Charter.
3. The Court may consider cases or transfer them to the Commission.

Article 7 Sources of Law

The Court shall apply the provision of the Charter and any other relevant human rights instruments ratified by the States concerned.

Article 8 Consideration of Cases

The Rules of Procedure of the Court shall lay down the detailed conditions under which the Court shall consider cases brought before it, bearing in mind the complementarity between the Commission and the Court.

Article 9 Amicable Settlement

The Court may try to reach an amicable settlement in a case pending before it in accordance with the provisions of the Charter.

Article 10 Hearings and Representation

1. The Court shall conduct its proceedings in public. The Court may, however, conduct proceedings in camera as may be provided for in the Rules of Procedure.
2. Any party to a case shall be entitled to be represented by a legal representative of the party's choice. Free legal representation may be provided where the interests of justice so require.
3. Any person, witness or representative of the parties, who appears before the Court, shall enjoy protection and all facilities, in accordance with international law, necessary for the discharging of their functions, tasks and duties in relation to the Court.

Article 11 Composition

1. The Court shall consist of eleven judges, nationals of Member States of the OAU, elected in an individual capacity from among jurists of high moral character and of recognized practical, judicial or academic competence and experience in the field of human and peoples` rights.
2. No two judges shall be nationals of the same State.

Article 12 Nominations

1. States Parties to the Protocol may each propose up to three candidates, at least two of whom shall be nationals of that State.
2. Due consideration shall be given to adequate gender representation in nomination process.

Article 13 List of Candidates

1. Upon entry into force of this Protocol, the Secretary-general of the OAU shall request each State Party to the Protocol to present, within ninety (90) days of such a request, its nominees for the office of judge of the Court.

2. The Secretary-General of the OAU shall prepare a list in alphabetical order of the candidates nominated and transmit it to the Member States of the OAU at least thirty days prior to the next session of the Assembly of Heads of State and Government of the OAU hereinafter referred to as "the Assembly".

Article 14 Elections

1. The judges of the Court shall be elected by secret ballot by the Assembly from the list referred to in Article 13 (2) of the present Protocol.
2. The Assembly shall ensure that in the Court as a whole there is representation of the main regions of Africa and of their principal legal traditions.
3. In the election of the judges, the Assembly shall ensure that there is adequate gender representation.

Article 15 Term of Office

1. The judges of the Court shall be elected for a period of six years and may be re-elected only once. The terms of four judges elected at the first election shall expire at the end of two years, and the terms of four more judges shall expire at the end of four years.
2. The judges whose terms are to expire at the end of the initial periods of two and four years shall be chosen by lot to be drawn by the Secretary-General of the OAU immediately after the first election has been completed.
3. A judge elected to replace a judge whose term of office has not expired shall hold office for the remainder of the predecessor's term.
4. All judges except the President shall perform their functions on a part-time basis. However, the Assembly may change this arrangement as it deems appropriate.

Article 16 Oath of Office

After their election, the judges of the Court shall make a solemn declaration to discharge their duties impartially and faithfully.

Article 17 Independence

1. The independence of the judges shall be fully ensured in accordance with international law.
2. No judge may hear any case in which the same judge has previously taken part as agent, counsel or advocate for one of the parties or as a member of a national or international court or a commission of enquiry or in any other capacity. Any doubt on this point shall be settled by decision of the Court.
3. The judges of the Court shall enjoy, from the moment of their election and throughout their term of office, the immunities extended to diplomatic agents in accordance with international law.
4. At no time shall the judges of the Court be held liable for any decision or opinion issued in the exercise of their functions.

Article 18 Incompatibility

The position of judge of the court is incompatible with any activity that might interfere with the independence or impartiality of such a judge or the demands of the office as determined in the Rules of Procedure of the Court.

Article 19 Cessation of Office

1. A judge shall not be suspended or removed from office unless, by the unanimous decision of the other judges of the Court, the judge concerned has been found to be no longer fulfilling the required conditions to be a judge of the Court.
2. Such a decision of the Court shall become final unless it is set aside by the Assembly at its next session.

Article 20 Vacancies

1. In case of death or resignation of a judge of the Court, the President of the Court shall immediately inform the Secretary General of the Organization of African Unity, who shall declare the seat vacant from the date of death or from the date on which the resignation takes effect.
2. The Assembly shall replace the judge whose office became vacant unless the remaining period of the term is less than one hundred and eighty (180) days.

3. The same procedure and considerations as set out in Articles 12, 13 and 14 shall be followed for the filling of vacancies.

Article 21 Presidency of the Court

1. The Court shall elect its President and one Vice-President for a period of two years. They may be re-elected only once.
2. The President shall perform judicial functions on a full-time basis and shall reside at the seat of the Court.
3. The functions of the President and the Vice-President shall be set out in the Rules of Procedure of the Court.

Article 22 Exclusion

If the judge is a national of any State which is a party to a case submitted to the Court, that judge shall not hear the case.

Article 23 Quorum

The Court shall examine cases brought before it, if it has a quorum of at least seven judges.

Article 24 Registry of the Court

1. The Court shall appoint its own Registrar and other staff of the registry from among nationals of Member States of the OAU according to the Rules of Procedure.
2. The office and residence of the Registrar shall be at the place where the Court has its seat.

Article 25 Seat of the Court

1. The Court shall have its seat at the place determined by the Assembly from among States parties to this Protocol. However, it may convene in the territory of any Member State of the OAU when the majority of the Court considers it desirable, and with the prior consent of the State concerned.

2. The seat of the Court may be changed by the Assembly after due consultation with the Court.

Article 26 Evidence

1. The Court shall hear submissions by all parties and if deemed necessary, hold an enquiry. The States concerned shall assist by providing relevant facilities for the efficient handling of the case.
2. The Court may receive written and oral evidence including expert testimony and shall make its decision on the basis of such evidence.

Article 27 Findings

1. If the Court finds that there has been violation of a human or peoples' rights, it shall make appropriate orders to remedy the violation, including the payment of fair compensation or reparation.
2. In cases of extreme gravity and urgency, and when necessary to avoid irreparable harm to persons, the Court shall adopt such provisional measures as it deems necessary.

Article 28 Judgment

1. The Court shall render its judgment within ninety (90) days of having completed its deliberations.
2. The judgment of the Court decided by majority shall be final and not subject to appeal.
3. Without prejudice to sub-article 2 above, the Court may review its decision in the light of new evidence under conditions to be set out in the Rules of Procedure.
4. The Court may interpret its own decision.
5. The judgment of the Court shall be read in open court, due notice having been given to the parties.
6. Reasons shall be given for the judgment of the Court.
7. If the judgment of the court does not represent, in whole or in part, the unanimous decision of the judges, any judge shall be entitled to deliver a separate or dissenting opinion.

Article 29 Notification of Judgment

1. The parties to the case shall be notified of the judgment of the Court and it shall be transmitted to the Member States of the OAU and the Commission.
2. The Council of Ministers shall also be notified of the judgment and shall monitor its execution on behalf of the Assembly.

Article 30 Execution of Judgment

The States Parties to the present Protocol undertake to comply with the judgment in any case to which they are parties within the time stipulated by the Court and to guarantee its execution.

Article 31 Report

The Court shall submit to each regular session of the Assembly, a report on its work during the previous year. The report shall specify, in particular, the cases in which a State has not complied with the Court's judgment.

Article 32 Budget

Expenses of the Court, emoluments and allowances for judges and the budget of its registry, shall be determined and borne by the OAU, in accordance with criteria laid down by the OAU in consultation with the Court.

Article 33 Rules of Procedure

The Court shall draw up its Rules and determine its own procedures. The Court shall consult the Commission as appropriate.

Article 34 Ratification

1. This Protocol shall be open for signature and ratification or accession by any State Party to the Charter.

2. The instrument of ratification or accession to the present Protocol shall be deposited with the Secretary-General of the OAU.
3. The Protocol shall come into force thirty days after fifteen instruments of ratification or accession have been deposited.
4. For any State Party ratifying or acceding subsequently, the present Protocol shall come into force in respect of that State on the date of the deposit of its instrument of ratification or accession.
5. The Secretary-General of the OAU shall inform all Member States of the entry into force of the present Protocol.
6. At the time of the ratification of this Protocol or any time thereafter, the State shall make a declaration accepting the competence of the Court to receive cases under article 5 (3) of this Protocol. The Court shall not receive any petition under article 5 (3) involving a State Party which has not made such a declaration.
7. Declarations made under sub-article (6) above shall be deposited with the Secretary-General, who shall transmit copies thereof to the State parties.

Article 35 Amendments

1. The present Protocol may be amended if a State Party to the Protocol makes a written request to that effect to the Secretary-General of the OAU. The Assembly may adopt, by simple majority, the draft amendment after all the State Parties to the present Protocol have been duly informed of it and the Court has given its opinion on the amendment.
2. The Court shall also be entitled to propose such amendments to the present Protocol as it may deem necessary, through the Secretary-General of the OAU.
3. The amendment shall come into force for each State Party which has accepted it thirty days after the Secretary-General of the OAU has received notice of the acceptance

ANNEX V

AU, African Charter on Democracy, Elections and Governance (2007)

Preamble[1]

We, the Member States of the African Union (AU);

Inspired by the objectives and principles enshrined in the Constitutive Act of the African Union, particularly Articles 3 and 4, which emphasise the significance of good governance, popular participation, the rule of law and human rights;

Recognising the contributions of the African Union and Regional Economic Communities to the promotion, nurturing, strengthening and consolidation of democracy and governance;

Reaffirming our collective will to work relentlessly to deepen and consolidate the rule of law, peace, security and development in our countries;

Guided by our common mission to strengthen and consolidate institutions for good governance, continental unity and solidarity;

Committed to promote the universal values and principles of democracy, good governance, human rights and the right to development;

Cognizant of the historical and cultural conditions in Africa;

Seeking to entrench in the Continent a political culture of change of power based on the holding of regular, free, fair and transparent elections conducted by competent, independent and impartial national electoral bodies;

Concerned about the unconstitutional changes of governments that are one of the essential causes of insecurity, instability and violent conflict in Africa;

Determined to promote and strengthen good governance through the institutionalization of transparency, accountability and participatory democracy;

Convinced of the need to enhance the election observation missions in the role they play, particularly as they are an important contributory factor to ensuring the regularity, transparency and credibility of elections;

---

1 African Commission on Human and Peoples' Rights, Accessed on 28 July 2021: https://www.achpr.org/legalinstruments/detail?id=29.

 | DOI:10.1163/9789004520646_015

Desirous to enhance the relevant Declarations and Decisions of the OAU/AU (including the 1990 Declaration on the political and socio-economic situation in Africa and the fundamental changes taking place in the world, the 1995 Cairo Agenda for the Re-launch of Africa's Economic and Social Development, the 1999 Algiers Declaration on Unconstitutional Changes of Government, the 2000

Lomé Declaration for an OAU Response to Unconstitutional Changes of Government, the 2002 OAU/AU Declaration on Principles Governing Democratic Elections in Africa, the 2003 Protocol Relating to the Establishment of the Peace and Security Council of the African Union);

Committed to implementing Decision EX.CL/Dec.31(III) adopted in Maputo, Mozambique, in July 2003 and Decision EX.CL/124(V) adopted in Addis Ababa, Ethiopia, in May 2004 respectively, by the adoption of an African Charter on Democracy, Elections and Governance;

HAVE AGREED AS FOLLOWS:

Chapter 1 Definitions

Article 1

In this Charter, unless otherwise stated, the following expressions shall have the following meaning:

"AU" means the African Union;

"African Human Rights Commission" means the African Commission on Human and Peoples' Rights;

"African Peer Review Mechanism" APRM means the African Peer Review Mechanism;

"Assembly" means the Assembly of Heads of State and Government of the African Union;

"Commission" means the Commission of the Union; "Constitutive Act" means the Constitutive Act of the Union;

"Charter" means the African Charter on Democracy, Elections and Governance; "Member States" means the Member States of the African Union;

"National Electoral Body" means a competent authority, established by the relevant legal instruments of a State Party, responsible for organizing and supervising elections;

"NEPAD" means the New Partnership for Africa's Development;

"Peace and Security Council" means the Peace and Security Council of the African Union;

"Regional Economic Communities" means the regional integration blocs of the African Union;

"State Party" means any Member State of the African Union which has ratified or acceded to this Charter and deposited the instruments for ratification or accession with the Chairperson of the African Union Commission;
"Union" means the African Union.

Chapter 2 Objectives

Article 2

The objectives of this Charter are to:

1. Promote adherence, by each State Party, to the universal values and principles of democracy and respect for human rights;
2. Promote and enhance adherence to the principle of the rule of law premised upon the respect for, and the supremacy of, the Constitution and constitutional order in the political arrangements of the State Parties;
3. Promote the holding of regular free and fair elections to institutionalize legitimate authority of representative government as well as democratic change of governments;
4. Prohibit, reject and condemn unconstitutional change of government in any Member State as a serious threat to stability, peace, security and development;
5. Promote and protect the independence of the judiciary;
6. Nurture, support and consolidate good governance by promoting democratic culture and practice, building and strengthening governance institutions and inculcating political pluralism and tolerance;
7. Encourage effective coordination and harmonization of governance policies amongst State Parties with the aim of promoting regional and continental integration;
8. Promote State Parties' sustainable development and human security;
9. Promote the fight against corruption in conformity with the provisions of the AU Convention on Preventing and Combating Corruption adopted in Maputo, Mozambique in July 2003;
10. Promote the establishment of the necessary conditions to foster citizen participation, transparency, access to information, freedom of the press and accountability in the management of public affairs;
11. Promote gender balance and equality in the governance and development processes;
12. Enhance cooperation between the Union, Regional Economic Communities and the International Community on democracy, elections and governance; and
13. Promote best practices in the management of elections for purposes of political stability and good governance.

Chapter 3 Principles

Article 3

State Parties shall implement this Charter in accordance with the following principles:

1. Respect for human rights and democratic principles;
2. Access to and exercise of state power in accordance with the constitution of the State Party and the principle of the rule of law;
3. Promotion of a system of government that is representative;
4. Holding of regular, transparent, free and fair elections;
5. Separation of powers;
6. Promotion of gender equality in public and private institutions;
7. Effective participation of citizens in democratic and development processes and in governance of public affairs;
8. Transparency and fairness in the management of public affairs;
9. Condemnation and rejection of acts of corruption, related offenses and impunity;
10. Condemnation and total rejection of unconstitutional changes of government;
11. Strengthening political pluralism and recognising the role, rights and responsibilities of legally constituted political parties, including opposition political parties, which should be given a status under national law.

Chapter 4 Democracy, Rule of Law and Human Rights Article 4

1. State Parties shall commit themselves to promote democracy, the principle of the rule of law and human rights.
2. State Parties shall recognize popular participation through universal suffrage as the inalienable right of the people.

Article 5

State Parties shall take all appropriate measures to ensure constitutional rule, particularly constitutional transfer of power.

Article 6

State Parties shall ensure that citizens enjoy fundamental freedoms and human rights taking into account their universality, interdependence and indivisibility.

Article 7

State Parties shall take all necessary measures to strengthen the Organs of the Union that are mandated to promote and protect human rights and to fight impunity and endow them with the necessary resources.

Article 8

1. State Parties shall eliminate all forms of discrimination, especially those based on political opinion, gender, ethnic, religious and racial grounds as well as any other form of intolerance.
2. State Parties shall adopt legislative and administrative measures to guarantee the rights of women, ethnic minorities, migrants, people with disabilities, refugees and displaced persons and other marginalized and vulnerable social groups.
3. State Parties shall respect ethnic, cultural and religious diversity, which contributes to strengthening democracy and citizen participation.

Article 9

State Parties undertake to design and implement social and economic policies and programmes that promote sustainable development and human security.

Article 10

1. State Parties shall entrench the principle of the supremacy of the constitution in the political organization of the State.
2. State Parties shall ensure that the process of amendment or revision of their constitution reposes on national consensus, obtained if need be, through referendum.
3. State Parties shall protect the right to equality before the law and equal protection by the law as a fundamental precondition for a just and democratic society.

Chapter 5 The Culture of Democracy and Peace Article 11

The State Parties undertake to develop the necessary legislative and policy frameworks to establish and strengthen a culture of democracy and peace.

Article 12

State Parties undertake to implement programmes and carry out activities designed to promote democratic principles and practices as well as consolidate a culture of democracy and peace.

To this end, State Parties shall:

1. Promote good governance by ensuring transparent and accountable administration.
2. Strengthen political institutions to entrench a culture of democracy and peace.
3. Create conducive conditions for civil society organizations to exist and operate within the law.
4. Integrate civic education in their educational curricula and develop appropriate programmes and activities.

Article 13

State Parties shall take measures to ensure and maintain political and social dialogue, as well as public trust and transparency between political leaders and the people, in order to consolidate democracy and peace.

Chapter 6 Democratic Institutions

Article 14

1. State Parties shall strengthen and institutionalize constitutional civilian control over the armed and security forces to ensure the consolidation of democracy and constitutional order.
2. State Parties shall take legislative and regulatory measures to ensure that those who attempt to remove an elected government through unconstitutional means are dealt with in accordance with the law.
3. State Parties shall cooperate with each other to ensure that those who attempt to remove an elected government through unconstitutional means are dealt with in accordance with the law.

Article 15

1. State Parties shall establish public institutions that promote and support democracy and constitutional order.
2. State Parties shall ensure that the independence or autonomy of the said institutions is guaranteed by the constitution.
3. State Parties shall ensure that these institutions are accountable to competent national organs.
4. State Parties shall provide the above-mentioned institutions with resources to perform their assigned missions efficiently and effectively.

Article 16

State Parties shall cooperate at regional and continental levels in building and consolidating democracy through exchange of experiences.

Chapter 7 Democratic Elections

Article 17

State Parties re-affirm their commitment to regularly holding transparent, free and fair elections in accordance with the Union's Declaration on the Principles Governing Democratic Elections in Africa.

To this end, State Parties shall:

1. Establish and strengthen independent and impartial national electoral bodies responsible for the management of elections.
2. Establish and strengthen national mechanisms that redress election- related disputes in a timely manner.
3. Ensure fair and equitable access by contesting parties and candidates to state controlled media during elections.

4. Ensure that there is a binding code of conduct governing legally recognized political stakeholders, government and other political actors prior, during and after elections. The code shall include a commitment by political stakeholders to accept the results of the election or challenge them in through exclusively legal channels.

Article 18

1. State Parties may request the Commission, through the Democracy and Electoral Assistance Unit and the Democracy and Electoral Assistance Fund, to provide advisory services or assistance for strengthening and developing their electoral institutions and processes.
2. The Commission may at any time, in consultation with the State Party concerned, send special advisory missions to provide assistance to that State Party for strengthening its electoral institutions and processes.

Article 19

1. Each State Party shall inform the Commission of scheduled elections and invite it to send an electoral observer mission.
2. Each State Party shall guarantee conditions of security, free access to information, non-interference, freedom of movement and full cooperation with the electoral observer mission.

Article 20

The Chairperson of the Commission shall first send an exploratory mission during the period prior to elections. This mission shall obtain any useful information and documentation, and brief the Chairperson, stating whether the necessary conditions have been established and if the environment is conducive to the holding of transparent, free and fair elections in conformity with the principles of the Union governing democratic elections.

Article 21

1. The Commission shall ensure that these missions are independent and shall provide them with the necessary resources for that purpose.
2. Electoral observer missions shall be conducted by appropriate and competent experts in the area of election monitoring, drawn from continental and national institutions such as, but not limited to, the Pan- African Parliament, national electoral bodies, national legislatures and eminent persons taking due cognizance of the principles of regional representation and gender equality.
3. Electoral observer missions shall be conducted in an objective, impartial and transparent manner.
4. All electoral observer missions shall present the report of their activities to the Chairperson of the Commission within a reasonable time.
5. A copy of the report shall be submitted to the State Party concerned within a reasonable time.

Article 22
State Parties shall create a conducive environment for independent and impartial national monitoring or observation mechanisms.

Chapter 8 Sanctions in Cases of Unconstitutional Changes of Government Article 23

State Parties agree that the use of, *inter alia,* the following illegal means of accessing or maintaining power constitute an unconstitutional change of government and shall draw appropriate sanctions by the Union:
1. Any putsch or coup d'Etat against a democratically elected government.
2. Any intervention by mercenaries to replace a democratically elected government.
3. Any replacement of a democratically elected government by armed dissidents or rebels.
4. Any refusal by an incumbent government to relinquish power to the winning party or candidate after free, fair and regular elections; or
5. Any amendment or revision of the constitution or legal instruments, which is an infringement on the principles of democratic change of government.

Article 24
When a situation arises in a State Party that may affect its democratic political institutional arrangements or the legitimate exercise of power, the Peace and Security Council shall exercise its responsibilities in order to maintain the constitutional order in accordance with relevant provisions of the Protocol Relating to the Establishment of the Peace and Security Council of the African Union, hereinafter referred to as the Protocol.

Article 25
1. When the Peace and Security Council observes that there has been an unconstitutional change of government in a State Party, and that diplomatic initiatives have failed, it shall suspend the said State Party from the exercise of its right to participate in the activities of the Union in accordance with the provisions of articles 30 of the Constitutive Act and 7 (g) of the Protocol. The suspension shall take effect immediately.
2. However, the suspended State Party shall continue to fulfill its obligations to the Union, in particular with regard to those relating to respect of human rights.
3. Notwithstanding the suspension of the State Party, the Union shall maintain diplomatic contacts and take any initiatives to restore democracy in that State Party.
4. The perpetrators of unconstitutional change of government shall not be allowed to participate in elections held to restore the democratic order or hold any position of responsibility in political institutions of their State.

5. Perpetrators of unconstitutional change of government may also be tried before the competent court of the Union.
6. The Assembly shall impose sanctions on any Member State that is proved to have instigated or supported unconstitutional change of government in another state in conformity with Article 23 of the Constitutive Act.
7. The Assembly may decide to apply other forms of sanctions on perpetrators of unconstitutional change of government including punitive economic measures.
8. State Parties shall not harbour or give sanctuary to perpetrators of unconstitutional changes of government.
9. State Parties shall bring to justice the perpetrators of unconstitutional changes of government or take necessary steps to effect their extradition.
10. State Parties shall encourage conclusion of bilateral extradition agreements as well as the adoption of legal instruments on extradition and mutual legal assistance.

Article 26

The Peace and Security Council shall lift sanctions once the situation that led to the suspension is resolved.

Chapter 9 Political, Economic and Social Governance Article 27

In order to advance political, economic and social governance, State Parties shall commit themselves to:

1. Strengthening the capacity of parliaments and legally recognised political parties to perform their core functions;
2. Fostering popular participation and partnership with civil society organizations;
3. Undertaking regular reforms of the legal and justice systems;
4. Improving public sector management;
5. Improving efficiency and effectiveness of public services and combating corruption;
6. Promoting the development of the private sector through, inter alia, enabling legislative and regulatory framework;
7. Development and utilisation of information and communication technologies;
8. Promoting freedom of expression, in particular freedom of the press and fostering a professional media;
9. Harnessing the democratic values of the traditional institutions; and
10. Preventing the spread and combating the impact of diseases such as Malaria, Tuberculosis, HIV/AIDS, Ebola fever, and Avian Flu.

Article 28

State Parties shall ensure and promote strong partnerships and dialogue between government, civil society and private sector.

Article 29

1. State Parties shall recognize the crucial role of women in development and strengthening of democracy.
2. State Parties shall create the necessary conditions for full and active participation of women in the decision-making processes and structures at all levels as a fundamental element in the promotion and exercise of a democratic culture.
3. State Parties shall take all possible measures to encourage the full and active participation of women in the electoral process and ensure gender parity in representation at all levels, including legislatures.

Article 30

State Parties shall promote citizen participation in the development process through appropriate structures.

Article 31

1. State Parties shall promote participation of social groups with special needs, including the Youth and people with disabilities, in the governance process.
2. State Parties shall ensure systematic and comprehensive civic education in order to encourage full participation of social groups with special needs in democracy and development processes.

Article 32

State Parties shall strive to institutionalize good political governance through:

1. Accountable, efficient and effective public administration;
2. Strengthening the functioning and effectiveness of parliaments;
3. An independent judiciary;
4. Relevant reforms of public institutions including the security sector;
5. Harmonious relationships in society including civil-military relations;
6. Consolidating sustainable multiparty political systems;
7. Organising regular, free and fair elections; and
8. Entrenching and respecting the principle of the rule of law.

Article 33

State Parties shall institutionalize good economic and corporate governance through, inter alia:

1. Effective and efficient public sector management;
2. Promoting transparency in public finance management;
3. Preventing and combating corruption and related offences;
4. Efficient management of public debt;
5. Prudent and sustainable utilization of public resources;
6. Equitable allocation of the nation's wealth and natural resources;
7. Poverty alleviation;

8. Enabling legislative and regulatory framework for private sector development;
9. Providing a conducive environment for foreign capital inflows;
10. Developing tax policies that encourage investment;
11. Preventing and combating crime;
12. Elaborating and implementing economic development strategies including private-public sector partnerships;
13. An efficient and effective tax system premised upon transparency and accountability.

Article 34

State Parties shall decentralize power to democratically elected local authorities as provided in national laws.

Article 35

Given the enduring and vital role of traditional authorities, particularly in rural communities, the State Parties shall strive to find appropriate ways and means to increase their integration and effectiveness within the larger democratic system.

Article 36

State Parties shall promote and deepen democratic governance by implementing the principles and core values of the NEPAD Declaration on Democracy, Political, Economic and Corporate Governance and, where applicable, the African Peer Review Mechanism (APRM).

Article 37

State Parties shall pursue sustainable development and human security through achievement of NEPAD objectives and the United Nations Millennium Development Goals (MDGs).

Article 38

1. State Parties shall promote peace, security and stability in their respective countries, regions and in the continent by fostering participatory political systems with well-functioning and, if need be, inclusive institutions;
2. State Parties shall promote solidarity amongst Member States and support the conflict prevention and resolution initiatives that the Union may undertake in conformity with the Protocol establishing the Peace and Security Council.

Article 39

State Parties shall promote a culture of respect, compromise, consensus and tolerance as a means to mitigate conflicts, promote political stability and security, and to harness the creative energies of the African peoples.

Article 40

State Parties shall adopt and implement policies, strategies and programmes required to generate productive employment, mitigate the impact of diseases and alleviate poverty and eradicate extreme poverty and illiteracy.

Article 41
State Parties shall undertake to provide and enable access to basic social services to the people.
Article 42
State Parties shall implement policies and strategies to protect the environment to achieve sustainable development for the benefit of the present and future generations. In this regard, State Parties are encouraged to accede to the relevant treaties and other international legal instruments.
Article 43
1. State Parties shall endeavour to provide free and compulsory basic education to all, especially girls, rural inhabitants, minorities, people with disabilities and other marginalized social groups.
2. In addition, State Parties shall ensure the literacy of citizens above compulsory school age, particularly women, rural inhabitants, minorities, people with disabilities, and other marginalized social groups.

Chapter 10 Mechanisms for Application

Article 44
To give effect to the commitments contained in this Charter:

1. Individual State Party Level

State Parties commit themselves to implement the objectives, apply the principles and respect the commitments enshrined in this Charter as follows:
(a) State Parties shall initiate appropriate measures including legislative, executive and administrative actions to bring State Parties' national laws and regulations into conformity with this Charter;
(b) State Parties shall take all necessary measures in accordance with constitutional provisions and procedures to ensure the wider dissemination of the Charter and all relevant legislation as may be necessary for the implementation of its fundamental principles;
(c) State Parties shall promote political will as a necessary condition for the attainment of the goals set forth in this Charter;
(d) State Parties shall incorporate the commitments and principles of the Charter in their national policies and strategies.

2. Commission Level

A. At Continental Level

(a) The Commission shall develop benchmarks for implementation of the commitments and principles of this Charter and evaluate compliance by State Parties;

(b) The Commission shall promote the creation of favourable conditions for democratic governance in the African

Continent, in particular by facilitating the harmonization of policies and laws of State Parties;

(c) The Commission shall take the necessary measures to ensure that the Democracy and Electoral Assistance Unit and the Democracy and Electoral Assistance Fund provide the needed assistance and resources to State Parties in support of electoral processes;

(d) The Commission shall ensure that effect is given to the decisions of the Union in regard to unconstitutional change of government on the Continent.

B. At Regional Level

The Commission shall establish a framework for cooperation with Regional Economic Communities on the implementation of the principles of the Charter. In this regard, it shall commit the Regional Economic Communities (RECs) to:

a) Encourage Member States to ratify or adhere to this Charter.

b) Designate focal points for coordination, evaluation and monitoring of the implementation of the commitments and principles enshrined in this Charter in order to ensure massive participation of stakeholders, particularly civil society organizations, in the process.

Article 45

The Commission shall:

(a) Act as the central coordinating structure for the implementation of this Charter;

(b) Assist State Parties in implementing the Charter;

(c) Coordinate evaluation on implementation of the Charter with other key organs of the Union including the Pan-African Parliament, the Peace and Security Council, the African Human Rights Commission, the African Court of Justice and Human Rights, the Economic, Social and Cultural Council, the Regional Economic Communities and appropriate national- level structures.

Chapter 11 Final Clauses

Article 46

In conformity with applicable provisions of the Constitutive Act and the Protocol Relating to the Establishment of the Peace and Security Council of the African Union, the Assembly and the Peace and Security Council shall determine the appropriate measures to be imposed on any State Party that violates this Charter.

Article 47

1. This Charter shall be open for signature, ratification and accession by Member States of the Union in accordance with their respective constitutional procedures.
2. The instruments of ratification or accession shall be deposited with the Chairperson of the Commission.

Article 48

This Charter shall enter into force thirty (30) days after the deposit of fifteen (15) Instruments of Ratification.

Article 49

1. State Parties shall submit every two years, from the date the Charter comes into force, a report to the Commission on the legislative or other relevant measures taken with a view to giving effect to the principles and commitments of the Charter;
2. A copy of the report shall be submitted to the relevant organs of the Union for appropriate action within their respective mandates;
3. The Commission shall prepare and submit to the Assembly, through the Executive Council, a synthesized report on the implementation of the Charter;
4. The Assembly shall take appropriate measures aimed at addressing issues raised in the report.

Article 50

1. Any State Party may submit proposals for the amendment or revision of this Charter;
2. Proposals for amendment or revision shall be submitted to the Chairperson of the Commission who shall transmit same to State Parties within thirty (30) days of receipt thereof;
3. The Assembly, upon the advice of the Executive Council, shall examine these proposals at its session following notification, provided all State Parties have been notified at least three (3) months before the beginning of the session;
4. The Assembly shall adopt amendments or revisions by consensus or failing which, by two-thirds majority;
5. The amendments or revisions shall enter into force when approved by two-thirds majority of State Parties.

Article 51

1. The Chairperson of the Commission shall be the depository of this Charter;
2. The Chairperson of the Commission shall inform all Member States of the signature, ratification, accession, entry into force, reservations, requests for amendments and approvals thereof;

3. Upon entry into force of this Charter, the Chairperson of the Commission shall register it with the Secretary General of the United Nations in accordance with Article 102 of the Charter of the United Nations.

Article 52

None of the provisions of the present Charter shall affect more favourable provisions relating to democracy, elections and governance contained in the national legislation of State Parties or in any other regional, continental or international conventions or agreements applicable in these State Parties.

Article 53

This Charter, drawn up in four (4) original texts, in Arabic, English, French and Portuguese languages, all four (4) being equally authentic, shall be deposited with the Chairperson of the Commission who shall transmit certified copies of same to all Member States and the United Nations General Secretariat.

ADOPTED BY THE EIGHTH ORDINARY SESSION OF THE ASSEMBLY, HELD IN ADDIS ABABA, ETHIOPIA,

30 JANUARY 2007

ANNEX VI

ECOWAS Protocol on Democracy and Good Governance (2001)

Preamble[1]

We, the Heads of State and Government of the Member States of the Economic Community of West African States (ECOWAS),

MINDFUL of the ECOWAS Treaty signed in Cotonou on 24th July 1993, notably its Article 58;

MINDFUL of the Protocol relating to the Mechanism for Conflict Prevention, Management, Resolution, Peacekeeping and Security signed in Lomé on 10 th December 1999;

CONSIDERING all the issues enumerated or reaffirmed in the preamble to the Protocol of 10th December 1999 referred to above;

MINDFUL of the principles set out in the OAU Solemn Declaration on Security, Stability, Development and Cooperation in Africa adopted in Abuja on 8 and 9 May 2000 and the Decision AHG. DEC 142 (XXV) on the framework for OAU'S reaction to unconstitutional change of government, adopted by Algiers in July 1999;

CONSIDERING the Harare Declaration adopted by the Commonwealth on 20 December 1991 and the Bamako Declaration adopted by the member countries of the Francophonie on 3 November 2000;

CONSIDERING also the Cotonou Declaration adopted on 6 December 2000 at the end of the 4th international conference on new or restored democracies;

RECALLING that women's rights have been recognized and guaranteed in all international human rights instruments, notably the Universal Declaration of Human Rights, the African Charter on Human and Peoples Rights and the Convention on the Elimination of all forms of Discrimination Against Women;

MINDFUL of the ratification of the African Charter on Human and Peoples Rights and other international human rights instruments by the majority of the Member States and their solemn commitment to eliminate all forms of discrimination and harmful practices against women;

CONCERNED about the increasing wave of international terrorism;

1 Office of the High Commissioner for Human Rights, A/SP1/12/01. Accessed on 28 July 2021. https://www.ohchr.org/EN/Issues/RuleOfLaw/CompilationDemocracy/Pages/ECOWASProtocol.aspx.

 | DOI:10.1163/9789004520646_016

CONCERNED also about the increasing incidence of conflicts caused by religious intolerance, political marginalisation and non-transparent elections;

HAVING OBSERVED that to become really effective, the Protocol of 10 December 1999 needs to be complemented through the incorporation of provisions concerning issues such as prevention of internal crises, democracy and good governance, the rule of law, and human rights;

HAVING DECIDED to enhance the ECOWAS Mechanism for Conflict Prevention, Management, Resolution, Peacekeeping and Security;

HAVE AGREED AS FOLLOWS:

Chapter 1 Principles

The provisions of this chapter complement and clarify the principles set out in Article 2 of the Protocol of 10th December 1999 .

Section 1 Constitutional Convergence Principles

Article 1

The following shall be declared as constitutional principles shared by all Member States:

a)
  - Separation of powers – the Executive, Legislative and Judiciary.
  - Empowerment and strengthening of parliaments and guarantee of parliamentary immunity.
  - Independence of the Judiciary: Judges shall be independent in the discharge of their duties.
  - The freedom of the members of the Bar shall be guaranteed; without prejudice to their penal or disciplinary responsibility in the event of contempt of court or breaches of the common law.

b) Every accession to power must be made through free, fair and transparent elections.

c) Zero tolerance for power obtained or maintained by unconstitutional means.

d) Popular participation in decision-making, strict adherence to democratic principles and decentralization of power at all levels of governance.

e) The armed forces must be apolitical and must be under the command of a legally constituted political authority; no serving member of the armed forces may seek to run for elective political.

f) Secularism and neutrality of the State in all matters relating to religion; freedom for each individual to practise, within the limits of existing laws, the religion of his/her choice everywhere on the national territory. The secularism shall extend to all parts of the State, but shall not deprive the State of the right to regulate, with due respect to human rights, the different religions practiced on the national territory or to intervene when law and order break down as a result of any religious activity.

g) The State and all its institutions belong to all the citizens; therefore none of their decisions and actions shall involve any form of discrimination, be it on an ethnic, racial, religion or regional basis.

h) The rights set out in the African Charter on Human and Peoples' Rights and other international instruments shall be guaranteed in each of the ECOWAS Member States; each individual or organization shall be free to have recourse to the common or civil law courts, a court of special jurisdiction, or any other national institution established within the framework of an international instrument on Human Rights, to ensure the protection of his/her rights. In the absence of a court of special jurisdiction, the present Supplementary Protocol shall be regarded as giving the necessary powers to common or civil law judicial bodies.

i) Political parties shall be formed and shall have the right to carry out their activities freely, within the limits of the law. Their formation and activities shall not be based on ethnic, religious, regional or racial considerations. They shall participate freely and without hindrance or discrimination in any electoral process. The freedom of the opposition shall be guaranteed. Each Member State may adopt a system for financing political parties, in accordance with criteria set under the law.

j) The freedom of association and the right to meet and organize peaceful demonstrations shall also be guaranteed.

k) The freedom of the press shall be guaranteed.

l) All former Heads of State shall enjoy a special status including freedom of movement. They shall enjoy special benefits compatible to their status as former Heads of State.

Section II Elections

Article 2

1. No substantial modification shall be made to the electoral laws in the last six (6) months before the elections, except with the consent of a majority of Political actors.
2. All the elections shall be organized on the dates or at periods fixed by the Constitution or the electoral laws.
3. Member States shall take all appropriate measures to ensure that women have equal rights with men to vote and be voted for in elections, to participate in the formulation of government policies and the implementation thereof and to hold public offices and perform public functions at all levels of governance.

Article 3

The bodies responsible for organizing the elections shall be independent or neutral and shall have the confidence of all the political actors. Where necessary, appropriate national consultations shall be organized to determine the nature and the structure of the bodies.

Article 4

1. Each ECOWAS Member State shall ensure the establishment of a reliable registry of births and deaths. A central registry shall be established in each Member State .
2. Member States shall cooperate in this area with a view to exchanging experiences and where necessary providing technical assistance to each other in the production of reliable voters' lists.

Article 5

The voters' lists shall be prepared in a transparent and reliable manner, with the collaboration of the political parties and voters who may have access to them whenever the need arises.

Article 6

The preparation and conduct of elections and the announcement of results shall be done in a transparent manner.

Article 7

Adequate arrangements shall be made to hear and dispose of all petitions relating to the conduct of elections and announcement of results.

Article 8

Member States shall use the services of civil society organizations involved in electoral matters to educate and enlighten the public on the need for peaceful elections devoid of all acts of violence.

Article 9

The party and/or candidate who loses the elections shall concede defeat to the political party and/or candidate finally declared the winner, following the guidelines and within the deadline stipulated by the law.

Article 10

All holders of power at all levels shall refrain from acts of intimidation or harassment against defeated candidates or their supporters.

Section II Election Monitoring and Ecowas Assistance

Article 11

The provisions of Article 42 of the Protocol of 10th December 1999 hereby complemented by the provisions under this section.

Article 12

1. At the request of any Member State, ECOWAS may provide assistance in the conduct of any election.
2. Such assistance may take any form.
3. Also, ECOWAS may dispatch a monitoring team to the country concerned for the purpose of monitoring the elections.

4. The decision in this respect shall be taken by the Executive Secretary.

Article 13

1. As elections in a Member State approach, the Executive Secretary shall dispatch a fact-finding Mission to the Member State conducting an election.
2. This mission may be followed by an exploratory Mission aimed at:
   - Collecting all texts governing the elections concerned;
   - Gathering all information on the conditions under which the elections shall be conducted;
   - Collecting all pertinent information relating to the contesting candidates or political parties;
   - Meeting all candidates, political party leaders, government authorities and other competent bodies;
   - Assessing the status of preparations for the elections;
   - Gathering any other useful information that may provide a clear picture of the situation.

Article 14

1. The Executive Secretary shall appoint the leader and the members of the Observer/Supervisory Mission, who shall be independent persons and Nationals of Member States other than the Member State conducting the Elections.
2. The Members of the Mission shall include women.
3. Staff of the Executive Secretariat shall be designated to assist the Mission .

Article 15

1. The Observer/Supervisory Mission, with the documents collected by the exploratory Mission and the report prepared by the Mission, shall arrive in the Member State concerned at least forty-eight hours prior to the conduct of the elections.
2. The Observer/Supervisory Mission may be preceded by ECOWAS Staff, who shall prepare the meetings to be held between the Mission and the national authorities.
3. The Mission shall be expected to hold consultations with the relevant authorities of the host government for an exchange of views and in order to determine the mode of deployment in the host Member State .
4. It may establish cooperation links with NGO or any other observer team while maintaining its autonomy.
5. The members of the Mission shall show restraint and refrain from making any individual statement. Any statement shall be made collectively and on behalf of the Mission by the team leader or a spokesperson appointed for this purpose.

Article 16

1. The Mission shall remain in the country throughout the election period and until the election results are announced.
2. The Mission shall also submit a report to the Executive Secretary.
3. The Report shall comprise:

- The Mission 's own observations;
- Statements by witnesses;
- Its assessment of the conduct of the elections from the point of view of the national laws governing the elections and the universal principles in electoral matters;
- Its recommendations for the improvement of the conduct of future elections and monitoring Missions.

Article 17

1. The Observer/Supervisory Mission 's report shall be signed by all Members of the Mission and submitted to the Executive Secretary by the Mission 's leader within fifteen (15) days with effect from the date of accomplishment of the Mission .
2. Before leaving the host country, the Mission shall convene a consultative meeting for the preparation of the report.
3. Any member of the Mission, who is unable to attend the meeting, shall submit a report in writing to the Mission 's leader before leaving the country.
4. ECOWAS Staff shall assist the Mission in the preparation of the report.

Article 18

The report shall be forwarded by the Executive Secretary, together with his own observations, if necessary, to the Mediation and Security Council for recommendations to be made to the country concerned and/or to all Member States, and for measures to be taken, where necessary.

Section IV The Role of the Armed Forces, the Police and the Security Forces in a Democracy

Article 19

1. The armed forces and police shall be non-partisan and shall remain loyal to the nation. The role of the armed forces shall be to defend the independence and the territorial integrity of the State and its democratic institutions.
2. The police and other security agencies shall be responsible for the maintenance of law and order and the protection of persons and their properties.
3. The armed forces, the police and other security agencies shall participate in ECOMOG missions as provided for in Article 28 of the Protocol.
4. They may also, on the decision of the constitutionally constituted authorities, participate in peacekeeping missions under the auspices of the African Union or the United Nations.
5. Members of the armed forces may be drafted to participate in national development projects.

Article 20

1. The armed forces, the police and other security agencies shall be under the authority of legally constituted civilian authorities.

2. The civilian authorities shall respect the apolitical nature of the armed forces and police. All political or trade union activities and propaganda shall be forbidden in the barracks and within the armed forces.

Article 21

The armed and security forces personnel as citizens, shall be entitled to all the rights set out in the constitution, except as may be stated otherwise in their special regulations.

Article 22

1. The use of arms to disperse non-violent meetings or demonstrations shall be forbidden. Whenever a demonstration becomes violent, only the use of minimal and/or proportionate force shall be authorized.
2. All cruel, inhuman and degrading treatment shall be forbidden.
3. The security forces, while carrying out investigations, shall not disturb or arrest family members or relations of the person presumed guilty or suspected of having committed an offence.

Article 23

1. The armed forces, the police and other security agencies shall during their training receive instructions on the Constitution of their country, ECOWAS principles and regulations, human rights, humanitarian law and democratic principles. In this regard, seminars and meetings bringing together members of the armed forces, Police and other Security agencies and other sectors of society shall be organized from time to time.
2. Joint training sessions shall also be arranged for members of the armed forces from different ECOWAS countries, the police, other security forces, university dons and members of the civil society.

Article 24

1. The Member States undertake to strengthen their national agencies responsible for preventing and combating terrorism.
2. In accordance with Articles 3(d) and 16(1) of the Protocol, the Department of Political Affairs, Defence and Security of the Executive Secretariat shall initiate joint activities for the national agencies of Member States in charge of preventing and combating terrorism.

Section VII: Rule of Law, Human Rights and Good Governance

Article 32

Member States agree that good governance and press freedom are essential for preserving social Justice, preventing conflict, guaranteeing political stability and peace and for strengthening democracy.

Article 33

1. Member States recognize that the rule of law involves not only the promulgation of good laws that are in conformity with the provisions on human rights, but also

a good judicial system, a good system of administration, and good management of the State apparatus.

2. They are also convinced that a system that guarantees smooth running of the State and its administrative and judicial services, contributes to the Consolidation of the rule of law.

Article 34

1. Member States and the Executive Secretariat shall endeavour to adopt at national and regional levels, practical modalities for the enforcement of the rule of law, human rights, justice and good governance.
2. Member States shall ensure accountability, professionalism, transparency, and expertise in the public and private sectors.

Article 35

1. Member States shall establish independent national institutions to promote and protect human rights.
2. The Executive Secretariat shall take measures to strengthen their capacities. The institutions shall be organized into a regional network. Within the framework of this network, each national institution shall systematically submit to the Executive Secretariat, any report on human rights violations observed on its territory. Such reports and reactions of governments shall be widely disseminated through the most appropriate means.

Article 36

Member States shall institutionalize a national mediation system.

Article 37

1. Each Member State shall work towards ensuring pluralism of the information sector and the development of the media.
2. Each Member State may give financial assistance to privately-owned media. The distribution and allocation of such assistance shall be done by an Independent national body or by a body freely instituted by the journalists Themselves.

Article 38

1. Member States undertake to fight corruption and manage their national resources in a transparent manner, ensuring that they are equitably distributed.
2. In this regard, Member States and the Executive Secretariat undertake to establish appropriate mechanisms to address issues of corruption within the Member States and at the Community level.

Article 39

Protocol A/P1/7/91 adopted in Abuja on 6 July 1991 relating to the Community Court of Justice, shall be reviewed so as to give the Court the power to hear, inter-alia, cases relating to violations of human rights, after all attempts to resolve the matter at the national level have failed.

Chapter II Modalities for Implementation and Sanctions

Article 44

1. This Article complements the provisions of Chapter V of the Protocol of 10th December 1999 .
2. In order to give full force to the provision of Article 28 of this Supplementary Protocol and in accordance with Article 57 of the Treaty, a legal convention Incorporating, if need be, Convention A/P1/7/91 relating to mutual assistance In criminal matters, and the Convention A/P1/8/94 on Extradition shall be Elaborated and adopted not later than twelve months after the entry into force Of this Supplementary Protocol.

Article 45

1. In the event that democracy is abruptly brought to an end by any means or where there is massive violation of Human Rights in a Member State, ECOWAS may impose sanctions on the State concerned.
2. The sanctions which shall be decided by the Authority, may take the following forms, in increasing order of severity:
   - Refusal to support the candidates presented by the Member State concerned for elective posts in international organizations;
   - Refusal to organize ECOWAS meetings in the Member State concerned;
   - Suspension of the Member State concerned from all ECOWAS decisionmaking bodies. During the period of the suspension the Member State shall be obliged to pay its dues for the period.
3. During the period of suspension, ECOWAS shall continue to monitor, encourage and support the efforts being made by the suspended Member State to return to normalcy and constitutional order.
4. On the recommendation of the Mediation and Security Council, a decision may be taken at the appropriate time to proceed as stipulated in Article 45 of the Protocol of 10th December 1999 .

Chapter III General and Final Provisions

Article 46

This Suppplementary Protocol shall form an integral part of the Protocol relating to the Mechanism for Conflict Prevention, Management, Resolution, Peacekeeping and Security, signed in Lome on 10th December 1999 .

ENTRY INTO FORCE

This Supplementary Protocol shall enter into force upon ratification by at least nine (9) signatory States in accordance with the constitutional procedures of each Member State .

Article 50

DEPOSITORY AUTHORITY

This Supplementary Protocol and all instruments of ratification shall be deposited with the Executive Secretariat which shall transmit certified true copies to all Member States and notify them of the dates of deposit of instruments of ratification by the Member States and shall register it with the Organization of African Unity (OAU)/ African Union (AU), as well as the United Nations (UN) and any other organization as may be decided by the Council.

IN FAITH WHEREOF, WE, THE HEADS OF STATE AND GOVERNMENT OF THE MEMBER STATES OF THE ECONOMIC COMMUNITY OF WEST AFRICAN STATES (ECOWAS) HAVE SIGNED THIS SUPPLEMENTARY PROTOCOL, IN SINGLE ORIGINAL IN THE ENGLISH, FRENCH AND PORTUGUESE LANGUAGES, ALL TEXTS BEING EQUALLY AUTHENTIC. DONE ATDAKAR ON THIS 21ST DAY OF DECEMBER 2001.

ANNEX VII

OAU Convention Governing the Specific Aspects of Refugee Problems in Africa

Preamble

We, the Heads of State and Government, assembled in the city of Addis Ababa,

1. *Noting with concern* the constantly increasing numbers of refugees in Africa and desirous of finding ways and means of alleviating their misery and suffering as well as providing them with a better life and future,
2. *Recognising* the need for an essentially humanitarian approach towards solving the problems of refugees,
3. *Aware*, however, that refugee problems are a source of friction among many Member States, and desirous of eliminating the source of such discord,
4. *Anxious* to make a distinction between a refugee who seeks a peaceful and normal life and a person fleeing his country for the sole purpose of fomenting subversion from outside,
5. *Determined* that the activities of such subversive elements should be discouraged, in accordance with the Declaration on the Problems of Subversion and Resolution on the Problem of Refugees adopted at Accra in 1965,
6. *Bearing* in mind that the Charter of the United Nations and the Universal Declaration of Human Rights have affirmed the principle that human beings shall enjoy fundamental rights and freedoms without discrimination,
7. *Recalling* Resolution 2312 (XXII) of 14 December 1967 of the United Nations General Assembly, relating to the Declaration on Territorial Asylum,
8. *Convinced* that all the problems of our continent must be solved in the spirit of the Charter of the Organisation of African Unity and in the African context,
9. *Recognising* that the United Nations Convention of 28 July 1951, as modified by the Protocol of 31 January 1967, constitutes the basic and universal instrument relating to the status of refugees and reflects the deep concern of States for refugees and their desire to establish common standards for their treatment,
10. *Recalling* Resolutions 26 and 104 of the OAU Assemblies of Heads of State and Government, calling upon Member States of the Organisation who had not already done so to accede to the United Nations Convention of 1951 and to the Protocol of 1967 relating to the Status of Refugees, and meanwhile to apply their provisions to refugees in Africa,

 | DOI:10.1163/9789004520646_017

11. *Convinced* that the efficiency of the measures recommended by the present Convention to solve the problem of refugees in Africa necessitates close and continuous collaboration between the Organisation of African Unity and the Office of the United Nations High Commissioner for Refugees,

HAVE AGREED as follows:

Article 1 Definition of the Term "refugee"

1. For the purposes of this Convention, the term "refugee" shall mean every person who, owing to well-founded fear of being persecuted for reasons of race, religion, nationality, membership of a particular social group or political opinion, is outside the country of his nationality and is unable or, owing to such fear, is unwilling to avail himself of the protection of that country, or who, not having a nationality and being outside the country of his former habitual residence as a result of such events, is unable or, owing to such fear, is unwilling to return to it.
2. The term "refugee" shall also apply to every person who, owing to external aggression, occupation, foreign domination or events seriously disturbing public order in either part or the whole of his country of origin or nationality, is compelled to leave his place of habitual residence in order to seek refuge in another place outside his country of origin or nationality.
3. In the case of a person who has several nationalities, the term "a country of which he is a national" shall mean each of the countries of which he is a national, and a person shall not be deemed to be lacking the protection of the country of which he is a national if, without any valid reason based on well-founded fear, he has not availed himself of the protection of one of the countries of which he is a national.
4. This Convention shall cease to apply to any refugee if:
   (a) he has voluntarily re-availed himself of the protection of the country of his nationality, or
   (b) having lost his nationality, he has voluntarily reacquired it, or
   (c) he has acquired a new nationality, and enjoys the protection of the country of his new nationality, or
   (d) he has voluntarily re-established himself in the country which he left or outside which he remained owing to fear of persecution, or
   (e) he can no longer, because the circumstances in connection with which he was recognised as a refugee have ceased to exist, continue to refuse to avail himself of the protection of the country of his nationality, or
   (f) he has committed a serious non-political crime outside his country of refuge after his admission to that country as a refugee, or
   (g) he has seriously infringed the purposes and objectives of this Convention.

5. The provisions of this Convention shall not apply to any person with respect to whom the country of asylum has serious reasons for considering that:
   (a) he has committed a crime against peace, a war crime, or a crime against humanity, as defined in the international instruments drawn up to make provision in respect of such crimes,
   (b) he committed a serious non-political crime outside the country of refuge prior to his admission to that country as a refugee,
   (c) he has been guilty of acts contrary to the purposes and principles of the Organisation of African Unity,
   (d) he has been guilty of acts contrary to the purposes and principles of the United Nations.
6. For the purposes of this Convention, the Contracting State of asylum shall determine whether an applicant is a refugee.

Article 2 Asylum

1. Member States of the OAU shall use their best endeavours consistent with their respective legislation to receive refugees and to secure the settlement of those refugees who, for well-founded reasons, are unable or unwilling to return to their country of origin or nationality.
2. The granting of asylum to refugees is a peaceful and humanitarian act and shall not be regarded as an unfriendly act by any Member State.
3. No person shall be subjected by a Member State to measures such as rejection at the frontier, return or expulsion, which would compel him to return to or remain in a territory where his life, physical integrity or liberty would be threatened for the reasons set out in Article 1, paragraphs 1 and 2.
4. Where a Member State finds difficulty in continuing to grant asylum to refugees, such Member State may appeal directly to other Member States and through the OAU, and such other Member States shall in the spirit of African solidarity and international co-operation take appropriate measures to lighten the burden of the Member State granting asylum.
5. Where a refugee has not received the right to reside in any country of asylum, he may be granted temporary residence in any country of asylum in which he first presented himself as a refugee pending arrangement for his re-settlement in accordance with the preceding paragraph.
6. For reasons of security, countries of asylum shall, as far as possible, settle refugees at a reasonable distance from the frontier of their country of origin.

Article 3 Prohibition of Subversive Activities

1. Every refugee has duties to the country in which he finds himself, which require in particular that he conforms with its laws and regulations as well as with measures taken for the maintenance of public order. He shall also abstain from any subversive activities against any Member State of the OAU.
2. Signatory States undertake to prohibit refugees residing in their respective territories from attacking any State Member of the OAU, by any activity likely to cause tension between Member States, and in particular by use of arms, through the press, or by radio.

Article 4 Non-discrimination

Member States undertake to apply the provisions of this Convention to all refugees without discrimination as to race, religion, nationality, membership of a particular social group or political opinions.

Article 5 Voluntary Repatriation

1. The essentially voluntary character of repatriation shall be respected in all cases and no refugee shall be repatriated against his will.
2. The country of asylum, in collaboration with the country of origin, shall make adequate arrangements for the safe return of refugees who request repatriation.
3. The country of origin, on receiving back refugees, shall facilitate their re-settlement and grant them the full rights and privileges of nationals of the country, and subject them to the same obligations.
4. Refugees who voluntarily return to their country shall in no way be penalised for having left it for any of the reasons giving rise to refugee situations. Whenever necessary, an appeal shall be made through national information media and through the Administrative Secretary-General of the OAU, inviting refugees to return home and giving assurance that the new circumstances prevailing in their country of origin will enable them to return without risk and to take up a normal and peaceful life without fear of being disturbed or punished, and that the text of such appeal should be given to refugees and clearly explained to them by their country of asylum.
5. Refugees who freely decide to return to their homeland, as a result of such assurances or on their own initiative, shall be given every possible assistance by the

country of asylum, the country of origin, voluntary agencies and international and intergovernmental organisations, to facilitate their return.

Article 6 Travel Documents

1. Subject to Article III, Member States shall issue to refugees lawfully staying in their territories travel documents in accordance with the United Nations Convention relating to the Status of Refugees and the Schedule and Annex thereto, for the purpose of travel outside their territory, unless compelling reasons of national security or public order otherwise require. Member States may issue such a travel document to any other refugee in their territory.
2. Where an African country of second asylum accepts a refugee from a country of first asylum, the country of first asylum may be dispensed from issuing a document with a return clause.
3. Travel documents issued to refugees under previous international agreements by State Parties thereto shall be recognised and treated by Member States in the same way as if they had been issued to refugees pursuant to this Article.

Article 7 Co-operation of the National Authorities with the Organisation of African Unity

In order to enable the Administrative Secretary-General of the Organisation of African Unity to make reports to the competent organs of the Organisation of African Unity, Member States undertake to provide the Secretariat in the appropriate form with information and statistical data requested concerning:
(a) the condition of refugees,
(b) the implementation of this Convention, and
(c) laws, regulations and decrees which are, or may hereafter in force relating to refugees.

Article 8 Co-operation with the Office of the United Nations High Commissioner for Refugees

1. Member States shall co-operate with the Office of the United Nations High Commissioner for Refugees.
2. The Present Convention shall be the effective regional complement in Africa of the 1951 United Nations Convention on the Status of Refugees.

Article 9 Settlement of Disputes

Any dispute between States signatories to this Convention relating to its interpretation or application, which cannot be settled by other means, shall be referred to the Commission for Mediation, Conciliation and Arbitration of the Organisation of African Unity, at the request of any one of the Parties to the dispute.

Article 10 Signature and Ratification

1. This Convention is open for signature and accession by all Member States of the Organisation of African Unity and shall be ratified by signatory States in accordance with their respective constitutional processes. The instruments of ratification shall be deposited with the Administrative Secretary-General of the Organisation of African Unity.
2. The original instrument, done if possible in African languages, and in English and French, all texts being equally authentic, shall be deposited with the Administrative Secretary-General of the Organisation of African Unity.
3. Any independent African State, Member of the Organisation of African Unity, may at any time notify the Administrative Secretary-General of the Organisation of African Unity of its accession to this Convention.

Article 11 Entry into Force

This Convention shall come into force upon deposit of instruments of ratification by one-third of the Member States of the Organisation of African Unity.

Article 12 Amendment

This Convention may be amended or revised if any Member State makes a written request to the Administrative Secretary-General to that effect, provided, however, that the proposed amendment shall not be submitted to the Assembly of Heads of State and Government for consideration until all Member States have been duly notified of it and a period of one year has elapsed. Such an amendment shall not be effective unless approved by at least two-thirds of the Member States Parties to the present Convention.

Article 13 Denunciation

1. Any Member State Party to this Convention may denounce its provisions by a written notification to the Administrative Secretary-General.
2. At the end of one year from the date of such notification, if not withdrawn, the Convention shall cease to apply with respect to the denouncing State.

Article 14 Registration with the United Nations

Upon entry into force of this Convention, the Administrative Secretary-General of the OAU shall register it with the Secretary-General of the United Nations, in accordance with Article 102 of the Charter of the United Nations.

Article 15 Notifications by the Administrative Secretary-General of the Organisation of African Unity

The Administrative Secretary-General of the Organisation of African Unity shall inform all Members of the Organisation:

(a) of signatures, ratifications and accessions in accordance with Article X;
(b) of entry into force, in accordance with Article XI;
(c) of requests for amendments submitted under the terms of Article XII;
(d) of denunciations, in accordance with Article XIII.

IN WITNESS WHEREOF WE, the Heads of African State and Government, have signed this Convention.

Adopted on 10 September 1969 by the Assembly of Heads of State and Government. CAB/LEG/24.3. It entered into force on 20 June 1974.

ANNEX VIII

UN Human Rights Committee General Comment [No. 29] on Article 4 of the ICCPR: States of Emergency

1. Article 4 of the Covenant is of paramount importance for the system of protection for human rights under the Covenant. On the one hand, it allows for a State party unilaterally to derogate temporarily from a part of its obligations under the Covenant. On the other hand, article 4 subjects both this very measure of derogation, as well as its material consequences, to a specific regime of safeguards. The restoration of a state of normalcy where full respect for the Covenant can again be secured must be the predominant objective of a State party derogating from the Covenant. In this general comment, replacing its General Comment No 5, adopted at the thirteenth session (1981), the Committee seeks to assist States parties to meet the requirements of article 4.
2. Measures derogating from the provisions of the Covenant must be of an exceptional and temporary nature. Before a State moves to invoke article 4, two fundamental conditions must be met: the situation must amount to a public emergency which threatens the life of the nation, and the State party must have officially proclaimed a state of emergency. The latter requirement is essential for the maintenance of the principles of legality and rule of law at times when they are most needed. When proclaiming a state of emergency with consequences that could entail derogation from any provision of the Covenant, States must act within their constitutional and other provisions of law that govern such proclamation and the exercise of emergency powers; it is the task of the Committee to monitor the laws in question with respect to whether they enable and secure compliance with article 4. In order that the Committee can perform its task, States parties to the Covenant should include in their reports submitted under article 40 sufficient and precise information about their law and practice in the field of emergency powers.
3. Not every disturbance or catastrophe qualifies as a public emergency which threatens the life of the nation, as required by article 4, paragraph 1. During armed conflict, whether international or non-international, rules of international humanitarian law become applicable and help, in addition to the provisions in article 4 and article 5, paragraph 1, of the Covenant, to prevent the abuse of a State's emergency powers. The Covenant requires that even during an armed conflict measures derogating from the Covenant are allowed only if and to the extent that the situation constitutes a threat to the life of the nation. If States parties consider

 | DOI:10.1163/9789004520646_018

invoking article 4 in other situations than an armed conflict, they should carefully consider the justification and why such a measure is necessary and legitimate in the circumstances. On a number of occasions the Committee has expressed its concern over States parties that appear to have derogated from rights protected by the Covenant, or whose domestic law appears to allow such derogation in situations not covered by article 4.[1]

4. A fundamental requirement for any measures derogating from the Covenant, as set forth in article 4, paragraph 1, is that such measures are limited to the extent strictly required by the exigencies of the situation. This requirement relates to the duration, geographical coverage and material scope of the state of emergency and any measures of derogation resorted to because of the emergency. Derogation from some Covenant obligations in emergency situations is clearly distinct from restrictions or limitations allowed even in normal times under several provisions of the Covenant.[2] Nevertheless, the obligation to limit any derogations to those strictly required by the exigencies of the situation reflects the principle of proportionality which is common to derogation and limitation powers. Moreover, the mere fact that a permissible derogation from a specific provision may, of itself, be justified by the exigencies of the situation does not obviate the requirement that specific measures taken pursuant to the derogation must also be shown to be required by the exigencies of the situation. In practice, this will ensure that no provision of the Covenant, however validly derogated from will be entirely inapplicable to the behaviour of a State party. When considering States parties' reports the Committee has expressed its concern over insufficient attention being paid to the principle of proportionality.[3]

5. The issues of when rights can be derogated from, and to what extent, cannot be separated from the provision in article 4, paragraph 1, of the Covenant according to which any measures derogating from a State party's obligations under the Covenant must be limited "to the extent strictly required by the exigencies of the situation". This condition requires that States parties provide careful justification not only for their decision to proclaim a state of emergency but also for any specific measures based on such a proclamation. If States purport to invoke the right to derogate from the Covenant during, for instance, a natural catastrophe,

---

1 See the following comments/concluding observations: United Republic of Tanzania (1992), CCPR/C/79/Add.12, para. 7; Dominican Republic (1993), CCPR/C/79/Add.18, para. 4; United Kingdom of Great Britain and Northern Ireland (1995), CCPR/C/79/Add.55, para. 23; Peru (1996), CCPR/C/79/Add.67, para. 11; Bolivia (1997), CCPR/C/79/Add.74, para. 14; Colombia (1997), CCPR/C/79/Add.76, para. 25; Lebanon (1997), CCPR/C/79/Add.78, para. 10; Uruguay (1998), CCPR/C/79/Add.90, para. 8; Israel (1998), CCPR/C/79/Add.93, para. 11.

2 See, for instance, articles 12 and 19 of the Covenant.

3 See, for example, concluding observations on Israel (1998), CCPR/C/79/Add.93, para. 11.

a mass demonstration including instances of violence, or a major industrial accident, they must be able to justify not only that such a situation constitutes a threat to the life of the nation, but also that all their measures derogating from the Covenant are strictly required by the exigencies of the situation. In the opinion of the Committee, the possibility of restricting certain Covenant rights under the terms of, for instance, freedom of movement (article 12) or freedom of assembly (article 21) is generally sufficient during such situations and no derogation from the provisions in question would be justified by the exigencies of the situation.

6. The fact that some of the provisions of the Covenant have been listed in article 4 (paragraph 2), as not being subject to derogation does not mean that other articles in the Covenant may be subjected to derogations at will, even where a threat to the life of the nation exists. The legal obligation to narrow down all derogations to those strictly required by the exigencies of the situation establishes both for States parties and for the Committee a duty to conduct a careful analysis under each article of the Covenant based on an objective assessment of the actual situation.
7. Article 4, paragraph 2, of the Covenant explicitly prescribes that no derogation from the following articles may be made: article 6 (right to life), article 7 (prohibition of torture or cruel, inhuman or degrading punishment, or of medical or scientific experimentation without consent), article 8, paragraphs 1 and 2 (prohibition of slavery, slave-trade and servitude), article 11 (prohibition of imprisonment because of inability to fulfil a contractual obligation), article 15 (the principle of legality in the field of criminal law, i.e. the requirement of both criminal liability and punishment being limited to clear and precise provisions in the law that was in place and applicable at the time the act or omission took place, except in cases where a later law imposes a lighter penalty), article 16 (the recognition of everyone as a person before the law), and article 18 (freedom of thought, conscience and religion). The rights enshrined in these provisions are non-derogable by the very fact that they are listed in article 4, paragraph 2. The same applies, in relation to States that are parties to the Second Optional Protocol to the Covenant, aiming at the abolition of the death penalty, as prescribed in article 6 of that Protocol. Conceptually, the qualification of a Covenant provision as a non-derogable one does not mean that no limitations or restrictions would ever be justified. The reference in article 4, paragraph 2, to article 18, a provision that includes a specific clause on restrictions in its paragraph 3, demonstrates that the permissibility of restrictions is independent of the issue of derogability. Even in times of most serious public emergencies, States that interfere with the freedom to manifest one's religion or belief must justify their actions by referring to the requirements specified in article 18, paragraph 3. On several occasions the Committee has expressed its concern about rights that are non-derogable according to article 4, paragraph 2,

being either derogated from or under a risk of derogation owing to inadequacies in the legal regime of the State party.[4]

8. According to article 4, paragraph 1, one of the conditions for the justifiability of any derogation from the Covenant is that the measures taken do not involve discrimination solely on the ground of race, colour, sex, language, religion or social origin. Even though article 26 or the other Covenant provisions related to non-discrimination (articles 2, 3, 14, paragraph 1, 23, paragraph 4, 24, paragraph 1, and 25) have not been listed among the non-derogable provisions in article 4, paragraph 2, there are elements or dimensions of the right to non-discrimination that cannot be derogated from in any circumstances. In particular, this provision of article 4, paragraph 1, must be complied with if any distinctions between persons are made when resorting to measures that derogate from the Covenant.
9. Furthermore, article 4, paragraph 1, requires that no measure derogating from the provisions of the Covenant may be inconsistent with the State party's other obligations under international law, particularly the rules of international humanitarian law. Article 4 of the Covenant cannot be read as justification for derogation from the Covenant if such derogation would entail a breach of the State's other international obligations, whether based on treaty or general international law. This is reflected also in article 5, paragraph 2, of the Covenant according to which there shall be no restriction upon or derogation from any fundamental rights recognized in other instruments on the pretext that the Covenant does not recognize such rights or that it recognizes them to a lesser extent.
10. Although it is not the function of the Human Rights Committee to review the conduct of a State party under other treaties, in exercising its functions under the Covenant the Committee has the competence to take a State party's other international obligations into account when it considers whether the Covenant allows the State party to derogate from specific provisions of the Covenant. Therefore, when invoking article 4, paragraph 1, or when reporting under article 40 on the legal framework related to emergencies, States parties should present information on their other international obligations relevant for the protection of the rights in question, in particular those obligations that are applicable in times

4 See the following comments/concluding observations: Dominican Republic (1993), CCPR/C/79/Add.18, para. 4; Jordan (1994) CCPR/C/79/Add.35, para. 6; Nepal (1994) CCPR/C/79/Add.42, para. 9; Russian Federation (1995), CCPR/C/79/Add.54, para. 27; Zambia (1996), CCPR/C/79/Add.62, para. 11; Gabon (1996), CCPR/C/79/Add.71, para. 10; Colombia (1997) CCPR/C/79/Add.76, para. 25; Israel (1998), CCPR/C/79/Add.93, para. 11; Iraq (1997), CCPR/C/79/Add.84, para. 9; Uruguay (1998) CCPR/C/79/Add.90, para. 8; Armenia (1998), CCPR/C/79/Add.100, para. 7; Mongolia (2000), CCPR/C/79/Add.120, para. 14; Kyrgyzstan (2000), CCPR/CO/69/KGZ, para. 12.

of emergency.[5] In this respect, States parties should duly take into account the developments within international law as to human rights standards applicable in emergency situations.[6]

11. The enumeration of non-derogable provisions in article 4 is related to, but not identical with, the question whether certain human rights obligations bear the nature of peremptory norms of international law. The proclamation of certain provisions of the Covenant as being of a non-derogable nature, in article 4, paragraph 2, is to be seen partly as recognition of the peremptory nature of some fundamental rights ensured in treaty form in the Covenant (e.g., articles 6 and 7). However, it is apparent that some other provisions of the Covenant were included in the list of non-derogable provisions because it can never become necessary to derogate from these rights during a state of emergency (e.g., articles 11 and 18). Furthermore, the category of peremptory norms extends beyond the list of non-derogable provisions as given in article 4, paragraph 2. States parties may in no circumstances invoke article 4 of the Covenant as justification for acting in violation of humanitarian law or peremptory norms of international law, for instance by taking hostages, by imposing collective punishments, through arbitrary deprivations of liberty or by deviating from fundamental principles of fair trial, including the presumption of innocence.
12. In assessing the scope of legitimate derogation from the Covenant, one criterion can be found in the definition of certain human rights violations as crimes against humanity. If action conducted under the authority of a State constitutes a basis for individual criminal responsibility for a crime against humanity by the persons

5 Reference is made to the Convention on the Rights of the Child which has been ratified by almost all States parties to the Covenant and does not include a derogation clause. As article 38 of the Convention clearly indicates, the Convention is applicable in emergency situations.

6 Reference is made to reports of the Secretary-General to the Commission on Human Rights submitted pursuant to Commission resolutions 1998/29, 1996/65 and 2000/69 on minimum humanitarian standards (later: fundamental standards of humanity), E/CN.4/1999/92, E/CN.4/2000/94 and E/CN.4/2001/91, and to earlier efforts to identify fundamental rights applicable in all circumstances, for instance the Paris Minimum Standards of Human Rights Norms in a State of Emergency (International Law Association, 1984), the Siracusa Principles on the Limitation and Derogation Provisions in the International Covenant on Civil and Political Rights, the final report of Mr. Leandro Despouy, Special Rapporteur of the Sub-Commission, on human rights and states of emergency (E/CN.4/Sub.2/1997/19 and Add.1), the Guiding Principles on Internal Displacement (E/CN.4/1998/53/Add.2), the Turku (Åbo) Declaration of Minimum Humanitarian Standards (1990), (E/CN.4/1995/116). As a field of ongoing further work reference is made to the decision of the 26th International Conference of the Red Cross and Red Crescent (1995) to assign the International Committee of the Red Cross the task of preparing a report on the customary rules of international humanitarian law applicable in international and non-international armed conflicts.

involved in that action, article 4 of the Covenant cannot be used as justification that a state of emergency exempted the State in question from its responsibility in relation to the same conduct. Therefore, the recent codification of crimes against humanity, for jurisdictional purposes, in the Rome Statute of the International Criminal Court is of relevance in the interpretation of article 4 of the Covenant.[7]

13. In those provisions of the Covenant that are not listed in article 4, paragraph 2, there are elements that in the Committee's opinion cannot be made subject to lawful derogation under article 4. Some illustrative examples are presented below.
    (a) All persons deprived of their liberty shall be treated with humanity and with respect for the inherent dignity of the human person. Although this right, prescribed in article 10 of the Covenant, is not separately mentioned in the list of non-derogable rights in article 4, paragraph 2, the Committee believes that here the Covenant expresses a norm of general international law not subject to derogation. This is supported by the reference to the inherent dignity of the human person in the preamble to the Covenant and by the close connection between articles 7 and 10.
    (b) The prohibitions against taking of hostages, abductions or unacknowledged detention are not subject to derogation. The absolute nature of these prohibitions, even in times of emergency, is justified by their status as norms of general international law.
    (c) The Committee is of the opinion that the international protection of the rights of persons belonging to minorities includes elements that must be respected in all circumstances. This is reflected in the prohibition against genocide in international law, in the inclusion of a non-discrimination clause in article 4 itself (paragraph 1), as well as in the non-derogable nature of article 18.
    (d) As confirmed by the Rome Statute of the International Criminal Court, deportation or forcible transfer of population without grounds permitted under international law, in the form of forced displacement by expulsion or other coercive means from the area in which the persons concerned are lawfully present, constitutes a crime against humanity.[8] The legitimate right to

7 See articles 6 (genocide) and 7 (crimes against humanity) of the Statute which by 1 July 2001 had been ratified by 35 States. While many of the specific forms of conduct listed in article 7 of the Statute are directly linked to violations against those human rights that are listed as non-derogable provisions in article 4, paragraph 2, of the Covenant, the category of crimes against humanity as defined in that provision covers also violations of some provisions of the Covenant that have not been mentioned in the said provision of the Covenant. For example, certain grave violations of article 27 may at the same time constitute genocide under article 6 of the Rome Statute, and article 7, in turn, covers practices that are related to, besides articles 6, 7 and 8 of the Covenant, also articles 9, 12, 26 and 27.

8 See article 7 (1) (d) and 7 (2) (d) of the Rome Statute.

derogate from article 12 of the Covenant during a state of emergency can never be accepted as justifying such measures.

(e) No declaration of a state of emergency made pursuant to article 4, paragraph 1, may be invoked as justification for a State party to engage itself, contrary to article 20, in propaganda for war, or in advocacy of national, racial or religious hatred that would constitute incitement to discrimination, hostility or violence.

14. Article 2, paragraph 3, of the Covenant requires a State party to the Covenant to provide remedies for any violation of the provisions of the Covenant. This clause is not mentioned in the list of non-derogable provisions in article 4, paragraph 2, but it constitutes a treaty obligation inherent in the Covenant as a whole. Even if a State party, during a state of emergency, and to the extent that such measures are strictly required by the exigencies of the situation, may introduce adjustments to the practical functioning of its procedures governing judicial or other remedies, the State party must comply with the fundamental obligation, under article 2, paragraph 3, of the Covenant to provide a remedy that is effective.

15. It is inherent in the protection of rights explicitly recognized as non-derogable in article 4, paragraph 2, that they must be secured by procedural guarantees, including, often, judicial guarantees. The provisions of the Covenant relating to procedural safeguards may never be made subject to measures that would circumvent the protection of non-derogable rights. Article 4 may not be resorted to in a way that would result in derogation from non-derogable rights. Thus, for example, as article 6 of the Covenant is non-derogable in its entirety, any trial leading to the imposition of the death penalty during a state of emergency must conform to the provisions of the Covenant, including all the requirements of articles 14 and 15.

16. Safeguards related to derogation, as embodied in article 4 of the Covenant, are based on the principles of legality and the rule of law inherent in the Covenant as a whole. As certain elements of the right to a fair trial are explicitly guaranteed under international humanitarian law during armed conflict, the Committee finds no justification for derogation from these guarantees during other emergency situations. The Committee is of the opinion that the principles of legality and the rule of law require that fundamental requirements of fair trial must be respected during a state of emergency. Only a court of law may try and convict a person for a criminal offence. The presumption of innocence must be respected. In order to protect non-derogable rights, the right to take proceedings before a court to enable the court to decide without delay on the lawfulness of detention, must not be diminished by a State party's decision to derogate from the Covenant.[9]

9 See the Committee's concluding observations on Israel (1998) (CCPR/C/79/Add.93), para. 21: "... The Committee considers the present application of administrative detention to be incompatible with articles 7 and 16 of the Covenant, neither of which allows for

17. In paragraph 3 of article 4, States parties, when they resort to their power of derogation under article 4, commit themselves to a regime of international notification. A State party availing itself of the right of derogation must immediately inform the other States parties, through the United Nations Secretary-General, of the provisions it has derogated from and of the reasons for such measures. Such notification is essential not only for the discharge of the Committee's functions, in particular in assessing whether the measures taken by the State party were strictly required by the exigencies of the situation, but also to permit other States parties to monitor compliance with the provisions of the Covenant. In view of the summary character of many of the notifications received in the past, the Committee emphasizes that the notification by States parties should include full information about the measures taken and a clear explanation of the reasons for them, with full documentation attached regarding their law. Additional notifications are required if the State party subsequently takes further measures under article 4, for instance by extending the duration of a state of emergency. The requirement of immediate notification applies equally in relation to the termination of derogation. These obligations have not always been respected: States parties have failed to notify other States parties, through the Secretary-General, of a proclamation of a state of emergency and of the resulting measures of derogation from one or more provisions of the Covenant, and States parties have sometimes neglected to submit a notification of territorial or other changes in the exercise of their emergency powers.[10]'Sometimes, the existence of a state of emergency and the question of whether a State party has derogated from provisions of the Covenant have come to the attention of the Committee only incidentally, in the course of the consideration of a State party's report. The Committee emphasizes the obligation

---

derogation in times of public emergency .... The Committee stresses, however, that a State party may not depart from the requirement of effective judicial review of detention." See also the recommendation by the Committee to the Sub-Commission on Prevention of Discrimination and Protection of Minorities concerning a draft third optional protocol to the Covenant: "The Committee is satisfied that States parties generally understand that the right to habeas corpus and amparo should not be limited in situations of emergency. Furthermore, the Committee is of the view that the remedies provided in article 9, paragraphs 3 and 4, read in conjunction with article 2 are inherent to the Covenant as a whole." Official Records of the General Assembly, Forty-ninth session, Supplement No. 40 (A/49/40), vol. I, annex XI, para. 2.

10 See comments/concluding observations on Peru (1992) CCPR/C/79/Add.8, para. 10; Ireland (1993) CCPR/C/79/Add.21, para. 11; Egypt (1993), CCPR/C/79/Add.23, para. 7; Cameroon (1994) CCPR/C/79/Add.33, para. 7; Russian Federation (1995), CCPR/C/79/Add.54, para. 27; Zambia (1996), CCPR/C/79/Add.62, para. 11; Lebanon (1997), CCPR/C/79/Add.78, para. 10; India (1997), CCPR/C/79/Add.81, para. 19; Mexico (1999), CCPR/C/79/Add.109, para. 12.

of immediate international notification whenever a State party takes measures derogating from its obligations under the Covenant. The duty of the Committee to monitor the law and practice of a State party for compliance with article 4 does not depend on whether that State party has submitted a notification.

Bibliography

Documents

OAU Convention Governing the Specific Aspects of Refugee Problems in Africa, 1969.
African Charter on Human and Peoples' Rights (Banjul Charter) 1981.
African Charter on the Rights and Welfare of the Child, 1990.
Treaty Establishing the African Economic Community (1991).
Protocol to the African Charter on Human and Peoples' Rights on the Establishment of the African Court on Human and Peoples' Rights, 1998.
Constitutive Act of the African Union, 2000.
ECOWAS Protocol on Democracy and Good Governance (2001).
Protocol Relating to the Establishment of the Peace and Security Council of the African Union, 2002.
Protocol to the African Charter on Human and Peoples' Rights on the Rights of Women in Africa, 2003.
African Union, African Charter on Democracy, Elections and Governance (2011).
General Comment No. 1 on Article 14(1)(d) and (e) of the Protocol to the African Charter on Human and Peoples' Rights on the Rights of Women in Africa, African Commission on Human and Peoples' Rights 2012.
General Comment No. 2 on Article 14.1 (a), (b), (c) and (f) and Article 14.2 (a) and (c) of the Protocol to the African Charter on Human and Peoples' Rights on the Rights of Women in Africa, African Commission on Human and Peoples' Rights 2014.
General Comment No. 3: The Right to Life: Article 4 of the African Charter on Human and Peoples' Rights. African Commission on Human and Peoples' Rights(2015).
General Comment No. 4: on the Right to Redress for Victims of Torture and Other Cruel, Inhuman or Degrading Punishment or Treatment (Article 5) in relation to the Robben Island Guide. African Commission on Human and Peoples' Rights (2017).
General Comment, in collaboration with civil society and partner NGOs, following the successful development of General comment No. 4 on the African Charter on Human and Peoples' Rights: the Right to Redress for Victims of Torture and Other Cruel, Inhuman or Degrading Punishment or Treatment (Article 5) in relation to the Robben Island Guide. African Commission on Human and People's Rights, 2017.
Joint General Comment of the African Commission on Human and Peoples' Rights (ACHPR) and the African Committee of Experts on the Rights and Welfare of the Child (ACERWC) on Ending Child Marriage (2016).
Guidelines on Freedom of Association and Assembly in Africa, 2017.
Guidelines on the Conditions of Arrest, Police Custody and Pre-Trial Detention in Africa, 2015.

Guidelines and Principles on Economic, Social and Cultural Rights in the African Charter on Human and Peoples' Rights, 2011.
Principles and Guidelines on the Right to a Fair Trial and Legal Assistance in Africa, 2003.
Resolution on Guidelines and measures for the Prohibition and Prevention of Torture, Cruel, Inhuman or Degrading Treatment or Punishment in Africa (Robben Island Guidelines), 2008.
Guidelines for African Union Electoral Observations and Monitoring Missions, 2011.
Guidelines on Access to Information and Elections in Africa, 2017.
Guidelines for the Policing of Assemblies by Law Enforcement Officials in Africa, 2017.
Principles and Guidelines on Human and Peoples' Rights While Countering Terrorism in Africa, 2016.
The Right to Nationality in Africa, 2014.
Basic Principles on the Use of Force and Firearms by Law Enforcement Officials, 2012.
Framework and Guidelines on Land Policy in Africa, 2012.
Declaration of Principles on Freedom of Expression and Access to Information in Africa, 2019.
Guidelines on the Right to Water in Africa, 2019.

Books and Journals

African Human Rights Law Journal, Vols 1–21 (2001–2021). Published by the Praetoria University Law Press.
African Human Rights Yearbook, Vols. 1–3. (2017–2019) Published for the African Union by Praetoria University Law Press (PULP).
African Yearbook on International Law, Vols. 1–23 (1993–2020) Leiden, Brill.
An-Naim Abdullah A. and Francis M. Deng (Eds.), Human Rights in Africa. Cross-Cultural Perspectives. Washington D.C., The Brookings Institution, 1990.
Ambrose, Brendalyn P. Democratisation and the Protection of Human Rights in Africa. Problems and Prospects. Westport, Connecticut and London, Praeger, 1995.
Ankumah, Evelyn Ama "Universality of Human Rights and the African Charter on Human and Peoples' Rights", in Universaliteit van Mensrechten. Leiden, Stichting NJCM-Boekrij (1992), 73 pp.
Annan, Kofi Interventions. New York, Penguin Press, 2012.
Babiker Mohamed Abdelsalam (Ed.), Constitution-making and Human Rights in the Sudan. London, Routledge, 2018.
Bosl Anton and Joseph Diescho, Human Rights in Africa. Legal Perspectives on their Protection and Promotion. Windhoek, Namibia, Macmillan Education Namibia, 2009.

Cornell Drucilla et al, The Dignity Jurisprudence of the Constitutional Court of South Africa. 2 Vols. New York, Fordham University Press, 2013.

Crwys-Williams, Jennifer In the Words of Nelson Mandela. Johannesburg, London, New York, Penguin Books, 1997.

Elias, Taslim OlawaleThe Evolution of Law and Government in Modern Africa, University of California, Los Angeles, African Studies Center, 1963.

Elias,Taslim Olawale New Horizons in International law. Alpen and Den Rijn, Sightjoff & Noordhoff, Dobbs Ferry, Oceana Publications Inc., 1980.

Freeman, Sandra Human Rights Transformed: Positive Rights and Positive Duties, Oxford: Oxford University Press, 2008.

Gutto,Shadrack B.O. Equality and Non-Discrimination in South Africa. The Political Economy of Law and law-Making. Claremount, South Africa, New Africa Books, 2001.

Heyns Chrystof and Magnus Killander (Eds.), Compendium of Key Human Rights Documents of the African Union. Pretoria, Pretoria University Law Press. Fourth Edition, 2010.

Human Rights Watch, Protectors or Pretenders. Government Human Rights Commissions in Africa. New York, Human Rights Watch, 2001.

A Compendium on the Legacy of the ICTR and the Development of International Law. https://unictr.irmct.org/en/compendium-legacy-ictr-and-development-international-law.

Jalloh,Charles C., Mamari M. Clarke and Vincent O. Nmehielle (Eds.) The Afrocam Court of Justice and Human and Peoples' Rights. Cambridge, University Press, 2019.

Maluwa, Tiyanjana International Law in Post-Colonial Africa. The Hague, Kluwer Law International, 1999.

Maluwa Tiyanjana (Ed.), Law Politics and Rights. Essays in Memory of Kader Asmal. Leiden, Martinus Nijhoffs Publishers, 2013.

Maluwa, Tiyanjana, Max duPlessis and Dire Tladi (Eds.), The Pursuit of a Brave New World in International Law. Essays in Honour of John Dugard. Leiden, Brill, 2017.

Mowbray, Alistair The Development of Positive Obligations Under the European Convention on Human Rights by the European Court of Human Rights. Hart, Oxford, 2004.

Murray, Rachel Human Rights in Africa: From the OAU to the African Union. Cambridge, University Press, 2004.

Murray Rachel and Malcolm Evans, The African Charter on Human and Peoples' Rights: The System in Practice 1986–2006. Cambridge, Cambridge University Press, 2008.

Nyong'o, Peter Anyang, Aseghedech Ghirmazion and Davinder Lamba, NEPAD. A New Path? Nairobi, Heinrich Boll Foundation, 2002.

Roux, Theunis The Politics of Principle. The First South African Constitutional Court, 1995. Cambridge, Cambridge University Press, 2013.

Shivji, Issa G. The Concept of Human Rights in Africa. London, African Books Collective, 1989.
Tistounet, Eric The UN Human Rights Council. A Practical Autonomy. Cheltenham, UK, Edward Elgar Publishing, 2020.
Viljoen, Frans International Human Rights Law in Africa. Oxford, Oxford University Press, 2012.
Yeshanew, Sisay Alemahu The Justiciability of Economic, Social and Cultural Rights in the African Regional Human Rights System: Theory, Practice and Prospect. Cambridge, UK, Intersentia, 2013.

Articles

Anyangwe, Carlson "The Normative Power of the Right to Self-Determination under the African Charter and the Principle of Territorial Integrity: Competing Values of Human Dignity", 11 African Human Rights Yearbook, 2018, pp. 47–71.
Derso, Solomon A. The Jurisprudence of the African Commission on Human and Peoples' Rights with respect to peoples' rights, African Human Rights Law Journal, Vol, 6, Issue 2, Jan. 2006, pp. 358–381.
Elias, Taslim Olawale "Freedom of Assembly and Association", in VIII Journal of the International Commission of Jurists, December, 1967, No. 2, pp. 60–73.
Imman Derek and others, "The (Un)willingness to Implement the Recommendations of the African Commission on Human and Peoples' Rights: Revisiting the *Endorois* and the *Mamboleo* Decisions", 11 African Human Rights Yearbook, 2018, pp. 400–426.
Maluwa, Tiyanjana "International Law-Making in Post-Colonial Africa: The Role of the Organization of African Unity", XLIX Netherlands International Law Review (2002-Issue 1), pp. 81–103.
Maluwa, Tiyanjana "Reassessing Aspects of the Contribution of African States to the Development of International Law Through African Regional Multilateral Treaties", 41 Michigan Journal of International Law, Issue 2, (2020), pp. 327–415.
Namwase, Sylvie "Inclusive Dialogue, Freedom of Speech in Rwanda and the Milestone Decision of the African Court in the matter of *Victoire Ingabire Umuhoza* v. Republic of Rwanda", 11 African Human Rights Yearbook, 2018, pp. 487–506.
Ngarhodjim, Nadjita F. "The African Charter on Democracy, Elections and Governance: A Critical Analysis". Published by the Open Society Institute, Africa Governance Monitoring and Advocacy Project. Undated. Accessed on the internet 27 June, 2020.
Ocheje, Paul "Exploring the Legal Dimensions of Political Legitimacy: A 'Rights' Approach to Governance in Africa, in E.K. Quashigah and O.C. Okafor (Eds.),

Legitimate Governance in Africa, The Hague, Kluwer Law International (1999), pp. 165–205.

Ramcharan, Bertrand G. "Co-operation between the UN and Regional/Sub-Regional Organizations in Internal Conflicts: The Case of Liberia", 4 African Yearbook of International Law (1996), pp. 3–18.

Ramcharan, Bertrand G. "Recourse to the Law in the Settlement of International Disputes: Western Sahara", 5 African Yearbook of International Law (1997), pp.205–224.

Ramcharan, Bertrand G. "The Protection of Minorities in Africa", in G. Alfredsson and M. Stavropoulou (Eds.) Justice Pending: Indigenous and Other Good Causes. The Hague, Kluwer Law International 2002, pp. 99–116.

Udombana, Nsongurua J. "Between promise and Performance: Revisiting States' Obligations Under the African Human Rights Charter", 40 Stanford Journal of International Law, No. 1, (2004), pp. 105–142.

Zewudie, Tilahun Adamu "Huma Rights in the African Union Decision-Making Processes: An Inside View of States' Reaction to the Activity Reports of the African Commission on Human and Peoples' Rights", 11 African Human Rights Yearbook, 2018, pp. 295–320.

Index

www.ingramcontent.com/pod-product-compliance
Lightning Source LLC
LaVergne TN
LVHW102227300926
849160LV00005B/46
9789004520639